GUIDE TO THE RECORDS OF MERSEYSIDE MARITIME MUSEUM VOLUME II

Edited by
Dawn Littler

Trustees of the National Museums and Galleries on Merseyside/International Maritime Economic History Association

St. John's, Newfoundland
1999

ISBN -0-9681288-7-4

Guide to the Records of Merseyside Maritime Museum, Vol. II

Published by
International Maritime Economic History Association
Maritime Studies Research Unit
Memorial University of Newfoundland
St. John's, NF
A1C 5S7

Cover Photo: The *Helen* arriving on the Mersey, c.1850. Photo courtesy of the Trustees of the National Museum and Galleries on Merseyside.

Contents

Introduction

The publication of this second volume of the *Guide to the Records of Merseyside Maritime Museum* completes the project begun in the early 1990s to provide a full and comprehensive survey of our collection of mercantile and shipping records. The first volume of the guide, published in 1995, summarised our holdings of records of official organisations connected to the history of the port of Liverpool, including the Mersey Docks and Harbour Board and shipping and trade organisations, as well as the Liverpool Statutory Registers of British Merchant Ships. It also included our substantial holdings of the records of Liverpool-based shipping companies.

The arrangement of the second volume is very similar to that of the first, since both have been designed to be used together. A cumulative index to both guides will be found at the end of the present volume. This book describes the collections omitted from the earlier work and covers a wide variety of subjects and records, including the collections relating to merchants, shipbuilding, slavery, emigration, maritime families, maritime charities and seafarers. With its concentration of personal and family archives, it covers the human dimension of the history of the port of Liverpool. A chapter has also been included on the special collections relating to two famous Liverpool-registered ships, *Titanic* and *Lusitania*, in response to the continuing popular interest in their tragic histories. Unfortunately, space does not permit the inclusion of every document or collection relating to other ships, or to seafarers or passengers, and researchers will need to consult the catalogues in the Maritime Archives and Library reading room for such records. For example, while it has not been possible to include every discharge certificate from our vast collection, the contents of the seafarers' chapter have been selected to provide a good cross-section of the careers and experiences of merchant seamen covered.

Similarly, the chapter on pictorial and audio records is only a summary of our holdings, and the collection of maps, charts and plans requires further arrangement and cataloguing. The reference library is described in its own chapter. A series of separate bibliographies have been published on emigration and slavery books. A short list of suggested reading has been included at the end of each chapter, and in many cases references to works on specific collections have been provided. It is recommended that researchers consult these published works before using the original archives.

The penultimate chapter of this volume describes the research, miscellaneous and non-maritime records. The miscellaneous section only includes our largest holdings, including the Bryson Collection of business and family ephemera. Many maritime-related items from this collection have been described in previous chapters, as have many items from the large DX/SAS miscellaneous accumulations. Many important items from the merchant or maritime family collections, particularly records of slavery and emigration, have been drawn from this source and are listed in greater detail in the specific chapter on each subject.

The Archives Department of the National Museums and Galleries on Merseyside, of which the Maritime Archives at the Merseyside Maritime Museum are a part, is also responsible for a large number of non-maritime business and other records. These have been included in this volume for the sake of completeness, and many of the collections contain items of maritime interest. Finally, reference has also been made to objects within the Merseyside Maritime Museum's collections, such as ship models or paintings, which may also be of interest to researchers.

Notes on Access and Use of the Archives

The majority of the collections described in this volume are available at the Maritime Archives and Library on the second floor of the Merseyside Maritime Museum, Albert Dock, Liverpool L3 4AQ (Tel: +44 [0]151 478-4418). The current opening times are Tuesdays-Thursdays, 10.30 am-4.30 pm, and there is a small admission charge. Every effort has been made to inform readers of the current access conditions of collections. To summarise, all of those collections described as being *available strictly by appointment*, are held at our reserve store at North Street, Liverpool, and an advance appointment is essential. Unless otherwise stated, collections without any access restrictions are available without prior appointment. Nonetheless, we recommend contacting the Maritime Archives and Library in advance of your visit to check on the availability of specific collections. This is particularly important for the pictorial and audio records since many of these collections require further cataloguing. As editor, I apologise in advance for any errors or inconsistencies in this volume.

Although we operate a free postal enquiry service, because of the large number of enquiries there may be some delay in our reply. We regret that we are unable to undertake detailed research. We therefore recommend that if possible readers make a personal visit to undertake research, but a list of freelance researchers is available upon request. Photocopying facilities are available for a small charge, but we reserve the right to refuse to reproduce any fragile or prohibited material. We also operate a photographic service, but as orders are processed in-house, there is a considerable waiting time.

Acknowledgements

The production of this guide has been a team effort, and the editor would like to acknowledge all members of the Archives Department for their contribution. In particular, I would like to thank Helen Threlfall for the time-consuming task of indexing both volumes; David Le Mare, Eileen Edwards, Margaret Evans and Anita Glynn for their work on numerous chapters; and Karen Howard and John Moore for their contributions to Vol. II chapters 9 and 12, respectively. Michael Stammers, Keeper of Merseyside Maritime Museum, has contributed in innumerable ways, but especially by compiling some of the introductions and entries, assisting with proofreading, and negotiating publication. Much of the groundwork for this volume was undertaken by J. Gordon Read, the former Curator of Archives. I would like to thank Tony Tibbles, Curator of Maritime History, for writing the introduction to the slavery chapter, and also for assistance in finding a cover illustration. Professor Lewis R. Fischer of Memorial University of Newfoundland has provided invaluable advice and support throughout, and Margaret Gulliver efficiently performed a number of tasks related to formatting and lay-out. Members of the Liverpool Nautical Research Society helped with the research for the merchant's chapter. I would like to express my gratitude to the Trustees of the National Museums and Galleries on Merseyside and the International Maritime Economic History Association for publishing this volume. Finally, I would like to thank Lynda Rea for typing the final manuscript and for cheerfully suffering the many revisions along the way.

Dawn Littler, BA, DAA
Curator of Maritime Archives
1999

Notes on the Editor

Dawn Littler took a first degree in history from Chester College and a postgraduate diploma in archive administration at the University College of North Wales, Bangor, and has been Curator of Maritime Archives at Merseyside Maritime Museum since 1992. She is a member of the Council of the Liverpool Nautical Research Society; the Academic Board of the Centre for Port and Maritime History, a joint initiative of NMGM and the University of Liverpool; and the Council of the Historic Society of Lancashire and Cheshire.

List of Illustrations

CHAPTER 1

MERCHANTS, SHIP BROKERS AND AGENTS, STEVEDORING AND WAREHOUSING COMPANIES

Merchants

Merchants played a vital role in the successful development of Liverpool in the eighteenth century. It was usual at this time for merchants to deal in a wide range of commodities and trading areas, and they were often involved in other business interests such as insurance, banking and brokerage, and shipowning and shipbuilding. For example, Bryan Blundell, was a master mariner and merchant engaged mainly in the transatlantic trade and the firm of T. & J. Brocklebank, were merchants as well as shipowners and shipbuilders until 1864. Other Liverpool merchant companies which also engaged in shipowning include John Holt, in trade with West Africa, and Sandbach, Tinne, whose interests included West Indian sugar plantations, shipowning, trade in rice, transportation of coolies from India and the sale of sugar in the United Kingdom.

From about 1800 merchants in Liverpool began to specialise in one particular area or commodity, the result of the increase in the volume of trade and the rising complexity of commercial mechanisms. Records of specialist merchants in Liverpool, held at the Maritime Archives & Library, include those of William Gardner & Co., provision merchants, and William Lowe (Grain) Ltd.

The records of merchants held in the Merseyside Maritime Museum are a varied sample of the mercantile activities undertaken in Liverpool and the particular archives described in this chapter are supplemented by the shipping company collections such as those of T. & J. Brocklebank and John Holt (see Vol. I, chap. 4). There is also important material to be found in the archives of families who were engaged in mercantile trade, such as the Cropper, Crosbie-Oates and Earle families (see Vol. II, chap. 6). In addition, the records of the various trade associations (see Vol. I, chap. 3) and those of the port authority, the Mersey Docks & Harbour Board (see Vol. I, chap. 2) contain much relevant material.

Ship Brokers and Agents

Ship brokers and agents can be best described as the middlemen of maritime commerce. Their work usually comprised of the bringing of a buyer and seller of goods and services together in return for a commission (which was usually a percentage of the agreed selling price). Ship brokers would arrange for the sale or purchase of ships on behalf of their clients, for example, Kellock & Co. of Liverpool and London (archives in the National Maritime Museum) operated a ship auction room in Water Street, Liverpool. Shipbroking could also involve the arranging of cargo for vessels, the firm of Gracie, Beazley & Co., as well as operating their own vessels to Australia and New Zealand, acted as loading brokers for other lines, including the White Star Line and Shaw Savill & Albion, on that route.

Many examples of charter parties, or legal agreements, for the hire of vessels can be found in the archives of the shipbroking firm of W.H. Stott & Co. who, as well as acting as agent to many important Liverpool merchants, branched into shipowning in 1876. The work of ship's agent was often closely linked to broking, with the agent representing the visiting ship owners' interest while his ship was in port, ensuring that such administrative routines as customs, port dues, crew's provisions, etc., were carried out as well as cargo handling services and repairs.

Stevedoring and Warehousing Companies

The term stevedoring has become synonymous with all the work of loading and unloading cargoes. However, in reality this operation is divided into actual *stevedoring*, the loading and unloading on board the ship, and *porterage*, the documenting, stacking and moving of goods on the quayside and in the transit sheds. Master stevedores and master porters were licensed by the Mersey Docks & Harbour Board, and as a result its archives, together with those of the National Dock Labour Board and the Port Employers' Association, contain much useful material on this subject.

Warehousing records are also found in various archives, because the warehousing capacity of the port was divided between the Mersey Docks & Harbour Board's own premises such as the Albert Dock and Stanley Warehouses, and private owners elsewhere in the dockside or nearby, such as Henry Diaper who, at one time, occupied part of Albert Dock. Towards the end of the nineteenth century the provision of warehousing became increasingly specialised with the setting up of specialist warehouses for the cold storage of commodities, such as meat, or the bulk storage of grain. The most important archive in this respect is that of the Liverpool Warehousing Co. which was the largest of its kind in Britain. Its principal commodity was cotton. Also of importance is the archive of the Liverpool Grain Storage & Transit Co., formed in 1883.

Very little published work exists on the companies whose records are described in this chapter. Much of the background research for this section has been undertaken by members of the Liverpool Nautical Research Society. However, many details about these companies, many now defunct, still remain elusive. The titles in the following introductory bibliography contain helpful information on the main areas, and much reference and archive material can also be found at the Liverpool City Record Office.

References

Anon. *The Ambassador of Commerce, Supplement to the Liverpool Daily Post & Mercury.* 7 July 1924.

Anon. *The House of Diaper 1860-1960.* Liverpool, 1960.

Baines, T. *History of Commerce and Town of Liverpool.* London, 1852.

Hyde, F.E. *Liverpool and the Mersey: The Development of a Port 1700-1970.* Newton Abbot, 1971.

Parkinson, C. Northcote. *The Rise of the Port of Liverpool.* Liverpool, 1952.

Taplin, E.L. *Liverpool Docks and Seamen 1870-1890.* Hull, 1974.

Thornton, R.H. *British Shipping.* Cambridge, 1945.

Todd, J.A. *The Shipping World.* London, 1929.

Williams, D.M. "Liverpool Merchants and the Cotton Trade 1820-1850." In J.R. Harris (ed.) *Liverpool and Merseyside, Essays in the Economics and Social History of the Port and its Hinterland.* London, 1969.

Records

Merchants

Anonymous Eighteenth-Century Merchant

Account book of an unidentified Liverpool merchant dealing in trade in sugar, tobacco, etc., with the West Indies. Deposited on loan by the Mercer's Co., London.

DX/653   1717-1727   1 Volume

Bryan Blundell (d. 1756)

Bryan Blundell was a merchant and master mariner operating mainly in the transatlantic trade in the late seventeenth and early eighteenth centuries. He founded the charity school, the Blue Coat Hospital in Liverpool in 1708. In his journal for the years 1686-1709 and illustrated with sketches of his ships, he recorded details of his trading activities and voyages. The original journal is held in the Lancashire Record Office, but a microfilm copy is available in the Maritime Archives & Library.

Microfilm Collection   1686-1709   1 Item

R.R. Douglas Ltd.

R.R. Douglas Ltd. were merchants and importers, and the surviving documents and papers cover the dates 1923-1965. Their offices for much of this time were at 11 Dale Street. Among the commodities handled were beeswax, coffee, palm oil, spices and limestone. These archives were rescued from their offices in the old Liverpool Stock Exchange in 1975, just before it was demolished.

Records

Financial

Ledgers, 1927-1936.
Correspondence including insurance and claims, 1931-1944.

Operations

Bills of lading, 1940-1947.
Cargo correspondence including claims, 1936-1939.

Correspondence

General correspondence, 1923-1946.
B/DO   1923-1965   54 Boxes

Everitt & Co., Ltd.

Everitt & Co., Ltd. of Tithebarn Street, Liverpool, was founded by Racster Everitt in 1878, to trade in the steel and metallurgical industry. The firm specialised in the import and export of minerals, chemicals, metals and alloys. In 1912 he was joined by G.E. Lewis and F.W. Dingwall who became partners in the firm, and in 1920 they were joined by J.E. White. It was through the efforts of F.W. Dingwall and J.E. White that a grinding mill in Bootle was opened to crush ore which was used by the glass bottling and battery trades. An important part of the business was with the steel and tinplate industry. Everitt's association with the various British steel works enabled them to introduce supplies of Ferro Alloys imported from Norway. In the past one hundred years, Everitt & Co. has continually added new products to its merchanting list and continues to trade in the metallurgical industry today.

Records

Brief history of Everitt & Co., Ltd., 1878-1978.
Passport of Racster Everitt (to Turkey, Georgia), 1884-1899.

Profile of Everitt & Co., Ltd., c.1980.
DX/675   1878-c.1980   3 Items

Fraser, Trenholm & Co.

This unique collection consists of correspondence and other documents of Fraser, Trenholm & Co., of 10 Rumford Place, Liverpool (1860-1866), and of Prioleau & Co., London (1867-1877). During the American Civil War (1861-1865) Fraser, Trenholm was a prominent commercial house in Liverpool. The firm's senior partner, Charles Kuhn Prioleau, was a naturalised Englishman, who had been brought up in Charleston, South Carolina, where most of his family still lived. It was the English branch of Fraser, Trenholm & Co., based in Charleston whose senior partner, George A. Trenholm, became Secretary to the Confederate States Treasury in 1864. The Liverpool firm made an enormous contribution to the war effort of the South, acting as banker to the Confederate Government and financing the supply of armaments in return for cotton.

Fraser, Trenholm & Co. also participated in blockade running, organising the building on the Mersey of ships such as the commerce-destroyer, *Alabama*, assisted in the floating of Confederate loans, and generally encouraged support in Europe for the South. The collection provides a unique insight into these activities. Many of the major protagonists in the Civil War are mentioned in the letter books and correspondence. The firm's role in the reconstruction of the South and involvement in world trade, especially in armaments, is also revealed.

Of the fourteen letter books in the collection c.1860-1877, the first, produced in Liverpool between 1862 and 1865, is by far the most important. It contains the correspondence of C.K. Prioleau with leading Confederates, references to blockade running and to other aspects of the war and business. Equally important are more than one hundred loose autograph letters which were sent to Prioleau between 1860-1869. These contain crucial correspondence with G.A. Trenholm, J.D. Bulloch (agent for the Confederate Navy), Major Caleb Huse (principal Confederate Army purchasing officer in Europe) and General C.J. McRae (C.S.A. Treasury agent in Europe). Personal correspondence of C.K. Prioleau includes letters from his wife, Mary, and many from civilians living in the South whose lives were being affected by the course of the war, including eye-witness accounts of the shelling of Charleston. There are also items relating to work undertaken by the Merseyside firms of Jones, Quiggin & Co. (Shipbuilders) and Fawcett, Preston & Co. (Engineers), the surviving archives of which are also held by the Archives Department of the Merseyside Maritime Museum (see Vol. II, chap. 5).

Records

200 letters to C.K. Prioleau, many from key characters in the Confederate States, with a few photographs. Subjects include blockade-running vessels, the raising of loans, ammunition and details of battles, etc., 1860-1869.
Letters and telegrams sent to/from C.K. Prioleau. Wide variety of subjects, over 600 documents, 1870-1876.
Letters re: mainly financial matters, cheque book stubs, 1871-1877.
Specifications for vessels including steel screw steamer *Phantom* (Fawcett, Preston & Co., Liverpool), 1862 and paddlesteamers *Rosine* and *Ruby* (Jones, Quiggin & Co., Liverpool), 1864-1867.
Drawing of proposed alterations to *Colonel Lamb* (Jones, Quiggin & Co.), 1864.
Correspondence re: "small arms," and tracings of torpedoes, 1862-1875.
Assorted bills, receipts and accounts re: cotton, turpentine and military stores, etc., 1869-1875.
Legal documents re: cases held in the New York Supreme Court, the Admiralty and Chancery Courts. Various subjects including the purchase of cotton, ownership of vessels, and Fraser, Trenholm's role as financial agent to the Confederate Government, 1862-1870.
Printed Parliamentary papers including extracts from correspondence with the U.S. Government re: the blockade and with the Customs Commissioners re: *Alabama*, 1861-1864.
Printed list of members of the Southern Independence Association, Manchester, 1862.
Telegram codebook belonging to G.A. Trenholm and lists of trade codes, c.1870.
Letter books of Charles Kuhn Prioleau with various correspondents, subjects include cotton, the *Alabama* and other vessels, blockade-running, Confederate loans, etc., 1862-1877.
(N.B. The first letter book, 1862-1865, is available on microfilm aperture cards.)
Letter books of J.R. Hamilton (Prioleau & Co.), 1868-1874 (3 volumes).
Account book sales no. 1, Prioleau & Co., 1869-1876.
B/FT   1860-1877   13 Boxes & 1 Roll

Reference

Nepveux, Ethel T.S. *George Alfred Trenholm & the Company that Went to War, 1861-1865*. Charleston, SC, 1973.

William Gardner & Co.

William Gardner & Co., provision merchants, were founder members of the Liverpool Provision Trade Association. This resulted in forty-three volumes of the firm's provision trade circulars surviving in the archives of the Provision Trade Association (see Vol. I, chap. 3). These records are an important source of information for the study of Liverpool trade during the latter half of the nineteenth century. These records are available *strictly by appointment only*.

Records

Provision trade circulars, incomplete run, 1847-1896.
B/WG   1847-1896   2 Boxes, 24 Volumes

Hampshire, Birrell & Hobbs

Hampshire, Birrell & Hobbs of 47 Naylor Street, Liverpool, were fish importers and exporters, and the firm was formed when Hampshire, Hobbs and Birrell amalgamated in 1927 to form Hampshire, Birrell & Co. The firm's subscribers were Louis Zollner, Consul for Denmark and Iceland, and Thorlakur Sigurasson from Newcastle-upon-Tyne. The firm operated from Liverpool, Hull, Grimsby, Aberdeen and Fleetwood. The records relate to various incarnations of the firm throughout its history, and to various fishing associations in which they were involved.

Records

Anglo-Newfoundland Fish Exporting Co., Ltd.

Articles of company, liquidators accounts, minute book, letter from directors to shareholders re: company's difficulties, notice of extraordinary general meeting re: winding up of company, 1900-1909.

A. & D. Birrell & Co., Ltd.

Letter re: new company, profit and loss sheet and balance sheet, financial record of company (also for Hampshire Hobbs Co.), private ledger, 1907-1918.

Hampshire Hobbs & Co.

Article of association and memorandum, report of company, 1909-1910.

Hampshire Birrell & Co. (Fish Exporters) Ltd.

Article of association, correspondence, financial records, statistics, 1917-1958.

Hampshire Hobb & Co., A. & D. Birrell

Balance sheet, 1911-1918.

Association of British Salted Fish Curers & Exporters

Proposal for association, minutes of meeting, correspondence, letterhead of association, notes to be raised with Sea Fish Commission, 1934-1959.

Bergen International Conference of Saltfish & Klipfish Exporters

Press release for conference, minutes of meeting, 1946.

International Salt Fish Association

Correspondence re: establishment of association, list of delegates and observers for conference, 1948.

Robert Isaac Ltd.

Letterhead, billhead, 1950s.

Miscellaneous

Fish importers notebook (photocopy), tender for fish, poultry, etc., from City of Liverpool Hospitals and Port Health Committee, Ministry of Food re: export of fish and export licences, fresh food ledger, White Fish Authority, UK, fish trade figures, 1885-1957.

DX/485   1900-1957   64 Items

H.C. Hawley & Co.

H.C. Hawley & Co. of Cleveland Square, Liverpool, was a firm of merchants and exporters in ceramics, glassware and cutlery, trading with West Africa. H.C. Hawley was founded in 1850, and the Pennington family, descendants of the local pottery dynasty, also joined the firm, P.S. Pennington being the last surviving partner. The business was wound up following his death in 1979. These records are available *strictly by appointment only*.

Records

Price lists (emphasis on West Africa trade), 1872-c.1914.
Whiston & Wigan Coal Co. reports and accounts, c.1877-1895.
Summaries, 1888-1923.
Account books, 1889-c.1970.
Ledgers, 1907-1928.
Wages books, 1916-1930.
Balance sheets, 1923-1943.

Partnership articles, 1923.
Tenancy agreements, 1924.
Profit and loss accounts, 1925-1951.
Catalogues, c.1930-1960.
Modern operational records, c.1960-1980.
Historical notes re: firm's history and miscellaneous local historical items, c.1832-1950.
B/HA   c.1832-1980   64 Boxes

William Lowe & Sons (Grain) Ltd.

William Lowe & Sons (Grain) Ltd., were grain merchants operating from premises in Fenwick Street, Liverpool, from c.1848. These records are available *strictly by appointment only.*

Records

Letter books, c.1851-1897.
Balance book, 1848-1934.
Profit and loss account, 1899-1918.
Ledgers, 1920-1935.
Journals, 1900-1957.
Customer's character book, c.1880.
DX/190/2   1848-1957   2 Boxes

Rankin, Gilmour & Co.

The merchant house of Rankin, Gilmour & Co., was founded by members of the Rankin and Gilmour families from Mearns, near Glasgow. The parent firm was Pollock, Gilmour, founded in Glasgow in 1804, importing timber and other products from the Baltic and later from Canada. Robert Rankin (I), a partner in the parent firm, set up the Liverpool house in 1838, developing it from an existing agency.

The Liverpool house developed a large business in cotton as well as timber, and engaged in agency, banking for colonial clients, and shipowning. Robert Rankin (II) was, like his senior namesake, a member of the Mersey Docks & Harbour Board, and chairman of PSNC at a time of financial crisis in 1890-1898. Sister houses in the USA at New Orleans and Mobile, Alabama, were opened in c.1843 and 1854, respectively, developing out of the Liverpool firm. However, both houses had to close because of the American Civil War in 1862.

In 1861 John Rankin, a member of the Canadian branch of the family, joined the Liverpool house, becoming chairman in 1906. He was also involved in the MDHB, PSNC, and was chairman of the Bank of Liverpool, Lloyd's

Registry of Shipping (Liverpool), and a member of the Council of Liverpool University. A number of his letters survive in the Danson archives (see Vol. II, chap. 6). He died in 1928. The shipping operation of the firm appears to have ceased about 1930.

Record

Account book containing details of the firm's stock, profit and loss accounts, interest accounts and commission due on cargoes. Also individual ships value accounts and cargo accounts for each company, c.1867-1873.
DX/726   c.1867-1873   1 Volume

Reference

Rankin, J. *A History of Our Firm – Being Some Account of the Firm of Pollock, Gilmour & Co. and its Offshoots and Connections, 1804-1920.* Liverpool, 1921.

Sandbach, Tinne & Co.

Sandbach, Tinne & Co. was founded in 1782 in Demerara (now part of Guyana), by James McInvoy as shipowners trading in sugar, coffee, molasses, rum and also *coolies*. In 1790 the company was joined by George Robertson, Charles Parker and Samuel Sandbach and became known as McInvoy, Sandbach & Co. From 1813 the company's headquarters were in Liverpool, and Samuel Sandbach, Mayor of Liverpool in 1831, appointed P.F. Tinne, who had been Governor's Secretary in Demerara under Dutch rule, as his partner in England. Although the company passed through a number of name changes, Sandbach, Tinne & Co. is the name by which the company is generally known. Branches of the company were opened in Glasgow (briefly), Montréal (West India Co.) and Trinidad. The Maritime Archives & Library has recently acquired the records of the more recent subsidiary companies.

Records

Correspondence, business letters to Samuel Sandbach from James McInvoy and Charles D. Parker re: administration, management, investment and purchase of sugar plantations. Others re: sugar and coffee cargoes, conditions of *coolies* and other labourers.
Letters from James Baines (Black Ball Line) re: shipments of *coolies*.
Plantation managers re: ships owned by the company, 1804-1908.
Agreements of partnership and sale of plantations, 1822-1891.
Deeds for land and property in Aigburth, Liverpool, 1825-1916.
Financial, profit and loss account (McInvoy Parker & Co.), balance sheets,

accounts of the proprietors of plantations, 1827-1885.

Plans, tracing plan re: abandoned land in Demerara, sketch of tanks at the Leonora plantation and coloured diagram at Carnels Ida plantation, 1767-1894.

Photographs of Demerara railway, Sandbach, Parker building at Georgetown, Guyana, sugar plantations and refinery, c.1890-c.1959.

Minute book (rough) with notes on financial matters and trading results of the West India Co., 1907-1948.

D/B/176/A-C   1767-c.1959   3 Boxes

Letter to Samuel Sandbach, McInroy, Parker & Co., from William McBean, McInroy, Sandbach & McBean Demerary [sic.] re: Negroes for Plantation Caledonia.

SAS/37A/1/3   1808   1 Item

Letters to Sandbach, Tinne & Co., from various business correspondents.

B/STI   1809-1876   14 Items

Recent Accrual

Sandbach, Tinne & Co.

Ledger of typed copied letters re: George Robertson writing from Granada re: new partners, health and family matters. Contract between George Robertson and Charles Parker. Sugar brokers, selling of sugar, staff, shareholders, 1790-1912.

Minute book of executors of Charles and Anne Parker with copy of their marriage settlement, 1868-1896.

Letter book re: business correspondence, 1870-1877.

Directors minute book, 1938-1964.

Ledgers re: taxation, accounts, management fees, profit and losses, 1938-1969.

Book of share certificates, 1956-1972.

Sandbach, Parker & Co.

Register of directors, members, transfers and charges, 1937-1944.

Directors minute books, 1959-1980.

Accounts, 1962-1974.

Demerara Co., Ltd.

Directors minute books, 1960-1976.

Accounts including papers re: Demerara Investment Trust in liquidation and Demerara Developments Co., Ltd. in liquidation, 1953-1981.

Registers of members, share capitals and debenture interests, c.1916-1978.

Ledger of company holdings, 1960-1974.
Files re: taxation notes, articles of association, business correspondence, annual general minutes, pensions, 1969-1978.

Caribbean Properties Ltd.

Memorandum and articles of association, 1957.

Diamond Rum Co., Ltd.

Minute book, 1969-1980.
Share register, 1969-1975.

Demerara Co. (Stocks) Ltd.

Directors minute book, 1958-1964.

Caribbean Distillers Ltd.

Directors minute book, including minutes of extraordinary general meeting re: winding up of the company, 1968-1981.
Register of members, 1958-1981.
Accounts, 1971-1972.
Agreements, 1971-1972.
Sales invoices for barrels of rum, 1971-1972.
Correspondence re: mortgage securities, rum prospects, company liquidation, Scottish & Newcastle Breweries Ltd., interest in part purchase of Caribbean Distillers Ltd., 1971-1979.
D/SAN   c.1790-c.1981   11 Boxes

Stitt Brothers

This firm of iron, and later, cotton merchants was extremely well known in its time. Founded as Acraman & Stitt in about 1824, it developed into a number of areas, including ship owning, stock broking, various forms of metal merchanting, chain cable manufacture, naval architecture and marine consultancy, investing its capital largely in marine insurance.

Records

Business correspondence and accounts referring to ships *Sutley, Carnatic* and *Canada*, new offices in Water Street, and the purchase of pig iron, c.1843-1863.
Personal correspondence (with some business), 1845-1860.
Correspondence with American agents, Bell & Mead, 1856-1861.

Investment papers, 1865-1888.

Papers re: partnership of J.C. Stitt and W.R. McKaig, naval architects and consulting engineers, including accounts, reports, ships surveys, agreements, legal papers, patent for improvement in steam generators of the tubular type, 1884.

Personal, estate and investment papers, 1873-1893.

Cash and letter books, minutes of Trustees of estate of J.J. Stitt and Samuel Stitt, Jr., 1854-1935.

D/B/115/B/1-4   1845-1935   4 Boxes

Daniel Williams

Daniel Williams (fl. c.1850) was involved in shipping animal products (salted hides, horsehair and meat) from South America to Liverpool. The surviving material is predominantly business correspondence written from Rio de Janeiro, Barcelona, London, Montevideo and Cadiz, relating to the shipping of outward cargoes of salt, coal and ironmongery from Liverpool, and the import of animal products. Although personal correspondence is limited, some details of family affairs, South American politics and civil unrest, may also be found.

Records

408 letters to Daniel Williams from various correspondents, the majority are written in English, but fifty are in Spanish and nine in French (summary transcripts available).

DB/175   1851-1876   1 Box

Williamson, Milligan & Co.

This firm of merchants was established in Liverpool by immigrant Scots and traded with South America, mostly with Argentina and Uruguay. The senior partner, John Williamson, endowed the Williamson Art Gallery in Birkenhead. His brother, Stephen, was a partner in Balfour, Williamson & Co., founded in 1851 in Liverpool, as merchants trading with Chile. Balfour Williamson ceased trading in Liverpool in the 1930s, but still operates from offices in London. Its records are held in the University College, London, and a list is available in the Maritime Archives & Library. The archives of Williamson, Milligan do not appear to have survived, except for the few documents described below. This collection is available *strictly by appointment only*.

Records

Letters to John Williamson from Scotland, including three from his uncle in Fife, re: personal and business affairs, including John Williamson starting work with his brother Stephen in Liverpool in 1849, 1847-1851.
Letters to John Williamson, c/o H.C. Smith & Co., Liverpool (South American merchants) from Stephen Williamson at New York and Valparaiso, re: business of the firm, 1851-1853.
Letter of introduction re: John Williamson from H.C. Smith & Co., Liverpool, to Messrs. Smith Brothers & Co., Montevideo, and letter to John Williamson, c/o H.C. Smith & Co., Liverpool, from Smith, Buenos Aires, 1852-1853.
Shipbuilding agreement John Reid & Co., Port Glasgow, and Williamson, Milligan & Co., Liverpool, for a four-masted steel sailing ship, 1886.
DB/108D   1846-1886   1 File

Ships Brokers and Agents

Bahr, Behrend & Co.

Bahr, Behrend & Co. was founded in 1793, and has remained both a private partnership and a family business, with a member of the fifth generation now being in the partnership. Since the end of World War II, it has increased its loading-brokerage activities considerably. By 1957 in addition to its traditional trade to West Sweden, the firm also loaded vessels to India and Pakistan, to the West Indies, to the Gulf ports of North America and to the Canary Islands. With branch offices at one time in Manchester, Bradford, Hanley and Sheffield, it still has an extensive organisation for freight-canvassing today. Its London office was established in 1913.

The founder of the firm was a Dane, Lorenz Hanson who, in 1793, became Danish Consul. By 1800 he was also Swedish Consul. In 1814 he took Charles Louis Bahr of Hanover into partnership, and in 1835 David Behrend, another Hanoverian, joined the firm. Throughout the nineteenth century the firm were brokers for ships sailing to many European and Mediterranean ports.

Unfortunately, the 1941 Blitz destroyed many of the firm's records. However, Arthur Behrend, a partner since 1924, and an accomplished writer, wrote the firm's history largely from oral sources. *Portrait of a Family Firm* (privately printed, Liverpool, 1970) conveys a vivid picture of nineteenth and twentieth century shipping practices. The Maritime Archives & Library holds a copy autographed by the author.

Records

Statement of average for the sailing vessel, *C B Pedersen*, 1930.
Legal papers re: Liverpool and London offices, 1941-1947.

Financial records including ledgers and balance sheets, 1935-1973.
Register of charter parties, 1939-1954.
Chartering and commission book, 1941-1969.
Position book no. 2 (West Indies) with details of loading and unloading cargo, 1960-1966.
Rate book, India, Ceylon and Burma conference, 1944.
File, re: freight rates, India and Pakistan, 1963.
Publicity ephemera, 1944-1982.
Staff pension reports, 1948.
Cricket club records, 1949-1962.
Diary of Royal Swedish Vice-Consulate at Liverpool, 1946-1980.
Miscellaneous export and trading ephemera, 1957-1966.
B/BB   1930-1980   5 Boxes, 2 Volumes

Reference

Behrend, A. *Portrait of a Family Firm: Bahr Behrend & Company, 1793-1945.*
    Liverpool, 1970.

James Chambers & Co., Ltd. and S.C. Chambers & Co., Ltd.

James Chambers began his career as a ship broker in Liverpool, c.1850. He developed an interest in shipowning when his sister, Annie, married an ambitious young shipowner called Henry Threlfall Wilson, who had recently founded the White Star Line with his partner, John Pilkington. James Chambers became first a shareholder, and in 1856 a partner, and the firm's style changed to Pilkington, Wilson and Chambers. However, in December of that year, Pilkington retired to manage his family's cotton-broking business, and the firm became known as Wilson & Chambers.

Henry Wilson proved a go-ahead but reckless partner, ordering bigger and faster sailing ships for the service to Australia. In 1865, Wilson and Chambers founded the Lancaster Shipowners' Co., Ltd. (see Vol. I, chap. 4). However, his partner's profligacy became a matter of concern to Chambers and he retired from the board of the White Star Line in December 1865. The collapse of the Royal Bank of Liverpool in 1867 also led to the bankruptcy of the White Star Line. With debts of £500,000, its ships were sold, and the name, trade and goodwill of the line sold to Thomas Henry Ismay for £1,000 (see Vol. I, chap. 4). James Chambers had by this time resumed trading under his old style, James Chambers & Co., but still remained on the board of the Lancaster Shipowners' Co., Ltd., and continued to manage its fleet. The firm moved to new premises at Nos. 2 and 5 King Street where it would remain for the next seventy-four years. Henry Wilson joined the firm as manager until his death in 1869 at the age of forty-four.

In 1876, James Chambers adopted the convention of naming his ships after English castles. This aroused the ire of Donald Currie, who had been using a similar convention for his Castle Line ships for some years. A compromise was reached where Currie was to name his ships after castles found south of a line drawn between the Wash and the Mersey, and those north of Hadrian's Wall, while Chambers was allotted those in between. After James Chambers' death in 1877, his eldest son Walter James Chambers, took control of the company. In 1887 the firm of S.C. Chambers & Co., Ltd., Ship brokers, was established under the chairmanship of James Chambers' younger son, Samuel.

In 1896 the Lancaster Shipowners' Co. was re-registered under the style of the Lancashire Shipping Co., Ltd., and after heavy losses during the World War II, its last four ships were sold in 1943. Chambers continued to manage three on behalf of the Ministry of War Transport. In 1946, James Chambers & Co., Ltd. ceased trading, but the brokering firm of S.C. Chambers & Co., Ltd. continued to flourish. In 1958, the brothers Kenneth and Robert Monroe of Kyle Shipping Co., Ltd. purchased a controlling interest, but in 1971 the Charente Steamship Co., Ltd. (Thos. & Jas. Harrison Ltd., managers) acquired forty percent of the shares, increasing their holding to fifty-one percent in 1985. Denholms of Glasgow own the remaining equity. Today S.C. Chambers & Co., Ltd., with offices at No. 1 Water Street, Liverpool, prospers as a firm of ship brokers specialising in the sale and purchase of ships of all types.

Records

S.C. Chambers, shipbroking accounts, 1897-1944.
Ledger, 1939-1941.
(Acquired as part of the Monroe collection).
D/MON   1897-1944   3 Volumes

Gracie, Beazley & Co.

Though the company assumed its name in 1882 when Edwin A. Beazley joined William Gracie, it traces its origins back to 1845 when it traded under the name of Edmund Thompson & Co., in whose service William Gracie entered as an apprentice in 1859. James Beazley founded the Beazley Line in 1845 owning twenty eight sailing ships between 1849 and 1875, making regular sailings from Liverpool to Australia and New Zealand. In 1864 he founded and managed the British Shipowners' Co., extending crossings to San Francisco and South America. In 1866 Edmund Thompson & Co., was renamed Thompson, May & Co., becoming Thompson, Gracie & Co., on the admission of William Gracie as partner in 1870, and subsequently renamed William Gracie & Co. Gracie, Beazley & Co., acted as loading brokers for the service of other lines to Australia and New Zealand, including White Star Line, Shaw Savill & Albion, Tyser Line Ltd., and Manchester Australia Shipping Co.

Records

Two volumes of sailing notices for steam and sailing vessels mainly to Australia and New Zealand, but including some to South America, including vessels of the White Star Line, Shaw Savill & Albion and other lines. Also plans of the crew and passenger accommodation on board steamships *Taramung* and *Konoowarra*, 1880-1925.
Letter book (wet copy), 1889-1904.
Newscuttings book with references to Captain A. Enwright of the Black Ball Line, and the wreck of the sailing ship *Dalgonar* in the South Pacific (1914), 1904-1922.
Book of hand-written freight charges from Liverpool to Australia, 1925-1934.
Newscuttings book with speeches on international maritime issues, by J.G.B. Beazley, M.C., T.D., as chairman of the Liverpool Steamship Owners' Association, 1933-1937.
B/GBE   1880-1937   3 Boxes

Hull, Blyth & Co., Ltd.

The firm of Hull, Blyth & Co., Ltd. was founded by E.C.P. Hull in 1875 as a coal exporting business. In 1877 he was joined by W.M. Blyth. The firm specialised in supplying bunker coal to depots at ports abroad, a vital service for steamship owners. By 1910 the firm had spread to Cardiff, West Hartlepool, Newcastle-upon-Tyne and Glasgow and had depots in the Canary Islands, Cape Verde Islands, Angola, Port Said, Colombo and St. Lucia. As British agents for local suppliers, Hull, Blyth & Co., Ltd. were able to contract for supplies at over forty ports world-wide.

In 1919 the firm became incorporated and a part of the Royal Mail Group. By this time the firm had sixteen subsidiary companies in many parts of the world. As a result of the depression in the 1930s, the firm was reconstructed under a new chairman, Frank Charlton, formerly chairman of Cunard. In 1935, William Cory & Sons acquired a large number of shares, along with Houlder Lines and Kaye, Son & Co. The company was absorbed into Ocean Cory, a subsidiary of Ocean Transport & Trading in 1978, and its records are to be found in the Ocean archive (see Vol. I, chap. 4).

Records

Secretarial

AGM minutes, 1919-1978.
Director's attendance book, agenda book and minute books, 1894-1978.
Managers' and AGM minute book (Port Said), 1910-1949.

Managers' minute book (Colombo), 1910-1948.
Articles of association, 1919.
Certificate of incorporation, reduction of capital and change of name, 1909-1949.
Agreements, 1893-1928.

Management

Managing director's reports, Angola, 1967-1972.

Investment

Register of members, share register, etc., 1919-1956.
Share certificates, 1919-1938.

Financial

Ledgers, 1913-1964.
Journals, 1947-1970.
Private journal, 1920-1963.
Cash book, 1894-1915.

Staff

Salary records, 1924-1946.
Wages books, 1939-1944.
OA/3001-3065   c.1894-1978   c.60 Items

McDiarmid, Greenshields & Co.

This firm of ship brokers managed the antecedents of the Canadian Freight
Secretariat and a number of other Conferences and Associations. In 1983, the
Canadian Freight Secretariat's archive absorbed the firm's archives and all
references will therefore be found under the entry for the Secretariat (see Vol. I,
chap. 3).

Monroe Bros. Co., Ltd. & Kyle Shipping Co., Ltd.

The Monroe family's first involvement in shipowning was in 1897 when William
Monroe bought the iron steamer *Vindomora* for shipping coal from South Wales.
In 1912 his cousin Kenneth Monroe, in association with two others, purchased the
steamer *Blairmore* (later *Ballater*), and began buying coal direct from the
collieries for export. Kenneth joined the army in World War I and in 1917 the
company's coasters were sold to J.C. Gould. In 1919, Kenneth set up Monroe
Shipping Co., Ltd., bought nine small coasters from J.S. Monks of Liverpool,

and opened an office at 30 Brunswick Street, Liverpool. In 1920 he was joined by his two brothers, Robert and William. Ships were registered under various company names, and the name of Monroe Shipping was wound up in 1925. In 1931 Monroe Bros. Co., Ltd. was formed and became the predominant registered company. By 1936 Monroe Bros. Co., Ltd. transferred all the steamers under their management to Kyle Shipping Co., Ltd. and all new acquisitions had the prefix "Kyle" in their names.

Between 1939 and 1944 the three brothers died, and the business was run for the following two years by Mrs. Ann Monroe, assisted by manager Hector Oliphant. In 1946 her son, Kenneth, was demobilised from the Royal Navy and took over the reins, to be joined in 1954 by his brother, Robert. This began a change in the 1950s and 1960s to larger vessels and increased continental and transatlantic trade using motor ships. In 1969 the Kyle Shipping Co., Ltd.'s last vessel was sold to the Stephenson Clarke Group and in the same year the Monroe Brothers activated the St. Vincent Shipping Co., Ltd., and became minor shareholders and managers of two deep-sea ships. This company was eventually wound up in January 1979 but with the Monroes remaining as ship brokers, managers and shipowners' advisers based in Old Hall Street, Liverpool (see also James Chambers & Co., Ltd.).

Records

Log books, deck and chief officers log books of the *Ana Ranata, Helen Miller* and *Susan Miller*, 1969-1978.
Maintenance records for the *Helen Miller*, 1947-1979.
General journal of Kyle Shipping Co., 1941-1967.
Monroe Bros. Ledger, 1939-1941.
Accounts ledger, 1930-1933.
Accounts ledger, 2 volumes, 1958-1959, 1962-1964.
Correspondence files, 1977-1979.
S.C. Chambers, ship brokers account books, 2 volumes, 1897-1912, 1914-1944.
Plans of vessels including the *Kylebute* and *Kylecroft*, c.1940-1950s.
B/MON   1897-1979   23 Boxes, 4 Volumes

Reference

Fenton, R.S. *Monroe Brothers Shipowners, World Ship Soc. Monograph No. 5.* 1982.

W.H. Stott & Co.

W.H. Stott was born in 1835 into a family active in several aspects of port services. He was apprenticed to the Liverpool shipbroking firm of Smith,

Edwards & Co., and in 1856 he joined Bahr Behrend & Co. as a chartering clerk. In 1860 he re-joined Smith, Edwards & Co. which, shortly after, took the title Allen & Edwards. He became a partner in that firm in 1862 and the name of the firm was altered to Edwards, Stott & Co.

In 1866 the firm of W.H. Stott & Co. was established, obtained the sole agency for several important merchants, and in 1876 branched into shipowning with two sailing vessels. They acquired their first steamer in 1886. About twelve vessels were owned over the next thirty years employed in trade between the Mersey and Baltic ports. In 1894 one of their vessels, the *Neva*, was the first vessel to carry cargo (wood pulp) to the port of Manchester via the Ship Canal before it was officially opened.

In 1895 Alfred Coker became a partner and the name of the firm was altered to Stott, Coker & Co. This lasted three years until, in 1898, Coker left to set up business as a shipbroker on his own account and the firm resumed its former name of W.H. Stott & Co. A year later W.H. Stott (II) was admitted as a partner with his father. The firm became a limited liability company in 1902 and two years later W.H. Stott (I) died. The Stott Line Ltd. was formed in 1906 to take control of the fleet, with W.H. Stott & Co. as the majority shareholder. The Stott Line operated regular services from Liverpool and Manchester to Baltic ports including St. Petersburg. In 1924 the line disposed of its last services with chartered tonnage until its interests were acquired by Ellerman Wilson Line of Hull, which adopted the style Ellerman's Wilson & Stott Line in 1931. W.H. Stott & Co., Ltd. continued to act as agents, representing amongst others, the Finland Steamship Co. and the Johnson Line of Stockholm. W.H. Stott & Co., Ltd. was dissolved in 1994.

Records

W.H. Stott & Co., charter party books, 1866-1908.
Stott Line charter party books, 1908-1924.
Miscellaneous material includes reference to the Russian trade and conferences at Stettin, and deck space for livestock carried from the River Plate to Rio de Janeiro, 1884-1900.
B/ST	1866-1924	23 Boxes

Reference

Carter, C.J.M. "Stotts of Liverpool," *Sea Breezes*. No. 262, Vol. 41 (October 1967), pp. 686-693.

Edward W. Turner & Son

Edward W. Turner (c.1840-1936) was born at Queensborough, Kent, and began his seafaring career in the Royal Navy. He left the Royal Navy in 1861 and qualified as a master in 1865. In the 1880s he became master of the barque *Mertola*, carrying copper ore from Portugal to Garston Docks. He bought the *Mertola* in 1882 and founded the business that bore his name in 1883. From being a sailing ship company it diversified into ship agency, brokerage, forwarding and surveying, all initially based at Garston.

In 1911 Edward took his son, C.E. Turner, into partnership, and in 1938, C.E. Turner made his elder son, J.C.E. Turner, a partner. After World War II the firm expanded and acted as loading brokers for a regular monthly deep-sea liner service and also developed an insurance and merchant business in Nigeria. In addition to the head office which had been opened in Liverpool in 1903, and the original office at Garston Docks, branch offices were also opened at Ellesmere Port, Preston and at Lagos, Nigeria. The firm also became involved in travel agency work and the canal pleasure boat business, and has now been absorbed into Vogt & Maguire.

The archives include a large number of personal and business papers, ranging from the age of sail to jet flight, and include a typescript history of the firm (c.1980) and Captain E.W. Turner's career papers for voyages to the West Indies and Russia.

Records

Personal Papers

Career papers of Captain E.W. Turner, including master's certificate, will, etc., 1865-1936.
Manuscript reminiscences of E.W. Turner re: Royal Navy service, West Indian and Russian voyages, etc., 1858-1864.
Papers of other members of the Turner family re: World War service, etc., c.1914-1945.

Administrative and Legal

Articles of partnership, 1911-1948.
Ministry of Shipping papers, 1916-1918.
Agreements for agencies and purchase of steamship service, Antwerp to Garston (1937), 1932-1976.
Tenancy agreements re: offices in Tower Buildings, Liverpool and Garston Docks, 1945-1958.
Agreement re: services, Liverpool and Manchester to Antwerp and Amsterdam, as Bristol Benelux Line, 1970.
Travel agency agreements, including airlines, 1946-1971.
Correspondence files including Svendborg Enterprise, North Delta Line, 1977-1983.

Correspondence with Bibby Line Ltd., re: joint proposal to form a private company to manage an offshore base at Morecambe Bay, 1982-1983.

Financial

Cash daybooks including crew wages, 1919-1941.
Annual statement and balance sheets, 1921-1933.

Investment

Correspondence re: investments, 1879-1951.

Operational

Mertola (I):
Log books, 1865-1885.
Voyage reports, 1865-1882.
Letters, receipts, etc., c.1860-1895.
Seamen's wage books, 1866-1877.
Rough books, 1880-1882.
Master's instructions, 1866.
Agreement for carrying stone from Lisbon to Gibraltar, 1871.
Insurance certificates, 1880.
Certificate of bill of sale, 1882.
Voyage account books, 1882-1885.

Mertola (II):
Insurance claim policies for MV *Mertola* (ex *Poortuilet*), 1960-1961.
Adjustment of average books, 1966-1968.
Survey report books, 1892-1919.
Time charter parties book, 1906-1953.
Correspondence re: chartered steamer *Ranheim*, 1948.
Time charter correspondence files, 1976-1983.

Photographs

Family and business, including the *Mertola* (II), c.1880-1950.
B/EWT   1858-1983   24 Boxes & 2 Volumes

Reference

Turner, E.H.E. "History of E.W. Turner & Son." Unpublished typescript, 131
   pp., c.1980.

Stevedoring and Warehousing Companies

W.H. Boase & Co., Ltd.

William Howard Boase (I), was born at Falmouth in 1822 and became a master mariner and shipowner. His son, W.H. Boase (II), born 1845, entered the retail trade in Liverpool. W.H. Boase (III), born 1869, was educated at the Liverpool Institute and upon leaving in c.1887, became a time-keeper for Williams & Jones, a stevedoring firm. By 1895 he was a partner in the firm Ryarson, Boase & Co., stevedores and wharfingers. This firm seems to have closed at the end of 1912.

In 1913 W.H. Boase (III) was working for Walter Nelson & Co., Ltd., for whom his son, William Paynter Boase, also worked. In the mid-1920s W.H. Boase (III) set up business on his own account and W.H. Boase & Co., Ltd. was formed in 1927. The firm thrived as master porters and stevedores to Alfred Holt, Elder Dempster, Booker Brothers and other well-known shipping companies. W.H. Boase (III) was, for many years, chairman of the Liverpool Master Porters & Master Stevedores Association and a member of the Port Employers' Association.

W.H. Boase (III) died in 1944 leaving his son, W.P. Boase, as chairman. V.T.O. Boase, W.H.B. (III)'s nephew, joined the firm in 1946 after war service. He was appointed to the board in 1963 just before the company was taken over by Alfred Holt & Co., and was retained as manager of the stevedoring firm until retiring, when Ocean Port Services was formed. In 1972 Ocean Port Services was taken over by the Mersey Docks & Harbour Co.

Records

Articles of association, 1927.
Letter book (Ryarson, Boase), 1901-1912.
Letter book (Nixon & Bruce), 1909-1912.
Bill books, 1897-1911.
Case book, 1904-1907.
Journal, 1906-1912.
Balance sheets, 1910-1912.
Wages book, 1911-1912.
Liverpool Steam Ship Owners' Association list of appropriated berths and statements of witnesses, 1938.
(Note: The family history information was supplied by V.T.O. Boase in February 1996.)
B/WHB   1897-1938   2 Boxes

Humphreys & Lambert

Humphreys & Lambert were stevedores and master lumpers established in Liverpool in 1960. Their business was the loading and unloading of cargoes which included coal, coke, stone, pharmacite, wheat and logs. They were hired by shipping companies and ship brokers on a regular basis, and details of vessels, cargoes and customers are recorded in the firm's job book. The firm was dissolved in 1967.

Records

Correspondence, 1959-1967.
Partnership agreement and M.D.H.B. licence, 1960.
Insurance policies, 1960-1962.
Job book, sales, journals, ledgers, etc., 1960-1967.
Accident book, 1960-1962.
Financial records, 1961-1967.
File re: tax settlement after dissolution of the partnership, 1966-1970.
DX/108   1959-1970   4 Boxes

Liverpool Stevedoring Ltd.

This company had a major trading connection with West Africa. Unfortunately, little is known about this company. The archive has an extremely interesting collection of photographs covering every aspect of cargo handling.

Records

Cargo notes, 1959-1967.
Handwritten monthly lists of ships and docks, 1936-1986.
Newscuttings, newspaper and Union circulars regarding the Devlin enquiry re: decasualisation of dock labour and dock strikes, 1963-1967.
West African trade study and West African port information file, 1982.
Photographs re: cargo handling, c.1970-1987.
B/LSL   c.1936-1987   5 Boxes

West Coast Stevedoring Co., Ltd.

In the 1940s, the Thames Stevedoring Co., Ltd., moved to Merseyside and was based at S.W. Alexandra Dock. It merged with the Booth Steamship Co. (the first of several mergers) in its early stages. By 1962, the company was known as the West Coast Stevedoring Co., Ltd., and had premises in Union House, Victoria Street, Liverpool. In 1965 there began a series of mergers with South End and Central Stevedoring, with West Coast acting as senior member of the merger. In

1966 the company merged with the Canadian Pacific Co., again as a senior partner, and moved to Bootle. Finally, the company merged with Cunard Stevedoring in April 1968.

The late 1960s were peak trading years for West Coast Stevedoring. During this period the company handled an average of 541 vessels per annum. This figure declined gradually until 1982 when only 114 ships passed through the company's hands. The company closed on 31 December 1982.

Records

Financial Records

Cash book, 1950-1964.
Journal, 1966-1976.

Staff and Wages

Booklet on working practices and conditions applicable to registered dock workers, c.1967-1971.
Piecework rules for loading into deep-sea vessels, 1968.
Coastwise trade bonus scales (Dock Labour Joint Committee), 1968.
Pamphlet: bonus tariffs and flat rate allowance to registered dock workers employed on deep sea general cargo operations, 1979.

Operational Records

Book of loading rates, 1961.
Log books re: berthing of vessels, 1961-1982.
Log books re: loading, 1971-1982.
Log book re: discharging, 1976-1982.
Log books re: berth cleaning and maintenance of Seaforth and Gladstone Docks, 1978-1981.
Log book re: arrival and commodities carried, 1982.
Instructions to checkers on import and export operations, 1975.
Folders of documents re: the stevedoring and porterage systems, 1979.

Sampled Operational Records

A number of complete sets of working documents has been preserved for incoming and outgoing cargoes. These include manifests, plans and reports for inward and outward movements for Brazil and the River Plate, Pakistan, Sudan, and the Far East; inward only for the West Indies and outward only for Ethiopia, Iran and South Africa, 1979-1982.

Photographs

Photographs showing palletisation, ship loading, etc., c.1960.

Miscellaneous

Advertising ephemera including booklet advertising the firm, c.1975.
Technical literature including Department of Trade codes of practices, 1930-1982.
MDHB master porterage, etc., 1937-1978.

Master Porters and Master Stevedores' Association

Financial records including cash book, balance sheets, 1902-1963.
Booklets re: trading conditions at Liverpool and handling goods from vessels arriving from foreign ports, 1974-1981.
B/WC   c.1902-1982   22 Boxes

Liverpool Grain Storage & Transit Co., Ltd.

The Liverpool Grain Storage & Transit Co., Ltd. was started in 1883 in one installation at Alexandra Dock. In its prime it had four, with facilities at Birkenhead, Brunswick, Coburg Docks and Alexandra Dock. The firm went into receivership in 1990. The records include minute books and operational records, and also a number of technical drawings which have yet to be sorted. These records are available *strictly by appointment only*.

Records

Minute books, 1883-1962.
Articles of association, 1883.
Correspondence, 1942-1973.
Operational records including stock books, rules, rates, discharge books, 1951-1983.
Miscellaneous papers relating to barges, fire damage, etc., 1954-1963.
Drawings and plans, c.1900-1988.
B/LGST   1883-1988   32 Boxes & Technical drawings

Liverpool Warehousing Co., Ltd.

The company was, for many years, the largest firm of warehouse-keepers in the United Kingdom. Its main commodity was cotton. In 1986 the firm became part of the Transport Development Group. In addition to the records of Liverpool Warehousing Co., Ltd., there are also records relating to fourteen subsidiary firms. These records are available *strictly by appointment only*.

Records

Director's minute books, 1901-1965.
Shareholders meetings, 1895-1965.
Report and accounts, 1944-1965.
Legal and investment records, 1900-1966.
Financial records, 1913-1969.
Operational records, 1951-1976.
Property records, 1947-1967.
Minutes of the United Warehouse Keepers Conference, and papers re: wage negotiations, 1922-1945.
Records of 14 subsidiary companies including:
Articles of association, 1900-1960.
Director's minute books, 1953-1966.
Stockholders register, 1948-1960.
B/LWC   1895-1983   77 Volumes & 21 Boxes

Compiled by M. Evans, A. Glynn, D. Littler, D. Le Mare, H. Threlfall and Members of the Liverpool Nautical Research Society.

CHAPTER 2

TRANSATLANTIC SLAVERY AND SLAVE TRADING

Although some individuals, such as Sir John Hawkins, engaged in the slave trade in the sixteenth century, British merchants did not begin large-scale slaving until the 1640s, when a number of private trading companies were established. The London-based Royal African Company, founded in 1663, was the most important of these and from 1672 had a monopoly of the British trade. Other merchants who wanted to enter this lucrative trade opposed the monopoly and it was ended in 1698.

In the early 1700s most of Britain's slave merchants were from London and Bristol. The first Liverpool vessel to enter the slave trade was the *Blessing*, which sailed for West Africa in August 1700. In subsequent years increasing numbers of ships from Liverpool followed her example to the extent that merchants from the town overtook all other participants. Although London, Bristol and other ports continued to send ships to Africa, Liverpool dominated the trade from about 1730 until its abolition in 1807. Indeed, Liverpool was the European port most involved in slaving during the eighteenth century and was responsible for transporting some one and a half million Africans across the Atlantic.

By the 1730s about fifteen ships a year were leaving Liverpool for Africa and this grew to about fifty a year in the 1750s, rising to just over a 100 in each of the early years of the 1770s. Numbers declined during the American War of Independence (1775-1783) but rose to a new peak of 120-130 ships a year in the two decades preceding the abolition of the trade in 1807. Probably three-quarters of all slaving ships at this latter period left from Liverpool.

Although Liverpool merchants engaged in many other trades and commodities, involvement in the slave trade pervaded throughout the whole port. Nearly all the principal merchants and citizens of Liverpool, including many of the mayors, were involved. Several of the town's MPs also invested in the trade and spoke strongly in its favour in Parliament. Generations of families such as the Tarletons, Cunliffes and Earles organised slaving voyages. The Earle family papers contain substantial references to the family's involvement in the trade, including the log of the *Unity* on a slaving voyage in 1769-1771. Outfitting a slaver was a complex and expensive business involving many tradesmen who provided goods for trading in Africa and supplies for the voyage. The surviving invoice books and correspondence provide evidence of this business, an excellent example being the account book for the *Enterprize* owned by Thomas Leyland & Co., trading to the Congo in 1794-1795.

The last British slave trader, the *Kitty's Amelia*, under Captain Hugh Crow, left Liverpool in July 1807. There is no evidence that Liverpool traders engaged in the illegal trade, though they may have supplied goods for others and as late as 1860 an American ship, *Nightingale*, which had been refitted in the port, was arrested for slaving.

The abolitionist campaign was relatively muted in Liverpool before 1807 but local involvement in the campaign for slave emancipation is covered in the Cropper family archives.

It would be wrong to attribute all of Liverpool's success to the slave trade but it was undoubtedly a major factor in the town's prosperity. Recent evidence suggests that slaving and related trades may have occupied a third and possibly a half of Liverpool's shipping activity in the period 1750 to 1807. The wealth acquired by the town was substantial and the stimulus it gave to trading and industrial development throughout the north-west of England and the Midlands was of crucial importance.

After abolition in 1807, Liverpool merchants continued to trade with West Africa, developing the palm oil trade, which they monopolised for most of the nineteenth century. Equally, trade with the Americas continued, particularly in cotton which was produced by slave labour until the 1860s.

The Transatlantic Slavery Gallery in the basement of the Merseyside Maritime Museum displays both original and copies of archival material and provides a comprehensive display on the history of the slave trade and slavery. Since the setting up of this gallery, a wide variety of relevant records and rare printed material has been acquired, in addition to the material held before then, which mainly related to slaving voyages. The slavery records held by the Maritime Archives & Library have been microfilmed and are now available commercially.

References

Anstey, R. *The Atlantic Slave Trade and British Abolition 1760-1810*. London, 1975.

Anstey, R. and Hair, P.E. *Liverpool, The African Slave Trade and Abolition*. Liverpool, 1976.

"Dickey Sam." *Liverpool and Slavery. An Historical Account of the Liverpool-African Slave Trade*. Liverpool, 1884. Reprinted Liverpool, 1986.

Equiano, Olaudah. *The Life of Olaudah Equiano*. Reprint, Essex, 1992.

Newton, J. (edited by Martin, B. and Spurrell, M.) *The Journal of a Slave Trader (John Newton) 1750-1754*. London, 1962.

Sanderson, F.E. *Liverpool & the Slave Trade – A Guide to Sources*. Liverpool, 1973.

Schwarz, S. *Slave Captain: The Career of James Irving in the Liverpool Slave Trade*. Wrexham, 1995.

Threlfall, H. *Slavery - A Bibliography of Works in the English Language held by the Maritime Archives and Library, Merseyside Maritime Museum, Albert Dock, Liverpool*. Liverpool, 1998.

Tibbles, A. *Transatlantic Slavery*. London, 1994.

Walvin, J. *Black Ivory: A History of British Slavery*. London, 1992.

Williams, G. *History of the Liverpool Privateers and Letters of Marque with an Account of the Liverpool Slave Trade*. London, 1897.

Slavery Records in Larger Collections

Liverpool Statutory Registers of British Merchant Ships

The most important registers relating to the slave trade are the volumes covering the years 1739-1807. These contain details of all the Liverpool slaving vessels, their owners, masters and the ultimate fate of the vessel, as well as their basic dimensions. (The registers for the years 1743-1784, known as the Plantation Registers are too fragile to be handled, so microfilms are available. For further details see Vol. I, chap. 1. All of the later registers are also now available on microfilm).

C/EX/L/2-6   1739-1807   5 Volumes

Earle Family and Business Archive

This important collection of family and business papers of the Earle family, a Liverpool family whose mercantile activities date back to the early eighteenth century, was acquired by the Merseyside Maritime Museum in 1993. The collection comprises some seventeen boxes of volumes and documents relating to the family's business, estate and personal affairs, especially their mercantile and shipping interests during the mid-eighteenth century, the period when Liverpool became the country's leading slave port. By this time the Earle family were in business as merchants and shipowners in a wide range of commercial ventures, including the slave trade. This gives special importance to these archives, which include a number of exceptionally interesting individual items in this connection.

Records

Letter of instructions to William Earle when captain of the *Chesterfield* for a voyage to Old Calabar, West Africa, in 1751.

D/Earle/1/1   1751   1 Item

Log of the *Unity* for a slaving voyage from Liverpool to Holland and across to Calabar, West Africa, in 1769. The log kept by the captain, Robert Norris, gives a valuable insight into life on board a slave ship. The voyage was eventful with numerous mentions made of deaths of slaves and insurrections.

D/Earle/1/4   1769   1 Volume & Microfiche

Letterbook of William Earle (1721-1788) who acted as managing owner for a number of vessels owned in partnership. The letterbook covers a period of eighteen months, from 23 January 1760 - 23 September 1761. Information on the activities undertaken, including the outfitting of the vessel with cargoes, the instructing of captains and correspondence with merchants and agents in Africa, West Indies and the American Colonies.

D/Earle/2/2   1760-1761   1 Volume

Articles of partnership for the trade in beads and arrangoes (another type of bead), commodities used for slave trading.

D/Earle/4/2   1766   1 Item

Bundles of correspondence and other documents relating to the administration of a plantation in Berbice, British Guiana (now Guyana), acquired by Thomas Earle (1754-1822) and William Earle (1760-1839), operating as the firm of T. & W. Earle & Co. in the 1830s. Includes documents relating to the use of slave and later free black labour.

D/Earle/5/1-11   1823-1899   11 Bundles

Volume of copies of deeds and other documents relating to property and slaves in Jamaica belonging to J. Knight, to whom the Earles were executors. Includes lists of slaves and details of their employment.

D/Earle/2/1   c.1667-1738   1 Volume

(Note: For further details of the Earle collection, see Vol. II, chap. 6).

Reference

Littler, D. *The Earle Collection: Records of a Liverpool Family of Merchants and Shipowners,* in *Transactions of the Historic Society of Lancashire & Cheshire.* Vol. 146, Liverpool, 1996.

Bryson Collection

A large and varied collection purchased in 1977, which includes:

Sandbach, Tinne & Co.

Under various styles, this firm operated in Demerara, now part of Guyana, from 1782, and exported sugar, coffee, molasses, rum, cotton and imported coolie labour (see also Vol. II, chap. 1).

Records

Documents re: Demerara cotton plantations, including a mortgage agreement and list of slaves.
D/B 176A/D/1-4   1807   1 Bundle

William Russell's report on conditions of coolie labour, 1870. Also letters from James Baines & Co. (Black Ball Line) to Sandbach, Tinne & Co., re: shipment of coolies from Calcutta to Demerara, 1863-1864.
D/B 176A/B/3-4   1863-1870   2 Bundles

Watercolour drawing of Cane Grove sugar plantation, Mahaica Creek, Demerara, property of George Booker.
D/B 176/C/1   1830   1 Item

NB: In the miscellaneous SAS collection there is a letter from William McBean, McInroy, Sandbach & McBean, Demerary (sic.) to Samuel Sandbach, McInroy, Parker & Co., re: Negroes for Plantation Caledonia and other commodities.
SAS/37A/1/3   1808   1 Original, 2 MS Copies

Cobham Family

Henry Cobham in Pennsylvania wrote letters to his cousin John Cobham at Liverpool, and referred to the American Civil War from a Unionist viewpoint and the reactions to, or fate of, Negro slaves. Please note that these records are available *strictly by appointment only*.

Records

Letters from Henry Cobham to John Cobham.
D/B/1   1863-1868   1 File

Cropper Family Archive

In the saga of the abolition of slavery, the name of Cropper is unfortunately, barely known. James Cropper (1773-1840) was a successful Quaker merchant. He and his collaborator and friend, Anglican Evangelical, Adam Hodgson, worked together for the abolition of slavery, using not only ethical arguments, but economic ones as well.

Harriet Beecher Stowe, author of *Uncle Tom's Cabin*, stayed at Dingle Bank, the home of John, son of James Cropper. James Cropper sent parcels of East Indies coffee and sugar to every MP, to demonstrate that these commodities could be produced without slave labour. He also had his crockery decorated with vignettes of slaves in iron with the caption: "Am I not a man/woman and a brother/sister?"

The archives include correspondence with Thomas Clarkson, William Wilberforce, Zachary Macaulay and others, and also contains many circulars and handbills.

Records

Correspondence between Thomas Clarkson and General Lafayette (1798). Also two letters from William Wilberforce (1822 and 1826).
D/CR/4/1-5   1798-1826   1 File

Letters, mostly re: Anti-Slavery Movement, one of which includes a description of the Spanish schooner, *Josefa Maracayera*, captured slave trading off Benin. (See D/CR/12/10 for an illustrated cross-section of the schooner).
D/CR/5/1-6   1822   1 File

Letter, James Cropper to Joseph Sturge, Birmingham, re: putting slave trade down by force.
D/CR/8/16   1835   1 Item

Letter book, which includes nine letters re: slavery abolition.
D/CR/10   1824-1835   1 Volume

Album containing mainly anti-slavery material, including:
A copy of the *Declaration of the objects of the Liverpool Society for Promoting the Abolition of Slavery*, 1823.
D/CR/11/15

Correspondence and pamphlets critical of the American Colonisation Society which established Liberia, 1832-1833.
D/CR/11/35

A juvenile poem by James Cropper Junior, grandson of James Cropper Senior, entitled "The Negro's Complaint," 1828.
D/CR/11/50

Declaration of the Anti-Slavery Convention, Philadelphia, 1833.
D/CR/11/21

Report of the Tropical Free Labour Company, 1826.
D/CR/11/54
D/CR/11   1785-1839   1 Volume

Album containing mainly anti-slavery material:

General Election Guide: candidates and electors giving their view on slavery, 1823.

D/CR/12/1

Hand-written list of individuals and towns receiving parcels of pamphlets, n.d. (c.1820s).

D/CR/12/2

Imaginative illustration re: slavery with verse caption, n.d. (c.1820s).

D/CR/12/3

Illustration of slaves with verse caption: "...we have no Slaves at home, why then abroad?" by W. Cowper, n.d. (c.1820s).

D/CR/12/4

Written extract from Exodus xxiv, 26, 27, and *Colonel Arthur's Letter* re: slavery, n.d. (c.1820s).

D/CR/12/5

Pamphlet: *The First Report of The Female Society for the Relief of the British Negro Slaves* (Birmingham and environs), 1826.

D/CR/12/6

Illustration of a slave at prayer, prose caption, n.d. (c.1820s).

D/CR/12/7

Illustration of a female slave with child, n.d. (c.1820s).

D/CR/12/8

Prayer of encouragement to the slave woman relevant to No. 8, n.d. (c.1820s).

D/CR/12/9

Illustrated cross-section of Spanish schooner, *Josefa Maracayera*, captured on the coast of Africa on 19 August 1822, with a cargo of 216 male slaves. Shows slaves stowed in hold.

D/CR/12/10

Supplement to the *Jamaica Royal Gazette*, Vol. XLV. Contains notices of slave sales and runaways, 14 June-21 June 1823.

D/CR/12/11

Additional postcript to the *Jamaica Royal Gazette*, with details of runaways, 14-21 June 1823.
D/CR/12/12

Article: *"Negro Slavery: Argument that the Colonial slaves are better off than the British peasantry"* – answered from the *Royal Jamaica Gazette* by Thomas Clarkson, M.A., originally appeared in *Christian Observer*, August 1824.
D/CR/12/13

Pamphlet: *No British Slavery, or An Invitation to people to put a speedy end to it*, London, 1824.
D/CR/12/14

Pamphlet: *What Does Your Sugar Cost – A Cottage Conversation*, re: British Negro slavery, 1826.
D/CR/12/15

Extract from *Reasons for the Abolition of Slavery, Clarkson's Reasons for the Abolition of the Slave Trade*, Vol. 2, 1808.
D/CR/12/16

Periodical: *Anti-Slavery Monthly Reporter*, No. 5, 31 October 1825.
D/CR/12/17

Criticism of slave conditions including advertisement re: sale of slaves from the *Jamaica Royal Gazette*, 4 August 1824, n.d. (c.1820s).
D/CR/12/18

Letter (copy) to the editor of the *Devizes Gazette* from "C.T." in Calne re: slavery in the West Indies, 10 September 1825.
D/CR/12/19

Article: The West Indies As They Are – "Or a Real Picture of Slavery, but more particularly as it exists in the Island of Jamaica," by the Reverend Richard Bickell, originally printed in *The Christian Observer*, March 1825.
D/CR/12/20

Pamphlet: *Account of A Shooting Excursion on the Mountains Near Bromilly Estate in the Parish of Trelawny and Island of Jamaica in the Month of October 1824* (to a settlement of runaway slaves), 1825.
D/CR/12/21

Illustration of slave driver and female slave with two line verse caption, n.d. (c.1820s).
D/CR/12/22

Prayer on "Africa's Weal & Woe," n.d. (c.1820).
D/CR/12/23

Pamphlet: "Verses on Slavery," by Jane Yeoman, Birmingham, March 1826.
D/CR/12/24

Chart of the World on Mercator's projection. Illustrative of the Impolicy of Slavery, coloured, n.d. (c.1820s).
D/CR/12/25

Periodical: *Anti-Slavery Monthly Reporter*, No. 16, 30 September 1826.
D/CR/12/26

Extract from a card of the Ladies Society for the Relief of Negro Slaves, explaining the contents of the Society's work bags, 2 pp., n.d. (c.1820s).
D/CR/12/27

Extract from the *Jamaica Royal Gazette* re: adverts of slave sales, 2 pp., 3 July 1824.
D/CR/12/28

Pamphlet: *Negro Slavery No. 13; Is Negro Slavery Sanctioned By Scripture?* (review of a pamphlet defending slavery), c.1820.
D/CR/12/29

(N.B. Items 30-32 are non-slavery)

List of names and addresses in England and Ireland for mailing of anti-slavery material to, n.d. (c.1820s).
D/CR/12/33

Printed sheet: *Questions to Professing Christians on the Use of Slave-Grown Sugar, Coffee, etc.*, Birmingham, n.d. (c.1820s).
D/CR/12/34

Hand-written list of anti-slavery pamphlets at R. Dickenson's, 16 February 1828.
D/CR/12/35

Hand-written list of anti-slavery pamphlets sent to R. Newton and to America, c.1828.
D/CR/12/36

(Item 37 is non-slavery)

Hand-written list of correspondence and places of residence of anti-slavery supporters in Great Britain, Ireland and America, 15 pp., n.d. (c.1820s).
D/CR/12/38

List of anti-slavery pamphlets circulated by the Liverpool Ladies Association, 1830-1831.
D/CR/12/39

(Item 40 is non-slavery)

Hand-written extract from the *York Chronicle* on the foundation of Liberia, n.d. (c.1832).
D/CR/12/41

D/CR/12/1-41	1808-1832	1 Volume

Album of anti-slavery newscuttings (indexed).

D/CR/13	1824-1826	1 Volume

Broadsheet: *Remarks on the Proposed Enormous Grant of Twenty Millions Sterling to the West-India Planters*.

D/CR/14/4	1830-1833	1 Item

(Note: For further details of the Cropper family archive, see Vol. II, chap. 6).

Reference

Conybeare, F.A. *Dingle Bank, Home of the Croppers*. Liverpool, 1925.

Danson Family Archive

J.T. Danson (1817-1898) was economic correspondent of *The Globe*, and his thoughts on slavery are recorded in his notes. Many pamphlets relating to slavery are included in the archive, which provided material for his writings. Please note that these records are available *strictly by appointment only*.

Records

Pamphlet: *The African Squadron Vindicated*, by Lieutenant Henry Yule.
D/D III/12/48   1850   1 Item

Published letter from Thomas Clegg, Cotton Merchant and Manufacturer of Manchester, to McGregor Laird, Chairman of the African Steamship Company, urging that African Chiefs should be encouraged to go in for cotton trading rather than tribal warfare and slave trading!
D/D III/12/85   1858   1 Item

J.T. Danson's manuscript notes re: slavery.
D/D III/14/2/17   n.d. (c.1890)   1 Item

Pamphlet: *The Administration of Governor Light in British Guiana* (re: emancipation of slaves).
D/D III/16/4/1   1848   1 Item

Pamphlet: *Economical Causes of Slavery in the United States and the Obstacles to its Abolition*, by a Southern Carolinian.
D/D III/16/20/1   1857   1 Item

Pamphlet: *The True State of the American Question: A Reply to Thurlow Weed*.
D/D III/20/3   1862   1 Item

Article in *The Globe* on slavery and cotton.
D/D III/17/11   1856   1 Item

Letter from J.W.W. Danson, Rangoon (Burma) to his father, J.T. Danson, referring to his father sending him a newscutting regarding the "slave trade" in female "slaves" for coolies, sold for 25 rupees each and the conviction of those engaged in it. He explains and, to an extent, defends the situation.
D/D IV/7   1890   1 Item

(Note: For further details of the Danson family archive, see Vol. II, chap. 6).

E.N. Clay Business Archive

This archive includes parchment deeds hoarded as curiosities by E.N. Clay, a local gold beater. These records are available *strictly by appointment only*.

Records

A mortgage of a plantation in Jamaica (with reference to slaves) and an assignment of the same, with a list of named slaves.

B/C/1/8-9   1789 and 1805   2 Items

Transfer of mortgages in a sugar plantation in Antigua, which contains a reference to emancipated slaves being no longer conveyed with the plantation.

B/C/1/33   1844   1 Item

Fraser, Trenholm & Co. Business Archive

Fraser, Trenholm & Co., were a firm of American cotton merchants based in Liverpool, whose senior partner, and naturalised Englishman, Charles Kuhn Prioleau, acted as agent for the Confederacy, purchasing armaments, participating in blockade-running and fund-raising activities.

Records

Letterbook of correspondence and original letters concerning the American Civil War from a Confederate viewpoint.

B/FT   c.1861-1863   1 Volume & 1 File

(Note: For further details of Fraser, Trenholm & Co. archives, see Vol. II, chap. 1).

Miscellaneous Original Manuscripts and Printed Texts

A large number of important documents relating to the slave trade are to be found in the miscellaneous, smaller collections of archives, known collectively as the DX and SAS collections. They include many important individual items.

Records

Printed volume: *Historical account of Guinea its situation, produce, disposition of inhabitants and inquiry into the rise and progress of the slave trade*, by Anthony Benezet, 1772. Includes references to a surgeon's journal for voyage from Liverpool, 1724, and a voyage account for a slave trader from Liverpool, 1749 (pp. 118-123). (Microfiche available.)

DX/1624/R   1724-1772   1 Volume

Facsimile copy of the *New England Weekly Journal*, with references to Negro slaves.

DX/1487   1728   1 Item

Account book for voyages to Old Calabar and Cameroons of the *Eadith*, *Chesterfield* and *Calveley*. Includes copy letter of instructions from William Davenport & Co., owners of the *Eadith*, to Captain James Mabin. The *Chesterfield* was under the command of William Earle, and his letter of instructions, 1751, can be found in the Earle family and business archive.
DX/169   1757-1761   1 Volume

Letter to William Davenport of Liverpool to Charles Margate, London, re: sale of arrangoes (beads used in slave trading).
DX/1555/R   1768   1 Item

Invoice book for the slaver snow *Aston*.
SAS/37A/1/4   1771-1773   1 Volume & Microcards

Articles of agreement and crew list of the *Liverpool Hero*, slaving vessel.
DX/1048   1783   1 Item

Printed volume: *Report of Lords of Committee of Council concerning the present state of the trade to Africa and particularly the trade of slaves*.
DX/1746   1789   1 Volume

Volume of newspapers including *The West Indian, Barbados Mercury and St. Vincent Gazette* with references to the sale of Negroes.
DX/1393   1789-1848   1 Volume

Will of Coleman O'Loghlan, surgeon's mate on the slaver *Christopher*.
DX/1711   1791   1 Item

Act of Parliament regulating slave ships.
DX/268/1   1791   1 Item

Printed volume: *Substance of the Report of the Sierra Leone Company*, includes maps of plantations and general comments on the slave trade.
DX/1550/R   1794   1 Item

Account book of slave ship *Enterprize*, owned by Leyland & Co., Liverpool. Includes descriptions of the taking of a Spanish privateer, and of a voyage to the Congo to collect slaves destined for Jamaica, and also a crew list, details of a slave sale, captain's instructions and voyage accounts.
DX/1732   1794-1795   1 Volume

Correspondence relating to the slaver *Kitty's Amelia*, the last Liverpool slave ship to sail from a West African port in 1807. Includes letters of instruction to Captain

Nuttall re: sale of slaves, and a crew list for a voyage in 1806. (An offprint of an article on the *Kitty's Amelia* by Charles Hand published in the *Transactions of the Historic Society of Lancashire and Cheshire*, 1930, and photocopies of the correspondence are available in SAS/37A/1/6 and 10).

DX/170   1804-1806   11 Items

Price list for Windward and Leeward Island produce at Liverpool.

SAS/37A/1/13   1805   1 Item

Voyage account of the slaver *Sally*, from the Cape Coast, Africa and list of seven slaves who died.

DX/1143   1806   1 Item

Printed volume: *The Life, History and Unparalleled Suffering of John Jea, African Preacher*. Portsea, 1810.

DX/1646   c.1810   1 Item

Receipt for the return of allowance paid to staff officer James Wilson, apothecary to forces at the garrison of Senegal, for a black servant.

DX/1543   1811   1 Item

Printed pamphlet: *Barbarity To A Female Slave*, and engraving *Inhuman Cruelty to an Innocent Female Slave, while in a State of Pregnancy*. London, 1817.

DX/1677   1817   2 Items

Printed letter: Adam Hodgson, Chairman of the Bank of Liverpool, on the *Comparative Expense of Free and Slave labour*.

DX/428/1   1823   1 Item

Letter from James Calley, manager of a plantation in Berbice, Guiana to proprietor Hugh McCalmont in Belfast. Details of estates, cotton, slaves, etc.

DX/1544   1826   1 Item

Journal compiled by Vernon Poole, surgeon on the *Kingston* of Liverpool, for a voyage to West Africa, includes references to conditions, natives and Spanish slaves (microfiche available).

DX/1175   1832   1 Item

Acts of parliament for the suppression of the slave trade in the British Colonies, and various treaties with foreign powers.

DX/1661   1837-1839   11 Items

Printed volume: *A Narrative of the Adventures and Escape of Moses Roper, from American Slavery*. London, 1843. His father was white and his mother half white.

Includes references to Liverpool after his arrival on the ship *Napoleon* from New York.
DX/1706/R   1843   1 Item

Printed volume: *Fifty Days Aboard A Slave Vessel*, by Reverend P.G. Hill. London, 1844. re: his experiences on board HMS *Cleopatra* visiting slave markets in Rio de Janeiro, and the pursuit and capture of a Brazilian brig slaver off the coast of Mozambique.
DX/1675   1844   1 Volume

Printed volume: *Interesting Memoirs and Documents relating to American slavery and the glorious struggle now making for complete emancipation* by Lewis Clarke. London, 1846. American Joseph Baker's travels through America witnessing the atrocities of slavery.
DX/1534   1846   1 Item

Extracts from the family journal of Peter Robinson McQuie, relating to the ship *Thomas* sailing from Africa with 375 slaves and the death of Captain Peter Robinson McQuie during an insurrection of the slaves, 1807.
DX/641/6/1   1846   1 Item

Framed notice of an auction of 25 Sea Island cotton and rice slaves, Charleston, U.S.A., and an agreement for sale of a female slave, New Orleans. (See fig. 1).
DX/1551   1852-1853   2 Items

Transfer of ownership of a slave, New Orleans, U.S.A.
DX/593   1855   1 Item

Pamphlet: *The American War*, by Newman Hall re: the American Civil War and the suffering of slaves, originally given as a lecture to working men, delivered in London in 1862.
DX/520   1862   1 Item

A collection of black ephemera including advertising leaflets and Christmas cards featuring black characters. Also glass magic lantern slides featuring illustrations of black characters in the Southern States of America.
DX/1779   c.1889-1920   1 Box

Article: "Misadventures of a slaver, Captain Baker and his ship *Princess*," by J.D. Spinney, *Blackwoods Magazine*.
DX/1664   1951   1 Item

Typescript re: Robert Bostock, master mariner, who was transported to Australia for slave trading in Sierra Leone in 1814.
DX/642   c.1980   1 Item

Compiled by A. Glynn and D. Littler. Introduction by A.J. Tibbles.

GANG OF 25 SEA ISLAND

COTTON AND RICE NEGROES,

By LOUIS D. DE SAUSSURE.

On *THURSDAY* the 25th Sept., 1852, at 11 o'clock, A.M., will be sold at RYAN'S MART, in Chalmers Street, in the City of Charleston,

A prime gang of 25 Negroes, accustomed to the culture of Sea Island Cotton and Rice.

CONDITIONS. — One-half Cash, balance by Bond, bearing interest from day of sale, payable in one and two years, to be secured by a mortgage of the negroes and approved personal security. Purchasers to pay for papers.

No.		Age.	Capacity.	No.		Age.	Capacity.
1	Aleck,	33	Carpenter.	16	Hannah,	60	Cook.
2	Mary Ann.	31	Field hand, prime.	17	Cudjoe,	22	Prime field hand.
3—3	Louisa,	10		3—18	Nancy,	20	Prime field hand, sister of Cudjoe.
4	Abram,	25	Prime field hand.				
5	Judy,	24	Prime field hand.	19	Hannah,	34	Prime field hand.
6	Carolina,	5		20	James,	13	Slight defect in knee from a broken leg.
7	Simon,	1½		21	Richard,	9	
5—8	Daphne, infant.			22	Thomas,	6	
				5—23	John,	3	
9	Daniel	45	Field hand, not prime.				
10	Phillis,	32	Field hand.	1—24	Squash,	40	Prime field hand.
11	Will,	9					
12	Daniel,	6		1—25	Thomas,	28	Prime field hand.
13	Margaret,	4					
14	Delia	2					
7—15	Hannah,	2 months.					

Figure 1:   Notice of a sale at Charleston, South Carolina of a gang of twenty-five slaves accustomed to the culture of Sea Island cotton and rice, 25 September 1852.

Source: Merseyside Maritime Museum, DX/1551.

CHAPTER 3

EMIGRATION

Liverpool played an important role in facilitating mainly the poor, the ambitious or the persecuted to seek a new and (hopefully) better life across the Atlantic in North America. Passengers, some of whom were emigrants or indentured servants, were carried regularly to North America and the West Indies from about 1660 onwards. Numbers began to increase with the growth of population in the early nineteenth century. Emigrants were also attracted not only from the north west but from other parts of the British Isles and later with the establishment of North Sea steamers and railway links from the mainland of Europe. This was because Liverpool had come to dominate North American trade especially from New York. The establishment of regular sailing packet lines from 1818 and the huge demand for North American raw materials by British industries especially cotton and timber, stimulated imports. Emigrants along with British manufactures provided a useful return cargo. Ship's 'tween decks could be easily converted to steerage accommodation by building temporary bunks. The Irish potato famine of 1846-1847 expanded the demand for emigrant passages and by 1851 it was the pre-eminent port in Europe with 159,840 passengers sailing to the United States, as against the second, Le Havre, with 31,859. In the same decade, it played a major role in the rush of emigrants seeking their fortune in the Australian gold fields. But this emigrant traffic and that of New Zealand that began to grow in the 1860s, was shared with other ports, especially London, Southampton and Plymouth.

Most early steamship lines including Cunard refused to carry emigrants until the 1860s with the exception of the Inman Line. As competition increased between the lines (and there were the Cunard, White Star, Allan, Inman, Guion and National Lines all sailing from Liverpool by the 1870s) emigrants were not only accepted but actively recruited through passenger agents in the United Kingdom and Europe. The shipping companies also provided accommodation ashore while the emigrants waited to board their ship because Liverpool and its "land sharks" had a notorious reputation for their exploitation of emigrants.

However, Liverpool's dominant position as the main transatlantic and as an emigrant transhipment port, was gradually eroded in the late nineteenth century by competition from Southampton and the German ports of Bremerhaven and Hamburg, all of which had great geographical advantages over Liverpool. This was compounded by the growth of emigration from Italy and the emigration of Austro-Hungarian gypsies via Mediterranean ports. By 1907, for example, Naples was the busiest emigrant port in Europe.

The restrictions on immigration imposed by the USA in 1926 and the two World Wars further diminished Liverpool's role. However, small numbers of emigrants sailed from Liverpool until the end of ocean passenger services in 1971.

The records of this huge movement of Europeans are scattered or have disappeared. Much can be found at their destinations where they became new citizens and were not in transit. There are no passenger lists for Liverpool except for the occasional lucky survival before 1889. This is a source of great frustration to family historians, and the former Curator of Archives, J. Gordon Read, went to great lengths to gather copies of emigrant diaries and other documents as case studies, together with lists of sources of emigrant records outside Liverpool. These are summarised in the entry on his research collection.

The Merseyside Maritime Museum's archives, library and artefact collections, and its permanent exhibition – *Emigrant to a New World*, can offer much detail and images of specific ships, sailing dates (for example through the microfilms of Lloyd's Lists) and an evocation of the trials of a nineteenth century emigrant taking passage from this port. The Museum also publishes a bibliography of emigration reference books based on its own holdings. (See also Vol. I, chap. 4, for shipping companies involved in the passenger trade and Vol. II, chap. 6 for the Cropper family's involvement in the New York-Liverpool Black Ball Line).

Official Records

Conditions on emigrant ships were covered by the series of Passenger Acts that started in 1842 which attempted to lay down minimum standards of accommodation, nutrition and welfare. The provisions were difficult to enforce because the emigration officers provided for by the Act were frequently too hard pressed to make more than a cursory inspection. The Government also established a Board of Emigration Commissioners in 1840 to oversee emigration but with a particular brief to encourage emigration to Britain's under-populated colonies. Assisted passages were paid for by the sale of land. The Commissioners also chartered their own vessels and charter parties detailing the conditions of carriage survive in the Museum's collections. But the core records of emigration – the passenger lists – have not been preserved between 1776 and 1889. One unpublished passenger and crew list survives for the Liverpool ship *Speedwell* for 1769, for a voyage from Liverpool to Philadelphia and Newfoundland in the Earle archive (see Vol. II, chap. 6).

Before 1820, the Genealogical Publishing Company of Baltimore, USA, has reprinted virtually all the surviving lists. This includes the Liverpool indentured passenger lists from the Town Books in the Liverpool Central Library (Archives Department) for 1697-1707; the T/47 series in the Public Record Office, 1773-1776, as well as much material found only in the USA. The Maritime Archives & Library holds most of these publications. Editions of nineteenth century lists most relevant to the Port of Liverpool have been acquired, namely *The Famine Immigrants* (New York port only) 1847-1851; lists for Baltimore 1820-1834; New Orleans (Irish only) 1815-1848; Philadelphia 1800-1819. Passenger lists from 1890 to 1956 are preserved at the Public Record Office. Specimen copies of lists for scattered dates, between 1851 and 1956 can be found in the Gordon Read research collection along with copies of case study records. Access to this research collection is by *prior appointment only*.

References

Charlwood, D. *The Long Farewell*. Victoria, Australia, 1981.

Coleman, T. *Passage to America*. London, 1972.

Erikson, C. *Invisible Immigrants*. Leicester, 1972.

Garrett, R. *The Search for Prosperity*. London, 1973.

Hawkings, D.T. *Bound for Australia*. Chichester, 1987.

Read, J.G. *Liverpool - Floodgate of the Old World*, in *Journal of American Ethnic History*. Vol. 13, No. 1, Fall 1993.

Read, J.G. & Rees, P. *The Leaving of Liverpool*. (document pack), Liverpool, 1986.

Tepper, M. *American Passenger Arrival Records*. Baltimore, MD, 1988.

Threlfall, H. *Emigration – A Bibliography of Works in the English Language held by the Maritime Archives & Library, Merseyside Maritime Museum*. Liverpool, 1996.

Official Records

H.M. Colonial Land and Emigration Commissioners

Tender and charter party issued by H.M. Colonial Land and Emigration Commissioners for the conveyance of emigrants on the ship *Bloomer* (James Baines & Co.) from Birkenhead to Australia, includes dietary scale, arrangements on board, articles supplied by the owners, method of payment, and list of medicines required for every 100 persons.

DX/1017a   1853   1 Item

Correspondence including copy of charter party between James Baines & Co. and H.M. Colonial Land and Emigration Commissioners about the outbreak of Cholera among the passengers on the ship *Conway*.

SAS/3/2/2   1854   6 Items

(see also Vol. I, chap. 4, pp. 87-88).

(Note: Other Colonial Office papers re: emigration are available in the Library microform collection, see Vol. II, chap. 10).

Mersey Docks and Harbour Board and its Antecedent

Emigrants were not permitted to board their ships until the day before or the actual day of sailing. This usually meant finding accommodation in Liverpool and transporting their trunks by steamer or gig boat to the ship at anchor off the Pier Head. This exposed them to exploitation by unscrupulous locals and the port authority gave serious consideration to building an emigrant depot. In 1851 John Bramley Moore, Chairman of the Dock Trust and Lord Mayor, in his evidence to the Commons Committee on Docks, estimated that the depot should be sited close to the terminal for the Irish steamers at Clarence Dock and would be capable of holding up to 4,000 people at one time. Estimates and plans were drawn up. The latter still survive in the M.D.H.B. plan collection. In the event the depot was not built but a depot for Australian emigrants opened at Birkenhead in 1852. Again, plans have survived and the M.D.H.B.'s unbound worked-up papers file MDHB/WUP/L/E7 and the unbound newscuttings file MDHB/NC/E7 cover emigration matters at Liverpool from c.1852 to 1904 and from c.1890 to 1913 respectively.

Commonwealth of Massachusetts

This document produced for would-be citizens of the U.S.A., includes much information on the history and political systems operating at various levels. It reveals considerable racial prejudice: "You cannot become a citizen of the United States if you are not of the white race" and elitism: "If you are not a person of good moral character." It was also stated that "You must have a general knowledge of the history and government of the United States." This document reflects the thinking behind the National Origins Act of 1924 which accorded strong preference under the Quota Systems' to Northern European immigrants.

Record

Printed copy of *The Constitution Of The United States Of America, with Suggestions For Those Preparing For Citizenship*, issued by the Commonwealth Of Massachusetts, Department Of Education, Division of Immigration and Americanization.
DX/1281   1927   1 Item

Reference

Kennedy, J.F. *A Nation of Immigrants*. London, 1964.

Business Records

Henry Boyd

Henry Boyd (d. 1858) was a passenger agent in Dublin Street, Liverpool, who actively encouraged migrants travelling from Ireland via Liverpool in the middle of the nineteenth century. He worked closely with Vere Foster, a notable philanthropist, and his brother Sir Frederick Foster in assisting Irish emigration. The collection of personal and business papers preserved by the executors of Henry Boyd provide a rare and valuable source of information on the practical aspects of emigration. They include surrendered passenger tickets of the type issued to emigrants to New York, Canada and Australia, and a number of letters between Henry Boyd, and Sir Frederick and Vere Foster.

Records

Passenger tickets, correspondence, etc.
SAS/3/1/1   1854-1859   24 Items

Reference

McNeill, M. *Vere Foster 1819-1900 An Irish Benefactor*. Newton Abbot, 1970.
Busteed, M.A. "A Liverpool Shipping Agent and Irish Emigration in the 1850s: Some Newly Discovered Documents," in *Transactions of the Historic Society of Lancashire and Cheshire*. Vol. 129, 1980.

Cunard Line

Founded as the British & North American Royal Steam Packet Co. to provide a transatlantic mail service in 1840, Cunard were operating a weekly service in each direction by 1847, and commenced a Mediterranean service in 1851. In 1859 the *Canada* inaugurated a fortnightly call at Queenstown (Cobh), outwards and homewards, and the New York mail steamers also called there from March 1860. Cunard did not carry emigrant steerage passengers until the 1860s, when the *Etna* and *Jura* were the first Cunarders to be fitted with steerage accommodation. The *Etna* sailed for New York on 26 June 1860 with 67 steerage passengers. J. Baines & Co., the sailing packet owners, were the Company's steerage passenger brokers in Liverpool (see Vol. I, chap. 4).

Records

Microfilms of 3 volumes of passenger lists of the Cunard Line from originals in the Cunard Archive at the University of Liverpool.
Microfilm Collection   1840-1853   1 Reel

Bound volume, possibly compiled by A.P. Moorhouse at Cunard Offices, Water Street, Liverpool, of indexed notes, statistics, sailing information, laws, regulations and agreements re: emigrant traffic of Cunard Line to Mediterranean ports; covers Europe, Levant and North Africa. The volume includes extremely important ethnic statistics and a breakdown of all British and European passenger statistics. The notes suggest that Cunard were making a determined effort to capture a larger slice of the Mediterranean trades.

SAS/3/1/4   1899-1909   1 Item

J. Jackson & Sons

J. Jackson & Sons, 18 Chapel Street and 9 James Street, Liverpool, were emigration agents for all the principal shipping lines, British and Continental Railways, and the Chicago, Milwaukee and St. Paul Railways, in the early twentieth century.

Record

Brochure containing details of shipping lines, sailing schedules, fares and illustrations of ships and ports.

DX/1584   1906   1 Item

E.F. Larsson

E.F. Larsson was one of the best known Swedish emigration agents working for British lines and operating from Stockholm.

Record

Unused emigrant through ticket issued by E.F. Larsson, covering the passage Gothenburg-Hull, rail journey on to Liverpool, and steerage passage on a Guion Line steamer to New York.

DX/1693   c.1890   1 Item

Richard Marcroft & Son

Richard Marcroft & Son were licensed emigration agents operating from premises at 38 Union Street, Liverpool, and specialised in travel to North America.

Record

Blank notice of sailing of emigrant steamers to New York or other destinations. Full advice regarding diet, luggage, clothing, prevention of sea sickness and warning regarding dangers of "imposition." With hand-written note commending the character of the agent.

DX/799   c.1870   1 Item

Guide for Emigrants, by J.B. Murray, 1843

Pamphlet produced as a guide for emigrants travelling to Canada.
DX/520   1843   1 Item

Emigrant Songs

A number of songs written for emigrants to the New World by Charles Mackay (1814-1899) and Henry Russell (1812-1909) which were used to publicise the Gibbs, Bright & Co. shipping line to Australia. One of the most influential songs, "To the West ..." was actually sung by Henry Russell at a concert hall in Lord Nelson Street, Liverpool, c.1855.

Records

Score and text of song - "To The West ..." words by Charles Mackay, music by Henry Russell, c.1855.
Extract from *The Quiver*, "Away to the West," 1894.
Article "Gone – Euston Station," from *The Graphic* re: departure of the emigrant train to Liverpool, 1876.
DX/639   c.1855-1876   3 Items

Practical Hints for Emigrants to our Australian Colonies, Liverpool 1858

This pamphlet was probably underwritten by the first White Star line of Australian packets, as all of its information and advertisements relate to that company. The pamphlet's covers are illustrated on the front with the entrance to Port Philip (Melbourne) and on the back with an advertisement for the White Star Line of British and Australian ex Royal Mail packets to Melbourne. It includes sections on: "Qualifications of an Emigrant; Liverpool as a Port of Departure; Preparations to be made before the Emigrant leaves home; Life on Ship-Board; Calms and Amusement of the Passengers," and includes descriptions of the Colonies of Victoria, New South Wales, South Australia, Tasmania and New Zealand, etc. (see figure 2).

Note that the only connection between the White Star Line above and the later, more famous, transatlantic steamer line of the same name, is that the latter firm bought the White Star name, flag and goodwill from the original owners after they went bankrupt in 1867 (see Vol. I, chap. 4).

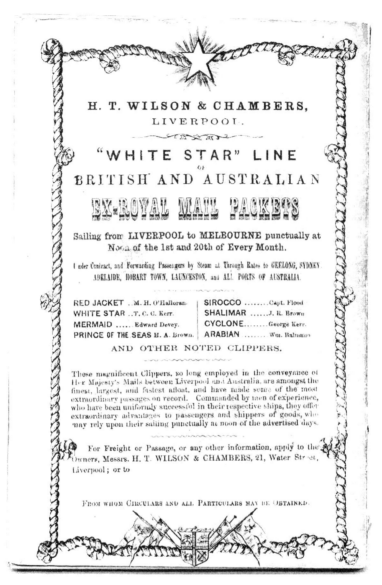

Figure 2:   Practical Hints for Emigrants to our Australian Colonies. This advertisement for the White Star Line of Australian packets features on the back page of a pamphlet for would-be emigrants to Australia, printed in Liverpool in 1858.

Source: Merseyside Maritime Museum, DX/507/1.

Record

Pamphlet for emigrants to Australia, 1858.
DX/507/1   1858   1 Item

Reference

Eight selected pages with the covers are reproduced in the teaching pack:
Read, J.G. and Rees, P. *The Leaving of Liverpool*. Liverpool, 1986.

Posters

The Guion Line or the Liverpool and Great Western Shipping Co., was established in 1866 by Stephen Guion, part-owner of the New York-Liverpool old Black Star Line of sailing packets and manager of Cunard's emigrant business (1862-1866). Guion Line ships carried many emigrants across the Atlantic until it was wound up in 1894.

The Allan Line or Montreal Ocean Steamship Co., was founded by Hugh Allan in 1854 to provide a regular steamship service from Liverpool to Canada. This company also attracted a large proportion of emigrant traffic due to its direct sailings from Glasgow and calls at Irish ports. Please note that a number of shipping company posters may be found in the poster collection of the Maritime History Department. (For further details of both of these shipping lines, see Vol. I, chap. 4).

Records

Guion Line poster (framed), c.1890.
Allan Line poster, 1911.
DX/596   c.1890-1911   2 Items

Illustrated London News

The *Illustrated London News* was a famous newspaper produced during the Victorian era, which contained news on politics, home affairs, advertisements and shipping news. It was renowned for its magnificent drawings and the ones illustrating its articles on emigration are an invaluable pictorial source for this subject.

Records

Illustrations and articles include:
Emigrants rescued from the brig *Charles Bartlett* by mail steamship *Europa*, 1849.

Emigration to U.S.A. & British Colonies, including embarkation at Waterloo Docks, Liverpool and searching for stowaways; an emigrant ship between decks and the emigration depot at Birkenhead, 1850.

The *Helena Sloman* steamship designed for conveyance of emigrants from Germany to U.S.A., 1850.

Section of emigrant ship *Bourneuf* showing the arrangement for government passengers to Australia, 1852.

Government emigrants' mess room, 1852.

Loss and wreck of the Australian packet-ship, the *Tayleur*, off Lambay Island, Dublin Bay, 1854.

Burning of the *James Baines* in Huskisson Dock, Liverpool, on morning after the fire, 1858.

Clipper ship *Great Australia* built for Baines & Co., Liverpool, 1860.

The *Eastern Monarch*, emigrant ship for New Zealand, 1874.

DX/287   1849-1874   10 Items

Passage Narratives and Related Documents

Anonymous Emigrant

Diary of a passage from Liverpool to Australia on the *Morning Light* (W. & R. Wright, Liverpool) departing 8 July 1856. Includes detailed references to activities on board, the Protestant Parson who addressed the emigrants before departure, and the number of officers, sailors, passengers, Roman Catholics and livestock. Vivid account of the unsuccessful, attempted rescue of a young saloon steward thrown overboard during bad weather, and the passengers being ordered on deck for fear that the *Morning Light* was sinking. The diary ends abruptly on 21 August before the ship reached her destination.

Record

Diary of a passage to Australia, 1856.

DX/908   1856   1 Item

Anonymous Emigrant

Scrapbook compiled by an anonymous emigrant who travelled on the Cunard liner *Campania* to Canada, c.1895. Contains newscuttings and magazine illustrations of the ship, its interior, on board leisure activities and emigrants on deck; also illustrations of Montreal, Ontario, Toronto; coloured map of the "Route of The Steamers" issued by the Richelieu & Ontario Navigation Co., and coloured map of the all-rail route to the Thousand Islands (Ontario) with the Rome Watertown & Ogdensburg Railroad.

Record

Scrapbook compiled during voyage to Canada, c.1895.
SAS/3/2/4 c.1895 1 Item

Anonymous Immigrant

Letter from a Canadian immigrant to his aunt in Newton-le-Willows describing his work threshing on farms in Manitoba. Also a postcard explaining that he "...did not get on very well in Vancouver ..." and had returned to Winnipeg.

Records

Letter and postcard from a Canadian immigrant, 1902-1904.
DX/1450 1902-1904 2 Items

Ann Bailey (1742-1825)

Ann Bailey of Virginia, U.S.A., was known as "Mad Ann" Bailey and lived as a scout and Indian fighter, rendering invaluable assistance to the first settlers of Virginia. She is now a legend in the U.S.A. and a Girl Scout camp is named after her.

Records

Photographs of sites associated with Ann Bailey; the Augusta Stone Presbyterian Church, Fort Defiance, Virginia where Ann married; stone commemoration plaque and road sign to the Girl Scout Camp in Virginia named after Ann Bailey, 1986.
DX/601 1986 3 Items

Clark Family

The Clark family emigrated from Liverpool to Canada on the SS *Montclare* (Canadian Pacific Line) in 1926. They settled on a farmstead at Caribou River, Nova Scotia.

Records

Photograph of the Clark family on board the *Montclare*, 1926.
Photographs of the Clark family on their farmstead, and agricultural scenes, 1926.
Tape of local radio interview with J. Clark, 1997.
DX/1415 1926 16 Items

J.T. Deighton (fl. c.1867)

J.T. Deighton, probably from Stretford, near Manchester, who appears to be young, single and well educated, compiled a beautifully written journal of his sailing ship voyage from Liverpool to Melbourne, Australia on board the *Fred Warren*, 1867. His comments about conditions on board, provisions, fellow passengers and crew are of great interest. He also refers to thefts on board and includes a genuine Cape Horn sailor's yarn.

Record

Journal of voyage on board the *Fred Warren*, Liverpool to Melbourne, March-July 1867. Full transcript available.
DX/651   1867-1868   1 Item

William Richard Dunn (fl. c.1856-1910)

Account of voyage of William Richard Dunn of Liverpool who, with his family, travelled to Toronto via New York on the SS *Nickerbocker* in 1856. A vessel of the Black Star Line carrying 500 passengers, the ship sprung a leak and landed in a bed of shingle during a hazardous journey. A U.S. vessel came to the rescue, which the passengers boarded with most of their luggage, and provided with food and sleeping quarters, eventually reached the emigrant depot at Castle Garden, New York. After sightseeing they took a steam boat up the Niagara River and journeyed by train to Toronto. He attended Trinity School, Toronto, and returned to England in 1862-1863.

Records

Hand-written and pictorial commonplace book giving detailed descriptions of journeys taken to Toronto and Yorkville via New York, poems written in French and anecdotes of the war of 1812, everyday life, and language of Negro workers, 1856.
Photographs of W. Dunn and his family, c.1910.
DX/608   1856   5 Items

James Farrell (fl. c.1851)

James Farrell is known from the passenger list of the ship *Princeton* to have been a young labourer from County Meath, Ireland, who emigrated alone from Liverpool to New York in 1851. His contract ticket is a rare survival, almost from the famine years, and is reproduced in the Merseyside Maritime Museum's education pack, *The Leaving of Liverpool*.

Record

Passenger's contract ticket for a steerage passage, Liverpool-New York on the *Princeton*, issued by John Taylor Crook, Waterloo Road, Liverpool, 1851.
DX/1673   1851   1 Item

Reference

G. Read and P. Rees, *The Leaving of Liverpool*, Liverpool, 1986.

Edward Garner (fl. c.1880)

Edward Garner of 8 Vine Grove, Toxteth, Liverpool, is believed to have emigrated to Saskatchewan in Canada, c.1880.

Records

Bible including family dates of birth, 1837.
Photograph of Edward Garner, c.1880.
DX/623   1837-c.1880   2 Items

George Gatheral (fl. 1900)

George Gatheral of Newcastle-upon-Tyne described in his notebook his voyage to, and from, New York on board the White Star liners *Cymric* and *Oceanic* in 1900.

Records

Hand-written notebook of ephemera which includes:
Memo of saloon log and passenger list of *Cymric*, Liverpool to New York, 1900.
Memo of log and saloon passenger list of *Oceanic*, New York to Liverpool, 1900.
Accommodation plans of *Cymric* and *Oceanic*, 1900.
Programme charity concert, *Oceanic*, 1900.
Postcards and other ephemera including saloon seat ticket, passenger list and menus, 1900.
Note of good wishes from the "Fifteen Liberal Club," Newcastle-upon-Tyne, 1900.
Brochures for New York and Niagara Falls including maps, 1900.
DX/316   1900   1 Item

William Culshaw Greenhalgh (fl. c.1853)

William Culshaw Greenhalgh left Liverpool in 1853 aboard the *Marco Polo* (James Baines & Co.) bound for Sydney. In his voyage diary, which he sent to his relatives in Bolton, he gives vivid descriptions of shipboard incidents: the brutal treatment received by a steward from the commander, Captain "Bully" Forbes, a number of men put in irons and fed bread and water, one for striking the captain, another for insulting the first mate, and the chief steward, baker and cook for being drunk and disorderly. He described how the third-class passengers, dissatisfied with the pea soup caused a commotion (one composed a song, "The Pea Soup Calamity") and includes other general remarks concerning weather conditions, sightings and daily activities. A full transcript is available in *The Passage Makers* (see below).

Record

Diary of William Culshaw Greenhalgh.
DX/1676   1853   1 Item

Reference

Stammers, M.K. *The Passage Makers, The History of the Black Ball Line of Australian Packets*. Brighton, 1978.

Thomas Gregory (fl. c.1841)

Thomas Gregory emigrated with his wife and daughter to Albany, New York from Finningley, Nottinghamshire in 1841, and wrote home to his mother and brother between 1841 and 1843. His first letter describes the voyage from Liverpool to New York, including diet, illness and deaths, and the English, Scots, Welsh and Irish passengers. The second letter gives his first impressions of Albany, and the remaining four letters were written two years later describing his life and work in Albany.

Records

Letters (with transcripts), 1841-1843.
DX/1168   1841-1843   6 Items

John Hedges (1828-1920)

John Hedges, a builder from Hampstead, London, and his wife and two young sons, Walter and Basil, were government assisted emigrants. In his diary, in the form of a letter to his mother, he described conditions during their stay at the

Birkenhead Emigrant Depot and their voyage on the *Admiral Lyons* to Sydney, New South Wales. There is much detail regarding health, hygiene, quality of provisions and hard work in Australia. His younger son Basil died in Sydney Harbour.

Records

Diary (of a letter to his mother), unfinished. Full transcript available (extracts used in publication cited below), 1858.
Photographs (black & white/colour) of John Hedges, his descendants, houses, and family grave in Waverley Cemetery, Sydney, c.1980.
Copies of official records, 1858-1920.
Family pedigree, 1986.
DX/243   1858-1984   17 Items

Reference

Read, J.G. and Rees, P. *The Leaving of Liverpool*. Liverpool, 1986.

H.J. Heinz (fl. c.1886)

H.J. Heinz, food manufacturer of Pittsburgh, PA, the son of German emigrants, sailed to Liverpool in the *City of Berlin*, and returned in the *City of Chester* in 1886. His diary describes his visit to Britain, including the Shipperies Exhibition in Wavertree Park, Liverpool. He also paid a visit to his family roots in Germany. His primary purpose, however, was to break into the British market, which he did with considerable success.

Records

Photographs of the text of his diary (part, 10 pp.), 1886.
DX/92   1886   10 Items

Reference

Alberts, R.E. *The Good Provider*. USA, 1973.

John Hooton (fl. c.1837-1858)

John Hooton, a sailor of Brandywine, PA, USA, wrote letters to his family who had emigrated to the USA, describing life on board ship during his voyages to USA, Germany and Cuba, where he died.

Records

Letter from emigrant Jacob Hooton, Brandywine, Pa., to his son John on board ship *Delaware*, mentions *Algonquin*, a Liverpool packet vessel, 1837.
Letters from John B. Hooton, to his mother re: his travels to Cuba and Germany, and outbreak of yellow fever on board ship, 1856.
Letter from Isaac Knight to Mrs. Simmonds re: John's death, 1858.
DX/526   1847-1858   4 Items

Paymaster Lieutenant Commander James M.P. Kirkness, R.N.R. (Fl. c. 1937)

Paymaster Lieutenant Commander J.M.P. Kirkness intended to emigrate with his wife and children to Australia, Canada or New Zealand in the 1930s-1940s. Papers include post war emigration plans for the three countries, and completed application forms for prospective citizenship in Ontario.

Records

Correspondence, application forms and curriculum vitae, 1937-1946.
DX/1181   1937-1946   29 Items

SS *Limerick* and SS *Rippingham Grange*

The *Limerick* and the *Rippingham Grange* were owned by Houlder Brothers of London, and from 1909 to 1912 were part of a passenger and cargo service to Queensland ports, Australia. This was run in co-operation with the Federal, Shire and British India Lines. The *Limerick* and *Rippingham Grange*, both built in 1898, carried 26 first-class and 230 third-class passengers. The records comprise photographs of passengers and crew on board both vessels on voyages from London to Brisbane, Australia.

Records

Photographs of stewards and stewardesses, a fancy dress ball, groups of passengers on deck, a boxing competition, a children's tea party, Church Army Boys (possibly emigrants sent out by the Church Army), Morgan's soldiers (fancy dress), and passage workers (i.e., emigrants working their passage as crew members).
DX/1279   c.1910   14 Items

John Lockett (Fl. c. 1935)

A well connected family with shares in major shipping companies. The archive contains letters regarding John Lockett's emigration to Sydney, Australia and

Santiago, Chile, with his wife, his lack of ability to find employment, his constant requests for financial aid and his eventual success employed in a school in Santiago, 1935-1938.

Records

Letters to, and from John Lockett's family, 1935-1938.
Share certificates for Cunard Steam Ship Co., Liverpool, 1919-1954, 1962.
Receipts for policies and bonds from Cunard Line, Mersey Steam Ship Co. and Papayanni & Co., Liverpool, and Armstrong Naval Yards, Newcastle-on-Tyne, 1899-1954.
DX/175   1935-1962   1 Box

Margaret McHugh (fl. c.1927-1937)

Margaret McHugh of Westport, Co. Mayo, Ireland, is believed to have emigrated to New York, USA c.1928, possibly on a vessel of the United States Lines, Roosevelt Steamship Company, Inc. She was assisted in her passage by various schemes, including the Irish Emigrant Society of New York, the Manhattan Savings Institution of New York City, and the Dry Dock Savings Institute. It is likely that her husband emigrated first and sent funds to these societies which would have arranged her passage through their Irish offices by charging him a commission. The society then paid the Irish or Liverpool broker out of the fund which ensured a safe channel for money to be received by poor relatives.

Records

Memoranda of money drafts and cheques of the Irish Emigrant Society of New York, to be drawn at Westport, Co. Mayo, Ireland, 1928-1937.
Cheques of Dry Dock Savings Institution, New York, in favour of Margaret McHugh, 1937-1939.
Cheque from the Manhattan Savings Institute, New York City, to be drawn on Munster & Leinster Bank Ltd., Westport, Ireland, 1935.
Bank drafts from the Irish Emigrant Society, 1936-1937.
Draft for £10 issued by United States Lines, Roosevelt Steamship Company Inc., 1934.
Money order receipts issued in New Rochelle, New York, c.1929-1931.
DX/582   1928-1939   34 Items

A. Nash (Fl. c. 1875)

A. Nash from Battersea, London, travelled from Liverpool to Toronto, Canada, on board the Allan Line's *Polynesian* in 1875.

Records

Printed letters from the Allan Line, James Street, Liverpool, regarding booking of passage, 1875.

Memorandums from the Allan Line to A. Nash re: passage of 8 days on *Polynesian*, fares for steerage class Liverpool to Toronto through ticket (£4. 7s. 6d.), and rail fare Quebec to Hamilton, (1ˢᵗ class, £2. 10s. 0d., emigrant class, £1. 5s. 6d.), 1875.

Verse (typescript) about escapade on iceberg and rescue by officers and crew of *Polynesian*, May 1875.

DX/571 1875 5 Items

National Childrens Home

Thomas Bowman Stephenson, a merchant minister, founded the National Childrens Home and directed its continuous growth for over thirty years. In 1873 Francis Horner accompanied the first of many parties of emigrant children to a Home in Hamilton, Ontario, Canada.

Records

Typed history of Childrens Home in Hamilton, Ontario, with account of voyage in SS *Polynesian*, 1873-1934.

Xerox extracts from *The Children's Advocate and Christian at Work*, with description of voyages to Canada, referring to SS *Polynesian, Texas, Ontario* and *Sarmation* and illustration of Home in Ontario, 1873-1874.

Publicity leaflets re: Children's Homes on Merseyside, c.1980.

Publicity leaflet entitled, *Roots and Branches*, c.1980.

Photographs of children waiting to embark for Canada, luggage marked "Hamilton," c.1900.

DX/444 c.1900-1980 24 Items

Nayler Family

Henry, Lucy and Edith Nayler of Doncaster, Yorkshire, emigrated to Illinois, USA, in 1831. In a letter to relatives in Doncaster they described the weather, taxes, economy, rents, shoemaking, tanning and farming. The letter strongly advised relatives to come to the "land of liberty."

Record

Letter (with transcript), 1843.

DX/1422 1843 1 Item

Richard Nuttal Preston (fl. c.1852)

Richard Nuttal Preston was an emigrant on the ship *Falcon* (Gibbs & Co., Liverpool) from Liverpool to Sydney in 1852. In his letters to his uncle and aunt, Mr. and Mrs. J. Greaves of Castle Street, Liverpool, he vividly describes the 110 day voyage, the conditions at sea, their arrival in Sydney and the death of his brother, whom he had encouraged to emigrate.

Records

Letters written by Richard Nuttal Preston to his aunt and uncle, 1852-1854.
SAS/3/1/12   1852-1854   6 Letters

G.B. Smith (fl. c.1856)

G.B. Smith, an emigrant to Illinois, USA, wrote to his brother in Doncaster, Yorkshire on the back of a large coloured map of Illinois. He relates how he sold his farm stock in Illinois and rode north to Jacksonville, contemplating taking a boat "up the river as I heard they were paying great wages in the north ... emigrants are flocking there by the thousands ..." He falls sick in St. Louis with fever, ultimately crossing into Canada and arriving at Edwardsburg on the St. Lawrence, which surpasses all his expectations, particularly to climate and prospects.

Record

Letter written upon the reverse of a map of Illinois published in New York, 1856 (with transcript), 1856.
DX/1456   1856   1 Item

Sarah Stephens (1850-1877)

Sarah Stephens, from Machynlleth, Montgomeryshire, Wales, emigrated on the sailing ship *Cardigan Castle* (R. & J. Evans, Liverpool) in 1876. She sailed from Gravesend, Kent to Lyttleton, South Island, New Zealand. She travelled with her widowed mother, her four younger sisters and her brother.

The diary is written in an excellent descriptive style in the form of a letter to an unidentified relative at home, probably the writer's elder brother. The ship carried many single, mostly Irish emigrant girls, supervised by a matron. References are made to problems with the matron, fighting amongst the girls and the organisation of the messes. A mutiny was reported on 13 December 1876, during which the captain was "knocked about very much."

Sarah's "Uncle Davies" was already at Tai Tapu, near Christchurch waiting to welcome them. The ship was affected by fever and on arrival, the passengers were quarantined for three weeks at Ripapa Island. The diary ends with a short account of Christchurch. Her brother was engaged by a local timber firm and Sarah had a job waiting for her in the "largest shop in Christchurch."

Records

Voyage diary (with transcript), 1867-1877.
Family history notes, including family tree compiled by Powys Family Historians. Photocopies of official documents, including commissioners' and surgeon-superintendent's report and part of a passenger list from the Archives of New Zealand.
Notes supplied by Canterbury Museum.
DX/1071/R   1876-1877   1 Volume

Isaac Whitehead (fl. c.1916)

United Stated Certificate of Naturalisation issued by the State of Ohio, 1874, initially heard in the Probate Court, City of Cleveland. It was finally granted to Isaac Whitehead in 1916, giving him citizenship, and the rights and privileges of a naturalised citizen.

Record

US Certificate of Naturalisation, 1874.
DX/867   1874   1 Item

Wray Family

The Wray family were Quakers from Derby who emigrated to New York State, where their grandmother Bowman, already lived in Monroe, Orange County. The father was a cabinet maker and the family finally settled in New York City, where there was more scope for his business. An interesting early example of well documented "opportunity" emigration recorded in a typescript memorandum which gives details regarding preparations and transport of the family and their belongings by canal from Altrincham, Cheshire, to Runcorn, by steam packet to Liverpool and the problem of finding lodgings in Liverpool. Also details of boarding and payment arrangements and the voyage of over six weeks on board the *James Monroe*, a Black Ball Line packet to New York, July-August 1818.

Records

Typescript of *Memoirs and remarks made during the voyage of myself and family from Derby in England to America*, written by Mr. Wray(?), 1818.
Typescript memorandum re: settlement, marriages and dispersal of the family over the next generation, n.d. [c.1820].
DX/562   1818-c.1820   2 Items

Emigration Records in Larger Collections

Much important material relating to emigration can be found in family or miscellaneous collections, which are described in detail in the appropriate chapters of this *Guide*. Details of some of these emigration documents are summarised below. The majority of these archives are available *strictly by appointment only*.

Danson Family Archive

For details of this family collection, see Vol. II, chap. 10. Access to this collection is *strictly by appointment only*.

John Towne Danson (1817-1898)

J.T. Danson, a one-time journalist specialising in economic and social affairs, was greatly interested in emigration and colonisation and amongst his indexed general correspondence and other papers, may be found many documents relating to these subjects.

Records

Correspondence re: his pamphlet, *The Commercial Progress of the Colonial Dependencies of the UK*, 1849.
Correspondence with the Colonial Office, 1843-1847.
Volume entitled, *Colonial Statistics*, c.1849.
Printed circular letter to Lord Ashley, M.P., from the "emigrant's friend," Mrs. Caroline Chisholm, entitled, *Family Colonisation Loan Society or A System of Emigration to the Colonies of New South Wales, Port Philip and South Australia*, August 1849 (reproduced in Read, J.G. & Rees, P., *The Leaving of Liverpool*, Liverpool, 1986).
DD/III/2/9 & 14: 11/17: 12/7   1843-1849   4 Files

Edward Chester Danson (1818-1898)

J.T. Danson's younger brother Edward emigrated from Liverpool to Sydney, Australia, on the *Elizabeth* in 1841. However, he did not make a success of his life as a shepherd in New South Wales, and was dependent on an annual allowance of £100 from his brother in England.

Records

Family correspondence prior to Edward's emigration (i.e. "what to do with Edward"), 1836-1841.
Letters from Edward Danson describing his voyage, life in Australia and the state of his financial affairs, 1841-1890 (transcripts of these letters are available).
Correspondence between Edward Danson and his nephew Francis Danson re: family affairs, and the former's recollections of the opening of the Liverpool-Manchester railway (1830), 1896-1898.
Probate papers re: Edward Danson's death and photographs of his tomb at Tamworth, New South Wales, Australia, 1896-1898.
DD/III/2/60, 63, 64: DD/V/2/3 & 10,
DX/1/64 (Photographs)   1841-1899   5 Files

Lockett Family

J.T. Danson married into the Lockett family of Llangollen, North Wales, and because of his financial and legal acumen, took charge of their affairs. The section of the Danson collection relating to the Lockett Trust includes an interesting group of papers concerning the emigration of J.G.W. Lockett and other members of the family.

J.G.W. (George) Lockett (1833-1878)

George Lockett emigrated with his wife to Victoria, Australia, in 1855. They sailed from London on the 30 March on the packet vessel *Hope*, and his wife gave birth to a baby daughter during the voyage.

Records

Letters re: J.G.W. Lockett's training as a surgeon at Guy's Hospital and the poor state of their financial affairs, 1853-1854.
Two posters for sailings to Australia, one for the Golden Line of Australian Packet Boats sailing from Liverpool, and the other poster for the *Hope* the first poster is reproduced in Read, J.G. & Rees, P., *The Leaving of Liverpool* (document pack), Liverpool, 1986.
Printed lists of necessaries required for a voyage, c.1855.

J.G.W. Lockett's personal log of the voyage (8 pp.), 1855.
Letter to J.T. Danson written on his arrival, stating his intention to be "off to the diggings," 1855.
Letters re: theft by J.G.W. Lockett and his poverty in Victoria, 1855.
Letters of administration, South Yarra, Victoria, 1878.
DD/VIII/1/2/1, 4, 5: 3/3/1-25   1853   17 Files

Edmund Lockett (1837-1908)

Born at Pen-y-Bryn Hall, Langollen, Edmund Lockett was educated in England with a view to following his uncle into the medical profession. He got into debt by misappropriating some of J.T. Danson's money, and by way of settlement was persuaded to emigrate to Canada. On the 5 May 1858, he sailed to Quebec, accompanied by his older sister. According to his obituary he became a respectable member of the local community as Postmaster at Bury, near Quebec, and a captain in the local militia.

Records

F.C. Danson's manuscript volume re: the Lockett Trust, contains notes on the dispersal of the family throughout North America, and Edmund's obituary from the *Montreal Star*, 1908.
J.T. Danson's commonplace book contains details of Edmund's emigration and debts, 1858.
Letters of administration, 1908.
DD/III/4/2/4, VIII/1/1/3, 1/2/4, 3/3/1-25   1854-1908   2 Volumes &
                                                           15 Files

Elizabeth Mary Lockett (1845-post 1861)

J.T. Danson arranged for Elizabeth Lockett to join her family in Canada after she had been involved in what he deemed to be an "unsuitable relationship" with a butcher's boy. She sailed to Montreal on the *Anglo Saxon* in 1861.

Records

Handbill advertising the voyage, newscuttings and letter from the prospective suitor, all in J.T. Danson's commonplace book, 1861.
DD/III/4/2/4 & 5   1854-1861   1 Volume & 1 File

Bryson Collection

This large collection of miscellaneous documents includes the papers of solicitors, among which, may be found many personal letters used as exhibits in court in connection with the administration of estates. Some emigration documents are also to be found in sections of the collection relating to a particular family or business. (For further details of the Bryson Collection, see Vol. II, chap. 11). Unless otherwise stated, these archives are available *strictly by appointment only*.

Battersby Family

A Liverpool Irish family, some of whom emigrated to America and Australia, whilst others remained in Liverpool and ran a successful coal trading business with a fleet of barges and flats. The collection includes extensive correspondence between members of the family at home and abroad. This collection is available *without an appointment* at the Maritime Archives & Library.

James Battersby (1820-1854)

James Battersby emigrated to the USA with his wife, Juliana, and their children, in 1850, and went to live in Cincinnati, Ohio.

Records

Correspondence with his brother, Richard Battersby, and family in Liverpool, describing his wife's desertion, their divorce, his application for American Citizenship, problems of employment, and life in Cincinnati, and following his death in 1854, the return of the children to England. Also letters to Juliana from her brother, William Reece, writing from New York re: the difficulties of life in America at a time of economic recession, and his inability to offer James Battersby any work or financial assistance, 1849-1855.
Specimens of Cincinnati business stationery, c.1895-1897.

Richard Battersby (fl. c.1852)

Richard Battersby, brother of James Battersby, sought to alleviate his financial difficulties by joining the "gold rush" to Australia in 1852. However, he was unsuccessful at making his fortune and returned home to Liverpool in 1853.

Records

Correspondence between Richard Battersby and his brother, James, re: his decision to go to Australia for 12-18 months, his life at the gold-fields and his relief at returning home, 1852-1854.

Frederick Battersby (fl. c.1833-1884)

Frederick Robert (James) Battersby emigrated to the USA in 1833, but went missing in November 1884.

Records

Correspondence of Colonel J.C. Battersby and others, concerning the search for Frederick Battersby, and his legal affairs, 1888-1899.
D/B/119/C & D   1844-1899   2 Boxes

(A selection of Battersby family documents have been reproduced in Read, J.G. & Rees, P., *The Leaving of Liverpool* [document pack], Liverpool, 1986).

Beakbane Family

The Beakbane family of Birkenhead and Liverpool were Quakers involved in the tanning industry. John emigrated to Montreal, Canada in 1883, after reading about the country in books at Birkenhead Free Library, and also to be re-united with his father, William, who had emigrated earlier. However, William had not made a success of his life and had become an alcoholic, which led him to take his life by drowning in the St. Lawrence River. John's brother, Thomas, emigrated to the USA but after being swindled by his employer, became destitute and enlisted in the US Army. John, however, appears to have made a success of life in Montreal.

Records

John Beakbane (fl. c.1865)

Letters to his family in Britain, expressing his hopes of a new life in Canada with his father, his father's death and finding work. The letters give a vivid description of emigrant life in a Canadian city, 1883-1884.

Thomas Beakbane (fl. c.1865)

Letters to family in Britain referring to his adverse situation and enlistment in the US Army, 1884.
D/B/102/AD   1881-1977   1 File & 1 Volume

(Three letters are reproduced in Read, J.G. & Rees, P., *The Leaving of Liverpool* [document pack], Liverpool, 1986).

Reference

Beakbane, R. *Beakbane of Lancaster, A Study of a Quaker Family*. Kidderminster, 1977.

Cobham Family

George Ashworth Cobham (1806-1870), a member of an old established Liverpool family, was committed to Lancaster Castle as a debtor. He had earlier married his sister-in-law, in breach of Canon Law, and thus his nephews became his stepsons. He escaped from prison and with his family, set sail from Le Havre for New York. They settled in Warren, Western Pennsylvania, where he built a house on virgin territory which still stands today.

The surviving records cover his financial and business affairs both prior to, and after his emigration, and include correspondence with his nephew John and lawyers in Liverpool. His letters at the time of the Civil War reveal his support for the Union, whilst his nephew John was influenced by Confederate opinion in Liverpool. George Ashworth, Jr., his stepson, died during the Battle of Peach Tree Creek in 1864. There are many papers relating to the extensive litigation concerning the will of George Cobham, Sr., the Lancashire estate, and genealogical material dating the family back to the sixteenth century.

Records

Letters, legal papers, deeds and family pedigrees, 1739-1925.
Probates of Cobham family wills, including George Cobham, merchant late of Liverpool, and then of Charlestown (Charleston), South Carolina, and the will and associated legal papers of G.A. Cobham, Sr., 1870.
Printed memoir of G.A. Cobham, Jr., 1864.
D/B/1/E & F   1739-1925   2 Boxes

Documents and photographs can also be found in the miscellaneous DX collection available without an appointment at the Maritime Archives & Library. These are:
Copies of articles relating to their emigration and settlement in Warren, and photographs of their family home.
DX/528   c.1855-1994   4 Items

Photographs of family portraits and heirlooms donated by a member of the family in 1987.
DX/630   c.1750-1920   37 Items

Reference

Toubkin, Lynne. *From Liverpool to Warren: Migration and Social Values in the Nineteenth Century*. PhD Thesis, University of Haifa, Israel, 1996.

Smaller Collections of Emigration Records in the Bryson Collection include:

J.M. Beckwith (fl. c.1891)

J.M. Beckwith of Rock Ferry, emigrated to the USA, c.1890, and became assistant manager of the Silver King Mining Co.'s mines in California.

Records

Deed of appointment as assistant manager, 1891.
Letters re: legal proceedings with the Silver King Mining Co., 1897.
D/B/111/M   1891-1897   1 Deed & 4 Letters

James Brightman (fl. c.1861)

James Brightman of Liverpool, emigrated to Victoria, Australia in 1861, and became manager of a quartz mine at Springdallah, Smythdales, near Ballarat.

Record

Letter to his cousin, Ellen in South Wales, describing the ships on which he has sailed, the *Sir Isack* (sic.), *Lyan* (sic.), *Goldsmith* and the *Golconda*, 1861.
D/B/105/C   1861   1 Item

Simpson and Walter Carruthers (fl. c.1894)

Simpson Carruthers of Ilkley, West Yorkshire, left the ministry of the Church of England on health grounds and with his younger brother, Walter, emigrated to Tasmania in c.1911. They bought an apple orchard at Back River, New Norfolk, and their letters home to their mother describe the problems of raising money to buy the orchard and the selling of the apple crop. Their mother later joined them in Tasmania.

Records

Letters home to their mother re: buying and operation of the apple orchard, etc., 1911-1913.
Invoice for shipping baggage on the SS *Afric*, 1912.
D/B/102/C   c.1911-1913   1 File

William Edgeley Duggan (fl. c.1883)

William Duggan of Liverpool, emigrated to Florida, USA in 1890, to work on an orange farm. He was forced to return to Liverpool because of ill health owing to the "Florida Fever" in 1891.

Records

Legal papers re: the administration of the estate of his father, William 1884-1893.
Letters of reference relating to F. Alston of Queensland, 1890.
Legal papers concerning his ill health, 1891.
Two advertising leaflets re: openings abroad for "young gentlemen," c.1890.
(One of the leaflets is reproduced in Read, J.G. & Rees, P., *The Leaving of Liverpool* [document pack], Liverpool, 1986).
D/B/102/A,D   1883-1900   1 File

Henry Holt (fl. c.1890)

Henry Holt of Liverpool was an architect who emigrated to New York and established a practice there. His letters home are very informative about his activities and apparent prosperity.

Records

Letters home to Liverpool, 1890-1901.
Business letters from contacts in various parts of the USA, 1890-1901.
D/B/104/A   1890-1901   1 File

John Keenan (fl. c. 1860)

John Keenan, an Irish emigrant, describes his proposed emigration with his family to an unspecified destination in a letter written to an unknown correspondent (possibly his solicitor).

Record

Letter discussing details of proposed emigration.
D/B/108/D   1860   1 Item

William Perkins (fl. c.1924)

William Perkins emigrated to the USA and discovered a rich vein of gold at a gold mine in "Robbins Mining District" at Idaho. In a letter to his friend J.S. Latham, he asks him to come out and collect his share, which will be waiting for him in New York.

Record

Letter from William Perkins, c/o Queen's Hotel, Halifax, Nova Scotia, to J.S. Latham, 1924.

D/B/108/D   1924   1 Item

Samuel Collins Radford

Samuel Collins Radford emigrated to Canada, leaving his mother, wife and children at Crosby, Liverpool. He travelled around with no fixed address, and eventually disappeared and was presumed dead.

Records

Letters home from Toronto, Ottawa and Winnipeg, some including references to strike breaking on the Grand Trunk Railway, and used in court proceedings re: the settlement of his estate, 1893-1930.

D/B/104/A   1893-1930   1 File

George Seddon (fl. c.1843)

George Seddon, a watchmaker originally from Liverpool, left Britain c.1843 on account of mounting debt. He became a seaman and travelled the world for six years, joining the Californian Gold Rush. He wrote home from San Francisco, to his brother-in-law, Ralph, describing his travels and later settled on the Sandwich Islands as a watchmaker.

Records

Letters from San Francisco, 1849-1850.
Papers re: administration of his estate, 1849-1850.

D/B/105/C   1849-1850   1 File

Stella Shaw

Stella Shaw (first Mrs. Ellicott, later Mrs. Goldsmith) emigrated to New Zealand with her brother and subsequently went to Australia where she spent thirteen months in hospital in Sydney suffering and recovering from meningitis, before returning to the UK.

Records

Letters and legal papers re: legacy from her grandfather, Jas. Fisher Jones, and reference to a manuscript of an unpublished novel, for which she sought a London publisher, 1910-1934.
Letters re: property in Hastings, Sussex, 1930-1934.
D/B/146/A,B   1910-1934   3 Boxes

Emigrant Hostel

A hostel for emigrants using White Star vessels was run by John Henrickson and William Rick at 2 Flint Street, Liverpool, c.1894.

Record

Partnership agreement between John Henrickson and William Rick, re: emigrant hostel, 1894.
D/B/111/U   1894   1 Item

N.B. Microfilms of voyage diaries of emigration held in other institutions, are available in the Library, see Vol. II, chap. 10.

Illustrations of Emigrant Ships

Requests for illustrations of ships, which carried emigrants, are frequent. The photographic collections have a reasonable coverage of steamships from about 1880 onwards. This includes the vessels owned by the major British transatlantic liner companies. The McRoberts collection (see Vol. II, chap. 9) has coverage of the Atlantic Transport, Allan, Anchor, Canadian Pacific, Cunard, Dominion, Guion, Inman, Leyland, National and White Star Lines.

There are no photographs of sailing emigrant ships but there are a number depicted in the paintings and models collections held by the Maritime History Department at the Merseyside Maritime Museum. These include a painting of the famous Australian emigrant clipper *Marco Polo* of 1851, and a model of a typical American transatlantic packet ship *Oxford* of 1836. Full details can be found in the Museum's catalogues of ship models and oil paintings.

Illustrations of the interiors of emigrant sailing ships can be found in selected copies of the *London Illustrated News*, examples of which are held in the archives collection (see Vol. II, chap. 3; DX/287).

Research Collections

Dr. B.P. Birch Research Collection on Mid-West Emigration to USA

Articles and photocopies presented by Dr. Brian P. Birch, Senior Lecturer in Geography at Southampton University, who has written many articles on emigration to the mid-western states of the USA.

Note that most of the material listed below is the copyright of the holder of the original manuscripts or of Dr. Birch.

Records

File entitled *Mid West Emigration*, includes title page of *The Emigrants Instructer on Wisconsin and the Western States of America*, Liverpool, 1844 (published by the British Temperance Emigration Society) with two lists of names of members of the British Temperance Society and Saving Fund, printed letter (1846) and report (1843), c.1842-1846.

All the above relate to the short-lived settlements of Gorstville and Reevesville (now Mazomanie and Arena), Wisconsin, established by the Society. Photocopied from the records held by the Wisconsin Historical Society. The file also contains letters (5) from Dr. Thomas Steel, emigrant from London to Genesee, Wisconsin, via New York, 1834-1845.

File containing diary of John Greening, emigrant farmer from Worcestershire (?) via Liverpool and New Orleans to Wisconsin and Minnesota, on the ship *Radius*, 1847-1849. (Photocopy of typescript, held by the Minnesota Historical Society).

File containing list of UK sources re: emigrants to North America, c.1985, and article entitled, "An English Approach to the American Frontier" in the *Journal of Historical Geography*, by B.P. Birch, 1982.

File containing typescript re: emigration of the Cowan brothers from Edinburgh to Iowa and Wyoming, USA and British Columbia, Canada, 1882-1899. Copied from original documents at the London School of Economics.

File containing typescript re: emigration from Hull to Sheppardsville, Clinton County, Iowa, USA on the ship *Columbus*, 1850; from Barrow-in-Furness and Scotland to Furness Colony, Wadena County and Minnesota, USA and from Somerset and Dorset to New Yeovil, Minnesota, USA George Sheppard (b. 1819), one-time newspaper editor from Hull, was the agent for these emigrations.

Article by B.P. Birch, entitled "The Pleasure and the Pain," in the *Journal of the Illinois State Historical Society*, Vol. 77, pp. 129-144, re: the emigration of Thomas Phipps, miller, on the ship *Connecticut*, from Liverpool to New York, 1851.

File containing short bibliography on Rural Settlement in the American Mid-West. Article by B.P. Birch, entitled "The Editor and the English," in *Annals of Iowa*, Vol. 42, pp. 620-642 (see reference to George Sheppard, above). Six other articles by Dr. Birch on emigration to Mid-Western States, written c.1980-1987.
DX/589   c.1834-1987   8 Files

Reference

Birch, B.P. "British Regional Emigration to Wisconsin around 1850s" in
    Regional Perspectives on Emigration from the British Isles. Liverpool, 1996.

J. Gordon Read Collection

J. Gordon Read, former curator of Archives at Merseyside Maritime Museum, was awarded a Churchill Travelling Fellowship in 1985 to tour record offices in Canada and USA to collect information on emigrant records. Since that date, he has assiduously amassed further information on other records in North America, Europe and Australasia. Access to this research collection *is by prior appointment only*.

Records

Churchill Fellowship report in 5 parts.
Albums of photographic prints.
Box files of brochures, articles, booklets and photocopies of original documents obtained from US State archives and museums during fellowship tour and to date. Emigration research files: articles, "case stories" relating to emigration from continental Europe, Britain and Ireland to the New World, Australasia and South Africa, containing photocopies of letters, diaries, etc., of emigrants and travellers c.1800-1960. Also relating to particular groups of emigrants, e.g. Irish, German, Scandinavian Jewish, Mormon, orphans and women.
Personal research files, lecture notes, etc., built up by J. Gordon Read through his research and his involvement with the Association of European Migration Institutions (founded 1992) and *Routes to the Roots*, USA emigrant tourism project, 1994.
J.G. Read Collection   c.1985-1998   c.40 Box Files & c.45 Boxes

Reference

Read, J.G. "Liverpool, Floodgate of the Old World." In *Journal of American Ethnic History*, Vol. 13, No. 1, 1993.

Compiled by E. Edwards, M. Evans, A. Glynn, D. Le Mare, D. Littler and M. Stammers.

CHAPTER 4

MARITIME CHARITIES, MISSIONS AND EDUCATIONAL ESTABLISHMENTS

In the mid-nineteenth century concerns about the incompetence of seamen through inadequate training led to the establishment of marine boards for the examination of masters or mates, and for enquiry into marine accidents. From a desire to improve the standards of ships, officers and men of the Mercantile Marine, Liverpool shipowners formed the Liverpool branch of the Mercantile Marine Service Association in 1857. One of the aims of the Association was to establish schools for the training of boys and men for careers in the Mercantile Marine, and in 1859 it founded the training ship HMS *Conway*. HMS *Conway* became a national institution for the training of future officers of the Merchant Navy, and its records are preserved at the Maritime Archives & Library.

The *Conway* was one of four training ships moored on the Mersey in the latter part of the nineteenth century. Two of these ships were reformatory ships, the *Akbar*, for the reform of Protestant boys, and the *Clarence*, for Roman Catholic boys. Unfortunately, none of the records of these institutions are held at the Maritime Archives & Library, although photographs of both ships can be found in the McRoberts photographic collection. The records of the *Akbar* are partly preserved at the Lancashire Record Office, Preston, as the records of Redbank School, Newton-le-Willows and Heswall Nautical School. The location of records of the *Clarence* is unknown, but enquiries should be made to the Nugent Care Society, 150 Brownlow Hill, Liverpool, L3 5RF.

The fourth training ship moored on the Mersey was the TS *Indefatigable*, a charitable institution founded in 1864, to give sea training to boys in poor circumstances. The TS *Indefatigable* merged with the Lancashire and National Sea Training Homes in 1945, and the records of both institutions are held at the Maritime Archives & Library.

Unfortunately, no records are known to survive of any Navigation Schools, but papers relating to the Association of Navigation Schools formed in 1917 in Liverpool survive. Occasionally, navigation exercise and textbooks can be found amongst the personal papers of seafarers (Vol. II chap. 7).

In the nineteenth century there was no welfare state for the relief of destitute sailors, their families, or their orphaned children. Liverpool shipowners and merchants were instrumental in raising the interest of the people of Liverpool in welfare provision for seamen and their families. The Liverpool Seamen's Friend and Bethel Union, founded in the 1820s, was one of the first institutions created to support seamen and their families. Liverpool's first Sailor's Home was opened in 1850 and provided much needed relief to seafarers, especially during the two World Wars, and its records are held at the Maritime Archives & Library. The archives of the Mersey Mission to Seamen, founded in 1856 to "minister to the spiritual, moral and temporal welfare of Merchant seamen," are held in the Liverpool City Record Office, but a number of annual reports can be found at the Maritime Archives & Library. From 1869 orphaned children of seafarers were cared for by the Royal Liverpool Seamen's Orphan Institution, and its extensive archives include both registers and confidential case papers.

From 1839 charitable provision for the relief of victims of shipwreck was provided by the Liverpool Shipwreck & Humane Society, and details of the many awards which the Society made to those who performed deeds of courage and rescue, are to be found in its annual reports. However, although national in their scope, these records may often disappoint those looking for graphic details of the disasters themselves, as they are only included in the records on account of the acts of courage performed on those occasions.

The archives of these institutions and training establishments reflect the importance attached to the supply of trained manpower for our merchant fleets, and also the recognition by the people of Liverpool of the many hazards, both physical and moral, of a sailor's life.

References

Evans, R. *Mersey Mariners*. Birkenhead, 1997. (re: sailor's charities, missions and training establishments).

Kennerley, A. *Seaman's Missions and Sailors' Homes: Spiritual and Social Welfare Provision for Seafarers in British Ports in the Nineteenth Century*. 1987.

Kennerley, A. "Sailor's Homes 1815 to 1970: Voluntary Welfare Provision for Seafarers." PhD Thesis, University of Exeter, 1989.

Masefield, J. *The Conway*. London, 1953.

Rimmer, J. *Yesterday's Naughty Children*, Manchester, 1986. (re: the history of the *Akbar* and successor institutions).

Smart, J. *The Forgotten Fleet*. (unpublished typescript), c.1950.

Charities and Missions

Liverpool Sailors' Home

The idea that seafarers should have special low cost accommodation separate from that available in boarding houses, was expressed publicly by the Reverend G.C. Smith of the Mariner's Club, London, in the early 1820s. Smith wished to found an establishment which would provide accommodation, banking and employment services for seafarers between voyages. The first Sailors' Home, in Well Street, London, opened in 1835.

It was at Liverpool that the first efforts to emulate the Sailors' Home in London were made. A number of shipowners, merchants and inhabitants held a meeting on the 25 February 1837, in the Underwriters committee room, but the provisional committee lapsed when the Corporation and Dock Trustees declined assistance. A reformed committee achieved subscriptions for £1800 by the 14 April 1841, but it was not until 10 May 1844, when the Council allocated land, that the plan proceeded. Temporary premises were opened in Bath Street in 1845, and the Liverpool Sailors' Home in Canning Place, was opened in 1850.

The Home provided much needed relief to seafarers in Liverpool, especially during the depression years and the two World Wars. Unfortunately, by the 1960s, the Home was unable to cater for the modern sailor, its accommodation being too basic, and with dwindling numbers, it was closed in 1969 and the Canning Place premises were demolished. However, the residential work of the Home continued in premises at Aigburth until 1975. In 1976 the Trustees formed the Liverpool Sailors' Home Trust which continues to support seafaring organisations on board ship and retired Liverpool seafarers in their own homes. Railings, other ironwork and a cabin from the Home are preserved in the collections of the Museum of Liverpool Life.

Records

Minutes, 1838-1954.
Account books, etc., 1845-1963.
Annual reports, 1933-1954 (broken series).
Miscellaneous correspondence and papers, c.1844-1947.
Daily record book of payments for board, 1967-1969.
Outfitting department accounts, 1951-1969.

| D/LH | 1838-1969 | 6 Boxes and 1 Volume |

Records Presented by the Charity Commissioners

Annual reports, 1911, 1923-1938 (incomplete series).
Statement of accounts, 1915.

| P/CC/LH | 1911-1938 | 1 Bundle |

Miscellaneous

Letter from Thomas Dismore & Son to unknown recipient, describing the silver trowel to be used by Prince Albert to lay the foundation stone of the Home.

| SAS/23B/1/1 | 1846 | 1 Item |

Newscutting from the *Illustrated London News* re: the opening of the Home by Prince Albert.

| SAS/23B/2/7 | 1846 | 1 Item |

Notices from the Home re: the hire of towels and the cost of playing billiards and snooker in the recreation room. Photograph of the interior of a room in the Home.

SAS/23B/1/3   c.1960   5 Items

Register of guests listing names, nationality, arrival and departures.

SAS/23B/1/4   1940-1969   1 Item

Headed notepaper of the Home, c.1950.
Contract of employment for cleaning room staff, c.1963.
Timesheet for employee, 1952.

SAS/23B/1/5   1950-c.1963   3 Items

Annual report with details of the history and gradual evacuation of the Home (1969), and exterior and interior photographs.

SAS/23B/1/6   1970   1 Item

Pamphlet issued by the Board of Trade as a guideline for mens, youths and boys sizes, and prices of outdoor clothing.

SAS/23B/2/1   1951   1 Item

Measurement book for HMS *Conway* cadets from the tailor's shop at the Home.

SAS/23B/2/3   1952-1956   1 Item

Cloth stock book from the tailor's shop at the Home, 1952-1954.
Receipts for cloth, 1959.
Letter re: material order from Tynwald Mills, Isle of Man, 1959.

SAS/23B/2/4   1952-1959   3 Items

Cutting book from the tailor's shop at the Home.

SAS/23B/2/5   1965   1 Item

Book of illustrations of company uniforms from the tailor's shop at the Home, including De Wolf, British India Steam Navigation Co., HMS *Conway* and Joseph Hoult & Co. Uniform regulations for commanders, chief officers, surgeons, engineers and midshipmen.

SAS/23B/2/6   c.1910   1 Item

Illustrations of uniform buttons and badges for all ranks, on card, produced by the tailor's shop at the Home, and approved by the Royal Mail Lines Ltd.

SAS/23B/2/8   c.1910   1 Item

Reference

Evans, R. *Mersey Mariners*. Birkenhead, 1997.

Liverpool Seamen's Friend Society and Bethel Union, Liverpool Seamen and Emigrants Friend Society and Bethel Union; Liverpool Seamen's Friend Society

Formed in Liverpool in 1820 as the Liverpool Seamen's Friend Society and Bethel Union, it was non-denominational and offered support to seamen, their families and departing emigrants, and also loaned portable libraries to ships. The Society also supplied religious publications in respective languages to emigrants at their boarding houses and at embarkation. The Society established the first floating chapel in Liverpool, on the *William*, sometimes called the "Bethel" ship, an ex-whaler built in 1775 and anchored at Salthouse Dock. In 1881 the Liverpool Seamen's Friend Society made its first move towards accommodating seafarers when it obtained a room in the Mariners Parade for use as a free sitting and reading room. In 1900 the Right Honourable Samuel Smith, M.P., erected and furnished a building as a memorial to mark the death of his son, J. Gordon Smith. The Gordon Smith Institute, Paradise Street, became the headquarters for the Liverpool Seamen's Friend Society, accommodating up to two hundred seafarers a night. In 1975 the Institute went into liquidation and the Liverpool Seamen's Friend Society ceased its operations.

Records

Liverpool Seamen's Friend Society and Bethel Union, annual report.

SAS/23D/1/1	1843	1 Item

Liverpool Seamen and Emigrants Friend Society and Bethel Union, annual report.

DX/1472	1871	1 Item

Liverpool Seamen's Friend Society, annual reports.

DX/1472	1904, 1911, 1940, 1947	4 Items
P/CC/SF/1-9	1916-1918, 1920, 1923-1927	9 Items

Liverpool Shipwreck and Humane Society

At the beginning of 1839, there were no specific charitable funds in Liverpool for the relief of sufferers from shipwreck. However, on the 7-8 January of that year, there occurred a hurricane which wrought havoc in the river and town, causing great damage to vessels moored in the Mersey and claiming many lives.

A number of liberal minded citizens of the town set about relieving the sufferers, most of whom were strangers passing through the port, and had lost most of their possessions and means of support. On 9 January a public meeting was held in the Underwriters Room "to concert measures for rewarding the intrepid persons who have been instrumental in saving…lives." James Aiken, merchant and shipbroker, proposed that a subscription fund and a permanent committee be established and be ready to act at a moment's notice, as well as to relieve those recently saved from the wrecks. Many of the survivors were assisted and able to return to their homes in Canada and America with the Society funding their passage.

At the first annual general meeting of the Society on 15 January 1840, it was resolved that the Society should be called the "Liverpool Shipwreck and Humane Society." It granted its first gold medal to Captain Clegg of the *Huddersfield*, who rescued ninety-three people on 12 January 1840 from the *William Huskisson* off Holyhead. Other notable awards include one to Matthew Webb, the Channel swimmer.

In 1884, the question arose of whether the Society should extend its responsibilities to providing relief to widows and children of mariners lost at sea. However, it was decided that its own limited funds needed to be reserved for relieving the widows and orphans of those who perished while attempting to save the lives of others.

Records

Minutes, 1839-1975.
Annual reports, 1901-1990.
D/LS   1839-1990   6 Boxes

Miscellaneous

Illuminated, framed certificates awarded to Commander A.W.V. Trant of the SS *Devonian* for rescuing sixteen crew from SS *West Point*, and for rescuing fifty nine passengers from the SS *Volturno* when on fire in mid-Atlantic.
DX/711   1910 and 1913   2 Items

Illuminated, framed certificate awarded to Captain Francis Edward Vincent of SS *Collegian*, for rescuing one hundred and twenty four passengers from the French ship SS *Euphrates*, wrecked on the east coast of Sokotre Islands.
DX/1036   1915   1 Item

Illuminated, framed certificate awarded to Idwal Wynn Hughes for attempting to save a man from drowning in Canning Dock.
DX/1037   1942   1 Item

Illuminated, framed certificate awarded to Thomas Hague for rescuing a man who had fallen into Huskisson Dock.

DX/1712   1905   1 Item

Illuminated certificate awarded to Captain Herbert Roberts and crew of steam tug *Bangarth* for rescuing the crew of MV *Lurcher*, sinking in the River Mersey off Canada Dock.

DX/1738   1961   1 Item

Reference

Sydney, J. *The Liverpool Shipwreck and Humane Society, 1839-1939*. Liverpool, 1939.

The Mersey Mission to Seamen

The history of The Mersey Mission to Seamen began in 1856 when W.H.G. Kingston, the Honorary Secretary of the newly formed Missions to Seamen (London), convened a meeting in Liverpool of the leading shipowners and influential merchants of the day. This meeting resulted in the establishment of the Liverpool branch. The objects of the Mission, "to promote and minister to the spiritual, moral and temporal welfare of Merchant Seamen," were clearly defined from the beginning and have changed little in a century and a half. The first permanent chairman was Christopher Bushell, who was succeeded by his son, and whose family were to serve the Mission for ninety six years. In 1873, the Mission assumed an independent and autonomous role under the title of "The Mersey Mission to Seamen." The Mission rented a number of rooms as meeting places for seafarers, including a room in Runcorn for the bargemen and flatmen using the canals, and a room in the Liverpool Sailors' Home as a rendezvous for seamen when ashore. In 1876 newly erected premises at Hanover Street were opened by Ralph Brocklebank which remained the headquarters of the Mission until 1957, when new headquarters were built in James Street and named Kingston House, in honour of the founder, W.H.G. Kingston. In 1984 the Mission moved to its present address at Colonsay House, Crosby Road, Crosby, where it still serves the needs of merchant seamen today. The majority of the Mission's records are held at Liverpool City Record Office.

Records

Annual reports.

DX/812   1952-1953, 1959   3 Items

Knitting pattern book for seamen, 1914.

Loose-leaf knitting pattern for sea-boot stockings, c.1941.

DX/1194   1914-c.1941   2 Items

Reference

Kingsford, M.R. *The Mersey Mission to Seamen, 1856-1956.* Abingdon, 1957.

Royal Liverpool Seamen's Orphan Institution

The first move to interest the people of Liverpool in the possibility of establishing an institution for the care of the orphaned children of seamen, was made by a group of leading Liverpool shipowners concerned by the increasing need for such provision. Members of the public were invited to attend a meeting held at the Mercantile Marine Service Association Rooms on the 16 December 1868, and the resolution to found such an establishment was proposed by Ralph Brocklebank and Bryce Allan, both leading shipowners and philanthropists. James Beazley, another leading shipowner, was invited to take over the chairmanship of the executive committee formed to further the plan to establish an orphanage. On 9 August 1869, the Liverpool Seamen's Orphan Institution opened in temporary accommodation in Duke Street, and by the end of that year there were sixty children in residence.

In 1870 Liverpool Town Council approved a resolution to give 7,000 square yards of land at the north-east side of Newsham Park to the committee to construct a Seamen's Orphan Institution. On the 31 January 1874, the children from the temporary home in Duke Street were transferred, together with forty-six newcomers. In addition to the children at the Orphanage, the committee also looked after children on an outdoor relief basis. In the Annual Report of 1899, it is recorded that there were 321 children in the orphanage, and 508 receiving outdoor relief.

The formal opening of the Institution took place on the 30 September 1874, the ceremony being performed by the Duke of Edinburgh, the "Sailor Prince," fourth son of Queen Victoria. In May 1886, the Queen herself visited the Institution, and granted the Orphanage the privilege of adding her name to the list of patrons. Royal patronage continued into the next century culminating in 1922, when the Institution was incorporated under Royal Charter.

At the outbreak of the Second World War, the Orphanage was evacuated to Hill Bark, Frankby, Wirral. In 1946, preparations were made for the return to Newsham Park, but the committee members were becoming increasingly concerned over the possible effect on the orphanage of the great expansion in the country's social services. These changes led to a gradual decline in the number of children living at the orphanage. Additional new legislation prohibited children under eleven years of age being educated at the same school as older children, and made it illegal for young children to live in a school of an institutional character. Hence the orphanage was closed on the 27 July 1949. However, the work of the Institution in providing for the relief and education of the orphaned children of seamen continues and in 1969 the Institution celebrated its centenary. Please note that searchers wishing to consult the registers of children or confidential case papers, must produce written permission from the Secretary of the Royal Liverpool Seamen's Orphan Institution, 3a Ground Floor, Tower Building, 22 Water Street, Liverpool, L3 1AB.

Records

Minute books and indexes, 1869-1963.
Executive committee draft minutes/supporting papers, 1869-1963.
Annual reports, 1869-1997.
Files of correspondence, reports, etc., c.1873-1919.
Registers of children, 1869-1949 (N.B. confidential – *written permission required*).
Bound volumes: account books, letterbooks, visitors book (Royal visit), school register, 1869-1974.
Letters, papers, etc., re: Orphanage Committee and staff, including James Beazley, c.1873-1916.
Miscellaneous papers and correspondence re: various subjects, including Royal patronage, outdoor relief scheme, staff, charitable bequests, World Wars I and II, c.1842-1969.
Personal case papers, arranged in alphabetical order, c.1880-1949 (N.B. confidential – *written permission required*).

D/SO	1869-1988	102 Boxes

Miscellaneous

W. Newman, Assistant Master of the Royal Liverpool Seamen's Orphan Institution, Newsham Park, Liverpool, 1892-1900.

Correspondence, 1886-1892.
Bye-laws: Liverpool Seamen's Orphan Institution, 1887.
Passenger list for the SS *Jebba*, African Steam Ship Co., 1899.
Photographs of orphanage dining hall and boys and girls races, football team, cricket, c.1900.

DX/66	1886-c.1900	25 Items

Prologue spoken at a concert given by Liverpool Pilots in aid of the Liverpool Seamen's Orphan Institution.

SAS/19D/2/5	1873	1 Item

Illustration of the Royal Liverpool Seamen's Orphan Institution from the *Illustrated London News*.
DX/887   1874   1 Item

Programmes for concerts held on board the *Umbria* and *Teutonic*, in aid of the Seamen's Orphan Institution.
SAS/29/8/20 and 21   1888 and 1914   2 Items

Programme for concert held on board the *Grampian*.
SAS/33C/1/2   1912   1 Item

Entertainment programmes for concerts held on board the *Lusitania* and *Mauretania*.
DX/728   1912   2 Items

Reference

Hughes, T. *The Royal Seamen's Orphan Institution A Century of Progress, 1869-1969*. Liverpool, 1969.

Miscellaneous Maritime Charities

Liverpool Homes for Aged Mariners

The Liverpool Homes for Aged Mariners at Egremont were opened by H.R.H. The Duke of Edinburgh in 1882, and provided for the maintenance of aged mariners (shipmasters, officers and seamen). It consisted of a central building and cottage homes where sixty-six inmates could be housed.

Record

Programme of fund-raising entertainment on RMS *Ambrose*, 1906.
DX/44   1906   1 Item

Liverpool Seamen's Pension Fund/Margaret Ismay Widows Fund, 1912

After the *Titanic* disaster of 1912, the existing Seamen's Pension Fund established by T.H. Ismay, founder of the White Star Line, was extended to provide pensions for seamen's widows.

Records

Correspondence re: J.B. Ismay's proposal for a fund for seamen's widows, 1912.
Correspondence re: Margaret Ismay Widows Fund, 1912.

Newspaper cutting re: *Titanic* relief fund, 1912.
Charities sub-committee of Mercantile Marine Widows Fund, n.d.
DX/504   1912   4 Items

Seamen and Boatmen's Friend Society

The north-western district of the Seamen and Boatmen's Friend Society was established in 1846. The Society originally had its premises at the Flatmen's Bethel, Mann Island, Liverpool, and later moved to Park Lane. It also had a branch at Seacombe. It was an interdenominational society, promoting the social, moral and religious welfare of seamen, especially flatmen, fishermen and canalmen. The records were presented by the Charity Commissioners.

Records

Annual reports, 1909, 1912, 1916, 1919, 1923, 1927-1935.
Abstracts of general annual report, 1937-1939.
P/CC/SB   1909-1939   17 Items

Educational Establishments

Association of Navigation Schools

A School of Navigation was established in the Royal Technical College, Glasgow, in 1910, and a course for marine cadets was started in 1912. Previous to this the Board of Trade had been approached by the College to obtain recognition of attendance at navigation classes, probably by a remission of sea service on lines similar to that given to other nautical institutions. This, and subsequent representations made to the Board of Trade for recognition of a cadet course and of senior courses, were turned down because the College was not a residential institution.

After the First World War, it was decided that official opposition might be broken down if all schools in England and Scotland took joint action. A meeting of teachers of navigation was held in Liverpool on the 9 November 1917 at the Central Technical School, Byrom Street. The ports of Bristol, Liverpool, London, Plymouth, South Shields, Aberdeen, Greenock and Glasgow were represented. The meeting resolved that the Board of Trade be requested to accept a period of not more than twelve weeks spent in a navigation school recognised for this purpose by the Board, as equivalent to the same period of sea service, for the purpose of qualifying for the Board's Certificates of Competency as Second Mate.

It was agreed that Shipowners' Associations and the Mercantile Marine Service Association should be asked for support. It was decided that the body should remain in existence and be named the "Conference of Navigation Schools," meeting on future occasions for the discussion of subjects of professional importance.

Mr. W. Merrifield of Liverpool was elected Chairman, and on the 8 June 1918 the Board of Trade agreed to recognise the schools. A course for cadets preparatory to going to sea was drawn up, after the conditions for the granting of a remission of sea service were announced by the Board of Trade in July 1919. The organisation was re-named the Association of Navigation Schools in 1933.

Records

File of papers re: Merchant Navy Training Board, 1947-1953.
File re: executive committee, 1935-1950.
Correspondence, etc., 1919-1969.
Ministry of Transport booklets, 1955-1961.
General circulars, nos. 1-315, 1950-1975.
Papers and correspondence on AGMs, 1919-1961.
D/ANS   1919-1975   4 Boxes

HMS *Conway*

On the 19 April 1858, a committee was formed by members of the Mercantile Marine Service Association to establish a training ship on the Mersey, to train boys to become officers in the Merchant Navy. The Admiralty offered the frigate *Conway*, a coastguard ship at Devonport which, on its arrival in the Mersey, was moored off Rock Ferry. The school opened on the 1 August 1859.

The original *Conway* was replaced after two years by HMS *Winchester* (re-named *Conway*), and in 1876 she was in turn replaced by HMS *Nile*, a vessel designed by Sir Robert Seppings, one of Britain's finest naval architects. Also re-named *Conway*, she remained in the Mersey until 1941 when she was moved to the Menai Straits to avoid the Blitz. In 1953, while being towed to Birkenhead for a re-fit, she was grounded near the Menai Suspension Bridge and broke her back. Soon afterwards she caught fire and had to be broken up.

From 1953-1974, the *Conway* flourished as a shore establishment, and in 1968 the school was given voluntary aided status. The British Shipping Federation took responsibility for the nautical training and placements, while Cheshire Education Authority assumed charge of the general education side. However, its closure was precipitated by the decline of Britain's merchant fleet, and on the 11 July 1974, the last eighty-five cadets laid up the Colours in Liverpool Cathedral. Eminent *Conway* cadets included John Masefield, who wrote its history in 1933 and 1953; Captain Matthew Webb, the first man to swim the Channel in 1875, and many eminent captains, commanders and admirals including four V.C.s, and Sir Arthur Rostron, Captain of the *Carpathia*, which picked up survivors of the *Titanic*.

Records

Annual reports, 1859-1894.
Monthly reports, 1881-1908.
Album of miscellaneous printed papers re: fund-raising, fitting out of cadets, 1858-1883.
Muster rolls, 1875-1959.
Wages books, 1882-1960.
Visitor books, 1934-1975.
Captain Superintendent's standing orders, 1949-1964.
Indexes to registers of cadets, 1859-1972.
Registers of cadets, 1859-1971.
Insurance stamp record books, 1953-1968.
Bound and loose volumes of the *Cadet Magazine*, 1889-1974 (1889-1966 are available on microfilm).
Photographs of cadets, sporting events, etc., 1891-1968.
Miscellaneous pamphlets and papers, 1897-1984.
D/CON   1859-1984   44 Boxes

Cadet Records

J.H.L. Allen (fl. c.1931)

Notebook, embossed HMS *Conway*, containing deck notes with drawings.
DX/1647   1931-1932   1 Item

John Craven (fl. c.1886)

HMS *Conway* bible, 1886.
The Sailors Handbook, presented for good conduct, *Conway* embossed on the front cover.
DX/1397 and DX/1649   1886-1887   2 Items

Thomas E.G. Holden (fl. c.1930)

Athletic sports day programme, 1930.
Rugby football fixtures, 1930-1931.
Dietary scales, 1930.
Typed unsigned report to Captain F. Richards, *Conway* president, re: collision between unknown steamer and *Conway*, 1930.

Menus illustrated with coloured flags and funnels for luncheon given by the Lord Mayor of Liverpool at the Town Hall, for John Masefield "and the boys of his old school," 1930.
Programme for thanksgiving service and laying up of the colours of the *Conway* at Liverpool Cathedral, 1974.
DX/858   1930-1974   1 Box

F. Martin (fl. c.1952)

Students workbook, with exercises on meteorology, ship magnetism, stability, engineering and cargo handling.
DX/774   1952-1953   1 Item

Wyndham Mortimer (fl. c.1920)

School report book, 1920.
Certificate for Second Mate qualification, 1922.
DX/1398   1920-1922   2 Items

Eric Sharrock (fl. c.1942)

School leaving certificate, 1944.
Letter home, 1942.
Hand-written uniform list with prices, bought from the Liverpool Sailors Home, 1942.
The *Cadet Magazine*, 1944.
Conway guide-book with application forms, 1965.
Photographs of *Conway* rugby and boxing teams, 1944-1945.
Conway cloth badges, 1942-1944.
Annual dinner menu, the Adelphi Hotel, 1954.
DX/897   1942-1954   1 Box

See also the collection of career papers of Captain R. Hammond (see Vol. II, chap. 7) and the recently acquired and uncatalogued papers of F.W. Vincent, O.B.E. (DX/1812), which includes correspondence with John Masefield re: the *Conway* Club and the career papers of Captain Eric Hewitt, the last captain of the *Conway* (see Vol. II, chap. 7).

Miscellaneous

What Company Should I Join? pamphlet for *Conway* cadets on completion of training, c.1950.
DX/1648   c.1950   1 Item

Photographs and 16mm film of *Conway* grounded in Menai Straits and photographs of *Conway* cadets, 1953.
DX/1717   1953   1 Box

Songsheet *"Carry On,"* the *Conway* school song, printed by James Smith & Sons, Liverpool.
DX/1118   n.d.   1 Item

The Ocean Steamship Co. undertook to re-fit the *Conway* in 1953, and plans connected with the projected re-fit can be found in the Ocean Archives.
OA 2083-C93   1953   c.60 Plans

Figure 3:   HMS *Conway*. This was the third and last vessel to serve as the Merchant Navy training ship, HMS *Conway*. Originally named HMS *Nile*, she was moored on the Mersey from 1876 until 1941 when she was moved to the Menai Straits to avoid the Blitz. In 1953 she became grounded, caught fire and was broken up.

Source: Merseyside Maritime Museum, McR/90/17.

References

Browne, T. *The Skyline is a Promise.* (Headmaster of HMS *Conway*), London, 1971.
Masefield, J. *The Conway from its Foundation to the Present Day.* London, 1933.
Masefield, J. *The Conway.* London, 1953.

TS *Indefatigable* (Liverpool Sea Training School for Boys)

In 1864 John Clint, a Liverpool shipowner, founded a charitable institution to train the sons of sailors, destitute and orphaned boys to become merchant seamen. The original definition was that it would cater "for the sons and orphans of sailors who are without means, preference being given to those whose fathers had been connected with the Port of Liverpool."

The first *Indefatigable* was loaned by the Admiralty, and was one of the last of the Navy's sailing frigates. Mr. James Bibby contributed £5,000 to transform her from a fighting ship into a training ship, and this was to be the start of a long association between the Bibby family and the school.

The *Indefatigable* was moored off Rock Ferry for over fifty years, until 1912 when it was declared unfit for further service. In 1913 HMS *Phaeton* was purchased from the Admiralty, and renamed the *Indefatigable*, remaining in use until 1941, when the bombing of Merseyside led to the ship being evacuated. The school became a shore-based training establishment, first in temporary accommodation in North Wales, and later in 1944 at Plas Llanfair, Anglesey. In 1945 *Indefatigable* was amalgamated with the Lancashire National Sea Training Homes for Boys, and renamed "The *Indefatigable* and National Sea Training School for Boys." The school celebrated its centenary in 1964, but closed in 1995 (see separate entry).

A terracotta bust of a boy sailor of the TS *Indefatigable*, a school uniform jacket and a figurehead from the TS *Indefatigable*, are held in the Merseyside Maritime Museum's collections.

Records

Committee registers, 1906-1949.
Minute books, 1913-1960.
Annual reports and accounts, 1901-1934, 1941-1988.
Correspondence, trust deeds, agreements and conveyances, 1901-1935.
Memorandums and articles of association, shareholder details of Phaeton Ltd., 1913-1952.
Centenary history pamphlet, 125th birthday, 1989.
Edition newsletter, 1989.

D/IND   1906-1989   4 Boxes

Bryson Collection

Bound volume of annual reports, 1st-17th, 1865-1881. Microfiche copy available. List of boys sent to join ships, includes name of vessel, company and date joined, 1949-1963.

D/B 115N   1865-1963   1 Volume & 1 File

Records Presented by the Charity Commissioners

Annual reports, 1902, 1980-1909, 1920, 1924-1925, 1927-1934.

P/CC IND   1902-1934   1 Bundle

Miscellaneous

Watercolour of *Indefatigable* boys at Deganwy summer camp, 1888 and colour postcard of *Indefatigable*.

DX/1516   1888   2 Items

Information file containing letters, receipts and accounts re: The King George's Fund for Sailors grants to the *Indefatigable* and National Sea Training School for Boys, 1930-1969.

SAS/23B/1/2   1930-1969   1 Box

Centenary brochure for the *Indefatigable* and National Sea Training for Boys, 1964.

SAS/23E/4   1964   1 Item

Records Held Elsewhere

After the closure of the school in 1995, its records were transferred to the Liverpool Record Office, 4th Floor, Central Library, William Brown Street, Liverpool, L3 8EW. These include:

Minute books, 1964-1984.
Register books, 1865-1990 (1950-1990 access closed).
Visitor report books, 1865-1978.
Punishment books, 1951-1995 (access closed).
Boys discharge book, 1961-1986.
Medical and dental registers, 1937-1970 (access closed).
Statistics, 1865-1949.
Photographs, c.1980-1990.

Reference

Centenary of the Indefatigable, 1864-1964. National Sea Training for Boys.
   Liverpool, 1964.

The Lancashire and National Sea Training Homes for Boys

This organisation underwent a number of changes of name and extensions of
activity. It began in 1896 as the Liverpool branch of the Navy League, and was
founded by Sir Alfred Jones, Vice President of the League's Liverpool branch.
From 1907-1908 the Home was called "The Lancashire (Navy League) Home for
Poor Boys." In 1913 the words "Navy League" were dropped, and the word
"Poor" was removed three years later. The name "Lancashire and National Sea
Training Home for Boys" was used until 1945 when they were merged with the
TS *Indefatigable* (Liverpool Sea Training School for Boys, see separate entry).
        The Homes were situated at Withens Lane, Wallasey and were available
to any British boy of good character, health and physique, however poor and
regardless of religious affiliation. It was claimed that the Home made a national
asset of what would otherwise be a public liability, and local authorities
throughout Britain awarded scholarships to the Home.

Records

Minutes, 1896-1937.
Subscription records, 1898-1945.
Treasury books, 1905-1945.
Sea registers, 1903-1945.
Miscellaneous financial records, 1913, 1938-1945.
D/NL   1896-1945   13 Boxes 14 Volumes

Miscellaneous

Colour calendar illustrations of ships *Garthpool* and *Cutty Sark*, produced to raise
money for the Lancashire and National Sea Training Home for Boys.
SAS/23E/1/3   c.1958   2 Items

Navy League minute book (Merseyside branch)
DX/208/5   1953-1963   1 Volume

Miscellaneous Educational Records

Seafarers' Education Service and College of the Sea

Founded in 1919, the Seafarers' Education and College of the Sea supplied books to merchant ships from its head office in London, each ship receiving a new library three times a year. Later, a library service was provided at Kingston House, head quarters of the Mersey Mission to Seamen (see separate entry). The service included a technical book loan scheme by which seafarers could borrow textbooks for professional studies, and this service continues today. Seafarers could write or visit for advice on many subjects besides nautical ones. Non-domiciled seafarers also sought the College's assistance.

Record

Annual report, 1959.
SAS/23D/1/5   1959   1 Item

Cookery Training Schools

Seaman's cookery book written by Alexander Quinlan, teacher of the Liverpool City Council seamen's cookery classes, and N.E. Mann, head teacher of the Liverpool Training School of Cookery.
SAS/23D/4/13   1894   1 Item

Cookery book for seamen written by Richard Bond, instructor to the City of Liverpool Technical Education Committee, 1907.
SAS/23D/4/12   1907   1 Item

Compiled by M. Evans, A. Glynn and D. Littler.

CHAPTER 5

SHIPBUILDING AND REPAIRING, ENGINEERING AND OTHER MARITIME TRADES

Shipbuilding developed at Liverpool in the late seventeenth century and was of national importance by 1800. However, by 1830 its prosperity was threatened by high labour costs and unrest, a lack of security of tenure and competition from low cost builders in Sunderland and Canada. The more far-sighted changed to building iron ships and four yards survived until the 1890s when lack of demand and the need to rebuild the South Docks ended shipbuilding in Liverpool. The Wirral shore and Garston also accommodated shipbuilding and the most successful firm was that of the Laird family. This firm was established as a boiler-making works in 1824 and became one of the major British yards. Ship repair was tackled both by shipbuilders and specialised firms and the Maritime Archives & Library's collection contains a cross section of firms involved in both ship repair and wider engineering activities. There are, however, gaps: there is little on boatbuilding or the major works such as those of Harland & Wolff, Cunard and White Star Lines. The ships of the port generated demand for other supplies and services including sails, hatch covers, rope and textiles for passenger accommodation, etc. The Handbook of Employments in Liverpool of 1916 demonstrates the huge number of jobs dependent on shipping. The collection also has a number of records of individuals and a sample is included in this section.

Details of ships built in Liverpool can be traced through the Liverpool Ship Registers for locally owned vessels and others through Lloyd's Registers. The latter has a helpful appendix after 1876 listing the output of individual shipbuilders. For earlier times, A.C. Wardle's lists of Liverpool shipbuilders in the Liverpool Nautical Research Society archive are useful (see Vol. II chap. 11).

References

Anon. *Thomas Royden and Sons, Shipbuilders, Liverpool, 1816-1893*. Liverpool, 1953.

Brown, R. Stewart. *Liverpool Ships in the Eighteenth Century*. Liverpool, 1932.

Burstall, A.R. *Shipbuilding in Liverpool, Sea Breezes*. Vol. XX (old series), 1936.

Neal, F. "Shipbuilding in Northwest England." In Ville, S. (ed.). *Shipbuilding in the United Kingdom in the 19th Century: A Regional Approach*. St. John's, Newfoundland, 1993, 75-112.

Rees, J.S. and Woods, E.C. "Seacombe Shipyards" in *Transactions of the Liverpool Nautical Research Society*. Vol. IX (1955-1961), 16-25.

Shipbuilding and Repairing

J. Gordon Alison & Co., Ltd.

James Gordon Alison established the Dock Engine Works at Birkenhead in 1875. Shortly after he was joined by Peter Duff as a partner who bought the business on Alison's death in 1894. Duff turned it into a limited liability company and it was liquidated to pay Duff's death duties. It was then reformed as a private company with the same name and in 1977 became a subsidiary of the Laird Group Ltd. In 1991 it traded as Gordon Alison & Co., Ltd., a subsidiary of the Pasec Group Ltd.

Records

Minutes, 1894-1927.
Cost books, 1883-1984, 1906-1907, 1909-1910.
Pocket books re: dry docking ships, 1915-1955.
Engineering drawings, c.1869-1969.
B/AL   c.1869-1969   1 Box

Advertisement with illustration of works, 1901.
SAS/25F/4/11   1 Item

Thomas and John Brocklebank Ltd.

Although shipbuilding at Whitehaven, the records of T. & J. Brocklebank Ltd. contain much detail on late eighteenth- and nineteenth-century shipbuilding business and technical practice (see Vol. I, chap. 4, pp. 91-96).

A. & R. Brown Ltd.

A. & R. Brown Ltd. (later Archibald Brown Ltd.) of 18-22 Porter Street, Liverpool, specialised in carrying out coppersmithing and brass founding for a wide range of industrial plant including sugar refining and industrial equipment, as well as marine work. The company merged with C. & H. Crichton Ltd., ship repairers and engineers in the early 1960s and this firm joined with Sandhills Engineering to form C.B.S. Engineering in 1972.

Records

Tally books, 1912-1927, 1940-1963.
Wages books, 1927-1956, 1966-1970.
Operational records including Charles Howson Ltd., Westminster Dredging Co., and Cunard Steam Ship Co., 1910-1076.
Finance and sales account ledgers, 1900-1972.
Miscellaneous including Trade Union rules, National Service register and Factory Act register, 1889-1952.
Mond nickel handbook, 1949.
Apprentice registers, 1927-1963.
B/AB   1899-1976   11 Boxes

Cammell Laird Shipbuilders Ltd.

William Laird emigrated from Scotland to set up a boiler making works at Birkenhead in 1824. He was joined by his son John in 1828 – the year of building their first iron boats – three lighters. They built their first steamer *Lady Lansdowne* in 1833, and the Merseyside Maritime Museum has a number of relics from her wreck.

John Laird's three sons took over and expanded the already well-established business in 1861. They built large merchant steamers and warships mainly for export. In 1903, they merged with the Sheffield steel makers, Charles Cammell & Co. and also expanded the yard, giving it the capacity to build large liners and battleships. In 1962, it acquired its neighbours Grayson, Rollo & Clover Docks Ltd. The shipbuilding and repair businesses were split up in 1972. The shipbuilding company became part of the nationalised British Shipbuilders in 1977 and was merged with Vickers Shipbuilding and Engineering Ltd. (of Barrow) in 1985 to concentrate on naval construction. Their last vessel was launched in 1993. Although the core of the yard was sold it continues to run under new management and specialises in ship conversions.

The main body of surviving Cammell Laird's records are held by Wirral Library Service at the Town Hall, Birkenhead. The Merseyside Maritime Museum's holdings are mainly ephemera, but include the important collection of family papers relating to MacGregor Laird (1808-1861), son of William Laird and pioneer of the West Africa trade (see Vol. II, chap. 6), and a number of Laird family letters and shipbuilding documents are available on microfilm.

Records

Dockyard sketch book containing drawings of vessel sections and construction details, c.1860-1870.
Folder of details of merchant ships built at Lairds, 1914-1949.
SAS/25G/1/6-7   c.1860-1949   2 Items

Notes on boiler design by H. Walker.
SAS/25D/1/26   1896-1925   1 Item

Publicity brochures including company "history" by anonymous author, *Builders of Great Ships*, 1959.
SAS/25/C/1-9   1912-1966   9 Items

Invitation cards, etc., for launches of HMS *Prince of Wales*, 1939, HMS *Ark Royal*, 1950, *Windsor Castle*, 1959, HMS *Campbelltown*, 1987 and HMS *Unseen*, 1989.
DX/879, 1006, 828, 889, 1043   1939-1989   10 Items

Reference

Warren, K. *Steel, Ships and Men*. Liverpool, 1998.

C.B.S. Engineering Co., Ltd.

C.B.S. Engineering Co., Ltd. was formed in 1972 by the amalgamation of Crichton Brown with the Sandhills Engineering Co., which was brought about by the decline of ship repairing on Merseyside. Crichton Brown Ltd. was a merger of C. & H. Crichton Ltd., ship repairers of Birkenhead and A. & R. Brown Ltd. (see separate entry). Four dry docks were leased from the M. D. & H. Co., as well as diversification into general engineering and building fishing vessels. The company was taken over by the Laird Group in 1974 and closed in about 1980.

Records

Services ledger, 1965-1967.
Scrap metal and timber purchases book, 1955-1974.
Register of material received for T. & J. Brocklebank Ltd., 1963-1971.
Ships awaiting book, 1966-1971.
Supplies inward book, 1970-1972.
Survey specifications for ship repairs mainly Ellerman Line, 1954-1977.
Apprentice registers, 1912-1934; (A. & R. Brown Ltd.), 1927-1963.
Estimate book, 1971-1973.
Photographs, c.1939-1968.
B/CB   1912-1974   1 Box

R. & J. Evans Ltd.

Established in 1840, R. & J. Evans Ltd. built ships from 1857 to 1894 and later continued as a ship repair business. It became a limited liability company in 1900, but was wound up in 1911 and later re-established under the same name in 1921. In 1934 it was taken over by Grayson, Rollo & Clover Docks Ltd. One of its products, the iron barque *Garland* of 1865, survives as a hulk in the Falkland Islands.

Records

Directors' meetings minutes, 1911-1921.
Articles of association, 1899-1900.
Combined share ledger, 1914.
Balance sheets, 1901-1908, 1916.
Legal papers, 1902-1904.
Liquidation papers, 1911.
Sail plans, 1870-1871.
Contract, 1893.
SAS/25A/2   1870-1911   1 Box

Specifications for iron work on deck and masts for sailing ships.
DX/1104   1873-1889   1 Volume

Reference

Hawkes, *G. Robert and John Evans of Liverpool, Shipbuilders: their contribution to the era of iron and steel sailing ships* in *Maritime Wales*. Vol. 18 (1996), 40-53 (includes list of ships built).

Grayson, Rollo & Clover Docks Ltd.

Grayson, Rollo & Clover Docks Ltd. were ship repairers based at dry docks at Woodside, Birkenhead. They were formed in 1928 from Grayson & Co. who had started as shipbuilders in Liverpool in 1766. Clover & Rollo was a combination of Clovers, first established as Liverpool shipbuilders in 1828 and David Rollo & Co., Ltd., marine engineers. They were taken over by Cammell Laird in 1962.

Records

Daybook.
SAS/25F/1/1   1927-1930   1 Volume

Grid iron book (Clover, Clayton & Co.).
SAS/25F/2/15   1902-1930   1 Volume

Publicity brochure for a new No. 1 dry dock at Birkenhead.
DX/815   1960   1 Item

Apprenticeship indenture for Thomas Rawlins, shipwright with Clover, Clayton
& Co.
DX/836   1918   1 Item

Shipbuilding book available on aperture cards only.
Microfilm Collection   1850   1 Item

Reference

Brooks, C. *Graysons*. Liverpool, 1956.

Jones, Quiggin & Co.

Jones, Quiggin & Co. was founded in 1855 when Josiah Jones bought into the
partnership of Jordan & Getty. The new partnership was called Jones, Getty &
Co., and in 1859 the firm became known as Jones, Quiggin & Co. with the
admission of William Quiggin as a partner. They formed the Liverpool
Shipbuilding Co., Ltd. in 1865 and although the shipbuilding ceased in 1875, the
repair work continued until 1880.

The firm of Jones, Quiggin & Co. was technically innovative and built
composite and iron ships early in its history, including sailing vessels, barges,
tugs, dredgers, yachts, paddle and screw steamers, and even iron lighthouses.
Much work was for customers abroad, and included commissions for the
Confederate Government during the American Civil War, arranged through the
commercial house of Fraser, Trenholm & Co. (see Vol. I chap. 4). Ships built at
this time include five blockade runners, one of which, the *Banshee*, became the
first steel ship to cross the Atlantic in 1863. The National liner *Egypt* of 4,670
gross tons, built in 1871, was the largest steamer then built, with the exception
of the *Great Eastern* (1858).

Records

Ship specification book: job nos. 1-159. (Fragile, photocopy available in search
room.)
DX/154   c.1855-1865   1 Volume

Specifications for paddle steamers *Rosine* and *Ruby*, and steam corvette *Danzig*, 1862-1867.
Drawing for proposed alterations to *Colonel Lamb*, 1864.
Advertisements, inventories and accounts, c.1860-1864.
Tracings of *Torpedoes* [sic.], n.d., c.1865-1870.
Bundles of letters re: small arms, 1869.
B/FT/4   c.1860 - 1870

Patent Grants

Joseph Hardwick of Liverpool, Gentleman – Improvements in Paddle Wheels, 1839.
Alfred Hardwick of Chatham Street, Liverpool – Improvements in Propelling Wheels, 1853.
DX/252   1839-1853   2 Items

J.W. Pickering & Sons Ltd

J.W. Pickering & Sons Ltd. was established at Garston in 1866 by John Worthington Pickering. In 1887 the firm moved to 41 Sefton Street, Liverpool, and was incorporated as a limited liability company in 1911. The company was dissolved in 1989. Work included ship repair, engineering, boiler making, copper and ship smithing, and iron and brass founding. Their customers included many well known shipping companies, including Pacific Steam Navigation Company.

Records

Diary (Blackwoods) of J.W. Pickering, 1874.
Estimate book – costs of materials and other purchases, 1884-1939.
Cash book containing list of employees and pay rates, and applications for apprentices, 1887-1916.
Index book – pay rates, prices, job costs, etc., including United Society of Boilermakers, Iron & Steel Shipbuilders, and wages rates, Mersey District, c.1890-1940.
Payment ledger, 1902.
Cash account book, c.1943-1962.
Ledger, 1911-1923.
Miscellaneous papers, 1855-c.1960.
DX/210   1874-1960   19 Items

Caleb & James Smith

Caleb & James Smith were established as shipwrights at Baffin Street, Queens Dock in 1818. They were involved in ship repair and boat building. James Smith died in 1836 and the business was continued by his brother until 1867.

Records

Apprenticeship indentures: Richard Worrall to Caleb & James Smith, master shipbuilders, for seven years, 1824; Edward Derby Worrall to William Rennie, James Johnson & William Rankin, shipwrights, Liverpool for seven years, 1854, and bankruptcy after twelve months service, 1855.
Certificate of service of Edward Derby Worrall, 1855.
Certificate of honourable discharge from William Rennie, James Johnson & William Rankin, shipwrights, per James Rankin, 1855-1861.
Liverpool Apprentice Shipwright's Association, membership ticket, 1858.
DX/155   1824-1858   5 Items

Joseph Steel & Sons

Joseph Steel (1780-1854), a Cumbrian, established a shipbuilding yard with two partners at Queens Dock, Liverpool in 1831. He and his son Joseph, who joined the firm in 1839, built, repaired, and from 1835 operated, wooden sailing ships until 1859. One, the *Jhelum* of 1849 survives as a hulk at Stanley, in the Falkland Islands, and has been extensively researched by M.K. Stammers, Keeper of Merseyside Maritime Museum.

Records

Transcripts of family records and survey of *Jhelum*.
D/JHE   c.1992   3 Boxes

Reference

Stammers, M.K. and Kearon, J. *The Jhelum A Victorian Merchant Ship*, Liverpool, 1992.

Engineering

Dunlop, Bell & Co., Ltd.

Dunlop, Bell & Co., Ltd. were established in the 1870s at Albert Engine Works, 46 Greenland Street, Liverpool. They specialised in building steam powered lifting machinery including colliery winding engines, cranes, cargo winches and anchor windlasses.

Record

Catalogue interleaved with number of items built, prices, names of customers, photographs of products and work's interior (fragile).

DX/841   1908   1 Volume

Fawcett, Preston Engineering Co., Ltd.

The firm known in its heyday as Fawcett, Preston Engineering Co., Ltd., was founded in 1758, by George Perry, as the Liverpool branch of the Coalbrookdale Foundry at Ironbridge. It became an independent company and built up an international reputation, particularly for sugar machinery. Its marine engines too were, in the early days, world famous, and these included those of the first Mersey steam ferry, *Etna* in 1817 and the *President*, the largest ship in the world in 1840. It was also a noted supplier of guns. In 1935 it moved away from its site at 177 Lydia Ann Street, Liverpool, to Bromborough and in 1947 became part of the Metal Industries Group. The records reflect its range of products up to the end of the Bromborough factory. Regrettably, some of the documents used for its bi-centenary history could not be found when the archives were acquired. However, photographs of some have survived. These records are available *strictly by appointment only*.

Records

Minute books, 1888-1963.
Deeds and legal documents, 1778-1920.
Financial records, 1905-1972.
Operational records, including engine books, drawings of machinery, guns, etc., 1813-1962.
Inventories, 1888-1947.
Sales records including catalogues, c.1910-1930.
Order books, 1872-1914.
Staff records, 1923-1952.
Photographs, 1910-1958.
Newscuttings, 1923-1958.
Visitor Books, 1942-1966.

B/FP   1778-1967   38 Boxes

Reference

White, H. *"Fossets." A Record of Two Centuries of Engineering*. Bromborough, 1958.

Jones, Burton & Co., Ltd.

Jones, Burton & Co., Ltd. was first established as electrical and mechanical engineers in 1891 at 19 Castle Street, Liverpool. From about 1911 they came to specialise in the sale of machine tools, engines, boats and launches. They published substantial illustrated catalogues which show that many of their wares were intended for export, especially to South America, and were manufactured by north western builders. The business appears to have been wound up about 1970. These records are available *strictly by appointment only*.

Records

Letterbooks, 1911-1914.
Operational records, 1896-1970.
Sales and services, 1896-1970.
Financial and legal, 1896-1970.
Catalogues, 1896-1970.
D/B 157   1896-1970   33 Boxes

Catalogue of machine tools.
Catalogue of steam and motor launches.
SAS/25B/2/89 & 25C/1/13   c.1930-1940   2 Items

M.E.P. (Liverpool) Ltd.

M.E.P. (Liverpool) Ltd. made hatch and grain shifting boards to prevent bulk grain from moving in a ship's hold. The older design of individual hatch boards was replaced by steel folding hatches from the 1960s, and the firm built their own design – "MEPCO" patent folding steel hatch covers. These records are available *strictly by appointment only*.

Records

Registers, 1946-1972.
Customer files, 1947-1970.
Ship records, 1958-1966.
Correspondence, 1951-1961.
Patents, 1936-1966.
Promotional items, c.1950.
Photographs and drawings, 1947-1974.
B/MEP   1936-1974   5 Boxes

Francis Morton & Co., Ltd.

Francis Morton & Co., Ltd. dates back to 1766 when John Morton established a chandler's business in Cable Street, Liverpool. By 1847 the firm was trading as the

"Galvanised Iron Merchants" and run by Francis and Henry Morton. In 1858 when Henry retired, Francis carried on alone and opened offices at 27 James Street and work premises in Bevington Bush. In 1863 additional works were acquired at Marybone.

Between 1863 and 1870, Francis Morton died, and to provide funds, the business was formed into a limited liability company, under the new Act of 1861, becoming one of the first firms in Liverpool to be so formed. The company prospered and built a new works in Naylor Street, and in 1880 took over the Windsor Iron Works, in Garston, run by Colonel Hamilton. These premises were ideal and Morton's expanded, increased production, and won orders from all over the world, for their fences, gates, iron schools, churches, railway buildings and bridges. One of the first contracts at the new site was for the main girders of the Liverpool Overhead Railway, work on which started in 1889. These records are available *strictly by appointment only*.

Records

Letter book of H.J. Morton, 1848-1853.
Sales catalogues, 1851-1900.
Newscuttings, 1886-1992.
Postcards with illustrations of Morton building, St. Helier, Jersey, 1893-1894.
Historical notes and articles re: Morton's and Garston's history, n.d.
B/FM   1848-1992   2 Boxes

Roby & Utley (Rainhill) Ltd.

Roby & Utley (Rainhill) Ltd. was an amalgamation of two Merseyside firms, John Roby Ltd., based in Rainhill, and Thomas Utley & Co., Ltd., with offices and works on Silverdale Avenue, Tuebrook in Liverpool. They were both brass founders, and made portholes, bells and other brass fittings for many famous ships, including the *Mauretania* and the *Titanic*.

The Rainhill works was closed in the 1970s, but the firm T.M. Utley (Offshore) Ltd. continues brass founding at St. Helens. An unpublished history of the Rainhill works by W. Tinker, is also available. These records are available *strictly by appointment only*.

Records

Sales documents including catalogues, 1929-1965.
Patents, abstracts of title and assignments, 1829-1962.
Financial documents, 1910-1965.
Correspondence, 1884-1965.
Will and trust documents, 1927-1934.
D/B 168   1829-1977   46 Boxes

Other Trades and Professions

John M. Gladstone

John M. Gladstone were sailmakers in Liverpool, c.1813-1859.

Records

Business and domestic bills and receipts, 1813-1859.
Family letters to and from the Williamson family, London, 1846-1848.
Miscellaneous letters and notes, including request to buy a ship's bell for school room in Isle of Man, 1843-1851.
DX/79   1813-1859   73 Items

(See also the letter book belonging to **Gladstone Nichols** who were also sailmakers in Liverpool, 1836-1846, DX/1775.)

Keizer Venesta Ltd.

Keizer Venesta Ltd. started in St. Anne Street, Liverpool in 1817, where Joseph Chiesa traded as "Carver, Gilder and Glass Merchant." By 1839, A. Greener had joined him in partnership. In 1842 L. Keizer joined Chiesa and Leopold Rohrer in partnership, who were now trading as "Carvers & Gilders, Looking Glass & Clock Makers & Dealers in Plate Glass."
        In 1902 on L. Keizer's death, the watchmaking business was sold off and the glass side, which continued trading as L. Keizer & Co., Ltd. developed rapidly. Larger premises on St. Anne Street were leased and the business was incorporated as a limited company. In 1967 the glass company was sold after 150 years in the business, but the name L. Keizer was retained. However, the woodworking side had expanded and concentrated on supplying plywood for the ship-building industry. They were so successful that by 1939, they claimed to have supplied plywood to the leading shipbuilders, for vessels such as *Empress of Britain*, *Queen Mary* and *Queen Elizabeth*. In 1965 the company merged with Venesta Plywood, after many years of co-operation, and became known as Keizer Venesta Ltd. These records are available *strictly by appointment only*.

Records

Director's minute books, 1903-1950.
Financial ledgers, 1903-1950.
Articles of association, 1903-1964.
B/KV   1903-1964   2 Boxes

Bills of lading for SS *Nora*.
Documents and correspondence re: consignment of Douglas Fir plywood from Seaboard Lumber Sales Co., Ltd., Canada, delivered to L. Keizer Co., Ltd., Liverpool, 1963.

DX/501	1963	27 Items

Reference

Wood, A.D. and Linn, T.G. *Plywoods Their Development, Manufacture and Application*. Edinburgh and London, 1942.

S. Matthews & Son

S. Matthews & Son, cotton waste dealers and bunting manufacturers, were established in the late nineteenth century, and by 1910 were based at 2 Wapping, Liverpool. There is no trace of this firm after 1930. Mary Millinger of 25 Strand Street, Liverpool was apprenticed in 1901 to S. Matthews as a flagmaker for three years, with her wages rising from 2/6d. to 9s. per week over that period.

Records

Apprenticeship indenture for Mary Millinger, 1901.

DX/116	1901	1 Item

William White

William White (1838-1921) was a sailmaker based in Liverpool.

Records

Sailmaker's work and account book of William Bartlett, 1860-1864 (photocopy).
Diary of William White, 1900-1902.
Photograph of Mr. & Mrs. White, c.1902.

DX/65	1860-1902	3 Items

Compiled by M. Evans, A. Glynn, D. Le Mare and M. Stammers.

CHAPTER 6

MARITIME FAMILIES

The acquisition of large collections of archives of maritime and mercantile families has never been a primary aim of the Merseyside Maritime Museum's collecting policy. The seven maritime family collections described in this chapter are all notable for their significance in different ways, and all contain much more than just family papers, many including papers of businesses (often for which no other records survive), and records of social and economic life for the periods which they cover. Other collections of family and estate papers of shipowners and merchants can be found amongst maritime business collections, for example, much family and genealogical material can be found in the shipping company archive of T. & J. Brocklebank, and also in the E.W. Turner mercantile collection (Vol. I, chap. 4 and Vol. II, chap. 1). Family papers can also be found amongst the career papers of seamen and officers, such as in the Bell collection relating to the family of three generations of Cunard engineers (see Vol. II, chap. 7), and amongst maritime solicitors' collections such as Alsop, Wilkinson and the Bryson accumulation (see Vol. I, chap. 11).

Two of the most notable collections of maritime family papers relate to Liverpool's involvement in the slave trade. The Cropper and Earle families represent the two opposing sides of the slavery issue, the Croppers worked for its abolition, and the Earle family were active participants in the trade during the mid-eighteenth century. Since few records of Liverpool ship-owning and mercantile partnerships survive for the eighteenth century, the Earle collection is of great importance. Both collections are notable for their bulk of correspondence and other papers relating to their family, business and social affairs, and both contain family estate deeds and papers dating from the seventeenth through to the nineteenth centuries.

Another collection which contains a large amount of genealogical and family material is the Crosbie-Oates archive, an outstanding family and maritime collection relating to early nineteenth century trade in palm oil with West Africa, life in Ireland, privateering and emigration to America. The largest collection of family papers held in the Archives Department is that relating to the Danson family which comprises over 216 boxes and volumes. The Danson family archive is an outstanding record of a professional middle-class dynasty, which combined the practice of law and marine insurance with wide public interests in both Liverpool and national affairs. The papers are a superb source of information containing much important material on shipping, trade, emigration and correspondence with important organisations in the commercial world, such as the

Mersey Docks & Harbour Board and the Chamber of Commerce.

The other smaller collections described in this chapter are the archives of the seafaring Stubbs family, the papers of William McQuie Mather and his family, and the personal letters of MacGregor Laird, pioneer of trade with West Africa.

References

Baines, T. *The History of the Town and Commerce of Liverpool*. London, 1852.
Chandler, G. *Liverpool*. Liverpool, 1957. (General history of the city mentioning major people and families.)
Orchard, B.G. *Liverpool's Legion of Honour*. 2 vols., Birkenhead, 1893.

(For details of other shipowning and merchant families, see Vol. I, chap. 4 and Vol. II, chap 1).

The Cropper Family

The Cropper family of Dingle Bank, Liverpool, were well known in Liverpool throughout the nineteenth century, especially for their charitable and philanthropic work. James Cropper (1773-1840) was brought up near Ormskirk, the son of a yeoman farmer. In 1790, he became an apprentice with the merchant partnership of Rathbone and Benson in Liverpool. In 1799, he joined Robert Benson as a shipowner to form Cropper, Benson & Co., and they became agents for the Black Ball Line of pioneering transatlantic sailing packets.

The Croppers were members of the Society of Friends (Quakers), and their relationships with fellow Quakers was largely responsible for the connection between Cropper, Benson & Co. and their counterparts in New York, Jeremiah Thompson and Benjamin Marshall, the founders of the Black Ball Line. In 1818, this firm initiated the running of a shipping line, which for the first time in history, ran on a fixed route, with or without a full cargo, and sailing from each place (Liverpool or New York) on a certain day every month, keeping to the terms of its advertisement. Thompson and Marshall imported vast quantities of cloth from England, in return for exports of large quantities of raw cotton to Liverpool. However, despite being described as the USA's largest shipowner and cotton dealer, the firm failed in 1827 because of imitation by rival lines in New York, Boston and Philadelphia.

Cropper, Benson, however, continued to prosper, and the Cropper family were able to devote their time to social issues, especially the campaign for the abolition of slavery (see Vol. I, chap. 2). James Cropper was particularly concerned with the economic conditions in Ireland, visiting the country in 1824 and making representations to the Government and persons of influence concerning the development of its trade and industry. He was also interested in the reformation of young offenders, setting up a farm school at Fearnhead, near

Warrington. His son, John, continued his involvement in this work, entertaining the boys from the reformatory ship *Akbar* (see Vol. II, chap. 4) and continuing the anti-slavery campaign on an international level. Harriet Beecher Stowe (authoress of *Uncle Tom's Cabin*) was entertained at Dingle Bank, the Cropper family home, when she visited Britain in 1853. The last member of the Cropper family left Dingle Bank in c.1920 and it became the site of an oil storage installation.

Records

Estate deeds and family papers, 1634-1845.
Business papers including apprenticeship indenture of James Cropper, 1790; Cropper & Benson agreement, 1799; dissolution of partnership, 1800 and 1833; draft letter to the Liverpool Dock Trustees, 1807.
Correspondence re: the Liverpool-Manchester Railway, 1825-1830.
Correspondence with William Wilberforce, Thomas Clarkson, George Stephens, Elizabeth Fry and Zachary Macaulay, et al, re: abolition of slavery, c.1798-1833.
Papers re: steam mill at Islington, Liverpool belonging to William Arrowsmith, 1800-1807.
Family correspondence, 1806-1840.
Correspondence with Eliza (née Cropper) and Joseph Sturge, of Birmingham, re: Quaker and business issues, James Cropper's reform school at Fearnhead, politics and other social issues, 1829-1839.
Liverpool Borough Bank and its liquidation, reports, etc., 1857-1860.
Letter book of Cropper family correspondence, 1791-1834.
Letter book containing correspondence and papers, re: business, religious and political affairs, including slavery, c.1790-1839.
Album containing letters, newscuttings, printed pamphlets, leaflets, etc., re: anti-slavery, c.1820-1832.
Album of anti-slavery newscuttings, 1824-1826.
Miscellaneous documents including John Cropper's account book, 1797-1799; drawings and plans of Dingle Bank, 1926.
D/CR   1634-1926   3 Boxes & 1 Parcel

References

Conybeare, F.A. *Dingle Bank, The Home of the Croppers*. Cambridge, 1925.
Albion, R.G. *Square Riggers on Schedule: The New York Sailing Packets to England and France and the Cotton Ports*. Princeton, 1938.

The Crosbie-Oates Family

An outstanding family and maritime collection relating to privateering, trade with the USA and Liverpool trade generally and palm oil trade with West Africa. It also contains details of Irish, ecclesiastical, political and domestic life, and the assassination of the British Prime Minister, Spencer Percival, in 1812. The archive contains an enormous amount of family and genealogical material and gives a fascinating contemporary insight into the national events of the nineteenth century.

One of the most interesting of the family affairs is the undocumented first marriage of Sir Edward William Crosbie, Bart., to Margaret Ferguson at Drogheda. After she had borne him three children, he deserted her for a wealthy widow c.1790, but in 1798 he paid with his life for his part in the Irish Rebellion. His eldest son was apprenticed to William Rathbone, and two years later his mother is recorded as keeping a boarding house in Lancelots Hey, Liverpool. Edward's only daughter, Elizabeth, married the Reverend Richard Oates in 1853, thus creating the Crosbie-Oates family.

The family were connected to James Otis, patriot of Boston and son of Samuel Oates who emigrated to America in 1724. Other notable names mentioned in correspondence with the Crosbie-Oates family are Aickin, Clare, Cronhelm, Forbes Smith, Gill, Halfpenny (this family emigrated to USA), Molyneux, Rea, Shaw, Singlehurst and Tardew.

Records

Two volumes of original letters: subjects include William Oates' trade in oil on board the barque *Sarah*, West Africa, (1856). National events and family news, eg Edward Crosbie's imprisonment in Mexico, (1854) and Sheldon's death on the *Lightning*, a vessel belonging to the King of Siam, in Bangkok (1838), 1778-1870 and 1819-1923. Letters of Marque against Spain and North America, 1779-1781.
Memorandums of Edward Crosbie, includes details of a voyage to Boston, USA, 1805-1906.
Crosbie Family Bible with dates of family events, etc., 1821-1826.
Account books (family, freight and household), 1831-1841, 1844 and 1860-1893.
Journals of Henry Crosbie re: family affairs, religion, politics, etc., 1840-1841, 1842, 1843 and 1844-1847.
Minute book for Christ Church Ragged School, Clare Street, Liverpool (1852-1856), given to Charles Robert Oates, ex Honorary Secretary on its closure, and used by him for recording family history notes, 1856-1878.
Journals of William J. Oates, trading master on voyages to Bonny, West Africa, including his first voyage on board the *Hants* of Liverpool, his return on the *Celma* (1852-1854), and his second voyage from Liverpool on board the *Charles Horsfall* (1856-1859), c.1852-1859.
Family scrap books, c. nineteenth to twentieth centuries.
Printed book, *The Trial and Execution of Sir Edward William Crosbie, Bt., 1798*, 1802.
Lease re: land in Holdingstown, Co. Wicklow, Eire, 1779.
D/O   1779-1923   3 Boxes

The Danson Family

This collection is a rare example of a complete middle-class archive. It begins in 1779 with the apprenticeship of John Danson (1766-1847) to a Liverpool barber and peruke-maker. John became Liverpool's leading barber and perfumer. His son, William Danson (1793-1844) became a rather unsuccessful lawyer. William's son, John Towne Danson (1817-1898), to whom the bulk of the archive belongs, had four distinct careers. He was a journalist specialising in economic affairs under Charles Dickens at the office of the *Daily News*, editor of the *Globe*, farmer, barrister and marine insurance underwriter. From about 1852 until his death in 1898, he kept all of his letters, diaries, accounts and bills, and also took photographs and sketched. His many interests included history, philosophy, economics, statistics, politics and science, and he wrote a number of books and pamphlets, perhaps the most significant being *Our Commerce in War*. He also wrote pamphlets and collected papers on the subjects of slavery, emigration (his brother, Edward, emigrated to Australia in 1841) and colonisation (see Vol. II, chaps. 2 and 3).

J.T. Danson had strong seafaring connections on his mother's side. His uncle, James Towne, was captain of an African trader owned by Sir John Tobin. In 1859 Danson wrote a pamphlet which showed that Liverpool handled fifty percent in value of Britain's exports, but he considered the local marine underwriting market to be quite inadequate. He proposed the formation of a joint stock marine insurance company, and on the 23 June 1860, "The Thames & Mersey Marine Insurance Co." was formed, with Danson appointed as secretary. In 1866 he became its underwriter, but retired in 1880 in disgust at the growing practice of dealing with brokers.

His son, Francis Chatillon Danson (1855-1926), was a leader in his profession of average adjusting, founding the firm of F.C. Danson. He was knighted in 1920 for his work as a member of the Admiralty Transport Arbitration Board in World War I. He was involved with various high profile organisations, including Liverpool University, Liverpool School of Tropical Medicine, Liverpool Chamber of Commerce and the Mersey Docks & Harbour Board. He was, at various times, Chairman of Birkenhead Conservative Party, the MD&HB Finance Committee, Liverpool Shipwreck & Humane Society and the Liverpool Association of Average Adjusters. He was also the Government Representative on the Liverpool & London War Risks Association. His letters survive in eleven wet-copy letter books covering 1884-1911 and 1925-1926, and his letters received date from 1872, beginning with a letter of advice from his father. From 1890 the series is almost continuous, comprising over 6,000 letters, and their subject matter can be gauged from the number of committees and organisations with which Sir Francis was involved. The correspondence relating to archaeology and the School of Tropical Medicine, are particularly useful since they were Sir Francis's major interests. His collection of antiquities was bequeathed to the National Museums & Galleries on Merseyside in 1978.

The archive also contains papers relating to Sir Francis's brother, John West Wood Danson (1853-c.1911), who took up residence in Burma as a timber merchant in 1876. The records include accounts relating to the *Pioneer*, a steam launch built for him by Halls of Aberdeen, his involvement in the early days of the Irrawaddy Flotilla Co., and Burmese ruby mines.

Sir Francis' two sons left no issue. Rudolph was killed at the Dardanelles in 1915. John Raymond (1893-1976), a confirmed bachelor served with distinction in both World Wars, earning the M.C. in the First, and as Lieutenant Colonel, commanding the 4th Battalion Cheshire Regiment at Dunkirk in the Second. He continued his father's patronage of the School of Tropical Medicine, becoming its Chairman, and also his father's interest in Egyptian antiquities. He retired in 1953 to the house at Grasmere, which his grandfather had built when he retired in 1880. Please note that access to this collection is *strictly by appointment only*.

Records

J.T. Danson (1817-1898)

Papers re: his father, William (1793-1844) and grandfather, John Danson (1766-1847), 1779-1847.

Letter books of J.T. Danson, 1852-1898.

Volumes of copy letters to his son, John West Wood Danson, 1876-1897.

Bundles of letters from various correspondents re: family, social and business affairs, 1833-1898.

Property papers and correspondence, 1853-1897.

Volumes of family and personal papers, 1839-1898.

Travel journals, papers, maps and plans, 1848-1895.

Investment and personal account books, etc., 1840-1898.

Career papers re: journalism, 1835-1850.

Legal papers including Liverpool New Exchange and MD&HB, 1822-1893.

Marine Insurance including Thames & Mersey Marine Insurance Co., 1842-1891.

J.T. Danson's published works, 1848-1901.

Economic papers and statistics, 1827-1891.

Antiquarian papers collected by J.T. Danson, 1822-1891.

Study notes on a wide range of subjects from geology to marine technology, c.1836-1896.

Study notes re: religion, philosophy, literature and poetry, 1817-1896.

Sketch books, 1852-1886.

Notes on photography, 1877-1878.

Miscellaneous papers re: membership of organisations, etc., including Liverpool elections, National Association for the Promotion of Social Science, Liverpool Institute, Oxford Political Economy Club, Queen's College, Liverpool, National

Education Union, Society of Antiquaries of London, Liverpool School of Science & Technology, Society for the Encouragement of Arts, Manufactures & Commerce, 1830-1898.
Printed pamphlets, geographical and topical, c.1823-1909.

John W.W. Danson (1853-c.1911)

Letters, accounts and miscellaneous papers re: life in Burma, including the steam launch, *Pioneer*, c.1861-1897.

Sir Francis C. Danson (1855-1926)

Copy letter books, 1884-1911.
Letters from various correspondents re: Association of Average Adjusters, archaeology, Chamber of Commerce, other subjects, etc., 1872-1926.

Edith Danson (c.1870-1950) (Wife of F.C. Danson)

Correspondence, 1896-1941.
Diaries, 1923-1947.
Newscuttings, 1926.

John R. Danson (1893-1976) (younger son of F.C. Danson)

Diaries, 1912-1974.
Correspondence, 1925-1972.
Papers re: financial and other interests, 1906-1975.
Philately, 1930-1970.
Receipts, reports and accounts, 1899-1976.

Lockett Trust

Correspondence, financial, legal and property papers, etc., re: the members of the Lockett family and their emigration to Australia and Canada, 1760-1912.
(see Vol. II chap. 3).

Photographs

Prints, negatives, slides and plates, 1820-1970.

Household

Diaries re: Dry Close, Grasmere, 1898-1971.
Family accounts, 1886-1955.

Miscellaneous

Maps, statistical graphs, sketches, plans, etc., c.1595-1915.
Oil painting of J.T. Danson, 1896.
Relics of the Danson family, 1879-1978.
D/D/I-XIII   c.1595-1978   216 Boxes, 12 Parcels & 25 Volumes

Reference

Anon. *A Short History of F.C. Danson and Co., 1879-1973*. Liverpool, 1973.

The Earle Family

Few records of Liverpool ship-owning partnerships and merchant businesses
survive for the period before the mid-nineteenth century. It was, therefore, a
momentous discovery when David Richardson of Hull University discovered the
family and business papers of the Earle family, a Liverpool family whose
mercantile activities date back to the early eighteenth century, on the Earle family
estate in Co. Limerick, Ireland. The present head of the family, Sir George Earle,
generously donated the collection to the Merseyside Maritime Museum in 1993.
          The collection comprises some seventeen boxes of volumes and
documents relating to the family's business, estate and personal affairs, especially
their mercantile and shipping interests during the mid-eighteenth century, the
period when Liverpool became the country's leading slave port. By this time the
Earle family were in business as merchants and shipowners in a wide range of
commercial ventures, including the slave trade. The archive includes some
outstanding individual items relating to trade and shipping such as letter books
and letters of instructions to captains. The slavery related papers have been given
a full description in the slavery section of this publication (see Vol. II chap. 2).
The Earles were also involved in the Mediterranean trade, and there is a
substantial number of papers relating to plantations which they owned in Berbice,
now part of Guyana. The collection also contains a wide range of estate and
family papers such as deeds, travel diaries, marriage settlements, wills and
correspondence dating from the early seventeenth century. The family held an
estate at Spekelands, Liverpool and later at Allerton Towers. Many of the
documents are in need of conservation suffering from the effects of mildew and
damp, and are currently being treated.

Records

Letter of instructions to William Earle, Captain of the *Chesterfield*, 1751.
Release for further claim of the *Eendragt* of Saardorn, Holland against the
privateer *Liverpool* of Liverpool, 1759.
List of crew and passengers of the *Speedwell*, Liverpool to Philadelphia and

Newfoundland, 1769.
Log of the *Unity* for a slaving voyage to Africa, 1769-1771
List of instructions to Captain Hayslam of the privateer *Enterprise*, 1779.
Articles for fitting out of the privateer *Mars* of Liverpool, 1779.
Release, crew list and letters re: *Harlequin* of Liverpool, 1781.
Bound volumes, letter books, etc., 1667-1761.
Business correspondence (includes personal correspondence of Joseph Denham, partner of Thomas Earle in Leghorn), 1751-1852.
Partnership papers, 1763-1836.
Berbice plantation papers, 1823-1895.
Estate deeds and papers, c.1644-1926.
Family correspondence, etc., 1723-1864.
Diaries (including travel diaries), 1775-1850.
Marriage settlements, 1753-1892.
Wills and probates, etc., 1758-1864.
Hodgson family papers, 1717-1833.
Horton family papers, 1679-1795.
Printed family histories, etc., 1889.
Family history research, c.1924-1930.
Miscellaneous notes re: local history, etc., 1889.
Photographs, slides of family portraits, c.1674-1994.
D/EARLE   1644-1930   17 Boxes

Reference

Littler, D. *The Earle Collection: Records of a Liverpool Family of Merchants and Shipowners*. In Transactions of the Society of Lancashire & Cheshire, Vol. 146, 1997.

MacGregor Laird & Laird Family

MacGregor Laird (1808-1861), a Liverpool-Scottish merchant, was, with his brother John, a pioneer of the iron steamship. They were both sons of William Laird (1780-1841), a Greenock rope maker who founded the shipbuilding firm of Laird, which later became known as Cammell Laird & Co., Ltd., at Birkenhead in 1824. MacGregor designed a fifty-five ton paddle steamer, the *Alburkah*, which in 1832 left Liverpool for Africa intending to open up the Niger trade. Although the expedition was a commercial failure, the expedition proved that it was possible to navigate the Niger River by steamship.

In 1874 he was one of the promoters of the British and American Steam Navigation Co., with the intention of running a steamship service between Britain and America. In 1838 the company's ship *Sirius* was the first steamship to cross the Atlantic entirely under steam. From 1844 he was actively engaged in developing the shipbuilding and engineering works of Laird Brothers, until 1848, when he moved to London to concentrate on developing trade with West Africa. He obtained the government contract to run a regular monthly service to West African ports and the African Steamship Co. was incorporated under Royal Charter in 1852. In 1875 the firm transferred its operations to Liverpool, and in 1890 it was taken over by Elder Dempster. (For further details see Vol. I, chap. 4). Please note that the archives of Cammell Laird Shipbuilders Ltd. are held at Wirral Archives Service. (See Vol. II, chap. 5)

Records

Letters from MacGregor Laird to his wife Nell, transcripts available, 1857-1860.
Typescript of letters addressed to Nell, 1848-1860.
Typescript of Laird family letters and reminiscences by Eleanor Bristow Laird, eldest daughter of MacGregor Laird, 1837-1899.
Letters and copies of letters re: memorial to, and research about MacGregor Laird, 1890-1953.
Copy of "Family Story," memoirs of Eleanor Bristow Laird, 1745-1837.
Photographs of MacGregor Laird and family, c.1833-1900.
Newscuttings, 1932-1946.
DX/258   c.1745-1953   140 Items

Printed Material

Plan for docks at Wallasey Pool, designed by William Laird, 1836.
Biographical sketch of John Laird, M.P., c.1870.
Notice re: gratuity awarded to workers at Birkenhead Iron Works on the occasion of the birth of the son of William Laird (J.W.P. Laird), 1874.
Pamphlet re: opening of Birkenhead Town Hall, 1887.
Pamphlet re: MacGregor Laird Centenary, Order of Service, St. John's Church, Westminster and also Liverpool Cathedral, 1932.
Birkenhead News (offprint) - Obituary of J.W.P. Laird, 1946.
DX/172   1836-1946   7 Items

N.B. A microfilm of Laird family papers (held in private hands), 1830-1860, is available in the Library. (See Vol. II, chap. 10)

Reference

Anon. *Builders of Great Ships*. Cammell Laird & Co. (Shipbuilders & Engineers) Ltd., Birkenhead, 1959.

The McQuie Mather Family

The McQuie family, originally from Galloway, Scotland, settled in Liverpool in 1790. The collection includes extracts from the journal of Captain Peter McQuie, who was a captain involved in privateering and the slave trade to the West Indies. He lost his life during an insurrection of slaves on board his ship, *Thomas*, on 2 September 1797. In 1857 several members of the family emigrated to Melbourne, Australia and to Illinois, USA.

In 1846 Peter Robinson McQuie compiled three volumes of family chronicles which were preserved with other family papers by his descendant, William McQuie Mather (1898-1963). Unable to pursue a career in the Royal Navy, William McQuie Mather served as a wireless officer in the Merchant Navy during World War I, and later joined the family business of chemical merchants. He was interested in maritime history and was involved in the foundation of the Liverpool Nautical Research Society and his bequest funds the Mather Fellowship, a research post at the Centre for Port and Maritime History. He was also an enthusiastic model-maker and his model of the HMS *Victory* is on display in the World of Models gallery at the Merseyside Maritime Museum, and is seen by many as one of the finest ever built.

Records

Family chronicles, hand-written with inserts and transcript, 1846.
Copies of wills, 1903-1911.
Photograph albums of family and scenic views, including cruising on the *Franconia*, c.1920-1940.
Photographs of W. McQuie Mather, c.1963.
Obituary of W. McQuie Mather, 1963.
Log of Southport Special Constabulary, 1940-1944.
Miscellaneous books and pamphlets produced by members of the Mather family, c.1872-1909.
DX/641   1857-1963   45 Items

Research collection compiled by William McQuie Mather re: model-making. Includes photographs of vessels (eg HMS *Victory*), ship models and correspondence with fellow model-making enthusiasts.
D/MTH   c.1930-1954   3 Boxes

The Stubbs Family

This archive consists of the maritime career and personal papers of Herbert Molyneux Stubbs (1879-1915) and his family. After serving his apprenticeship as a maintenance fitter with a Liverpool engineering firm, Herbert Stubbs was employed as 1st and 2nd engineer on numerous vessels belonging to the W. & C.T. Jones Steamship Co., Ltd. and the Cork Steamship Co., Ltd. In 1911 he took part in the Messina earthquake rescue, for which he received recognition from the Italian Government. He tragically lost his life in World War I during the sinking of the *Royal Edward* in 1915. His daughter, Lillian (1912-1967), continued the family's seafaring tradition by sailing as a stewardess on cruise liners of the Booker Line, Canadian Pacific and Lamport & Holt.

Records

H.M. Stubbs

Personal and career papers, including school reports, apprentice indentures, certificates of discharge and letters of recommendation, correspondence and newscuttings re: Messina earthquake and sinking of the *Royal Edward*, etc., 1879-1915.

Lillian Stubbs

Personal papers including school reports, postcards and Women's Institute membership, 1912-1967.
Maritime ephemera, etc., re: Booker Line, Canadian Pacific and Lamport & Holt Line vessels, including menus, passenger literature, staff newspapers, postcards and photographs, etc., 1932-1967.
D/STU   1879-1967   3 Boxes

Compiled by A. Glynn, D. Le Mare and D. Littler.

CHAPTER 7

SEAFARERS & OTHER INDIVIDUALS

The British have a long tradition as a seafaring nation and it would be unusual for a family not to include at least one member who went to sea amongst its ranks. The importance of Liverpool as at one time the second largest port of the British Empire and its long connection with the Merchant Navy is reflected in the vast number of collections of career and personal papers of seafarers held at the Maritime Archives & Library. It is important to stress, however, that no official records of a seaman's career are held at the Maritime Archives & Library, but information sheets are available on sources held elsewhere. There are many types of records held nationally for tracing a seafarer's career, although they can often take perseverance to track their location down.

The majority of official records began from 1835 onwards when central government started to take an interest in merchant seamen from a desire to improve their conditions and to help man the Navy in time of war. This interest resulted in the formation of the Register General of Shipping & Seamen, the historical records of which can now be found at the Public Record Office. These include registers of seamen, register tickets 1835-1856 and 1913-1941, and also indexes of apprentices 1824-1953.

In 1747 the earliest ship's muster rolls were compiled, but unfortunately, these muster rolls or crew lists survive for very few ports for the eighteenth century, and those for Liverpool begin in 1772. From 1835 they were known as *crew lists*, but their distribution is rather diverse to say the least. The Public Record Office kept all of the lists from 1835-1860, a ten percent sample for the years 1861-1938 and those for "celebrated vessels." The National Maritime Museum holds the remaining ninety percent for the years 1861, 1862, 1865 and every ten years to 1975. Local record offices hold crew lists up to 1913 for ships with Ports of Registry within their area, for example, Liverpool Record Office holds several hundred and the Maritime Archives & Library holds about seventy examples (see Vol. I chap. 1). A few survive in shipping company archives such as the British and African Steam Navigation Co. (see Vol. II, chap. 4). The Maritime History Archive, Memorial University of Newfoundland, Canada, holds the remaining majority of crew lists for 1861-1938 and 1951-1976, and the Registrar General of Shipping & Seamen, Cardiff, holds crew lists from 1939-1950 and from 1977 to date.

In 1845 a system of voluntary examinations of competency for those intending to become masters or mates of foreign-going British merchant ships was introduced. It was made compulsory in 1850 and extended to masters and mates of home trade vessels. Details of the award of certificates of competency and service were recorded in registers 1845-1921 which are now kept at the Public Record Office, the original certificates issued before 1900 are kept at the National Maritime Museum arranged by certificate number. For masters operational between 1854-1945, the certificate number can be found from Lloyd's Captains' Registers (Guildhall Library, Aldermanbury, London) which contain biographical and career details. A microfilm copy for the years 1874-1887, is available at the Maritime Archives & Library. Examinations of competence were extended to engineers in 1862.

Many examples of masters, mates and engineers certificates can be found amongst the career papers of seafarers held at the Maritime Archives & Library, together with other official documents such as radio proficiency and gunnery course certificates, as well as apprenticeship indentures. The Maritime Archives & Library holds many important collections relating to seafarers of all ranks, including captains, officers, engineers, boatswains, surgeons, stewards and stewardesses, pursers, carpenters, ordinary seamen and apprentices. Many seafarers have left extensive collections of papers, including not only official but personal documents, such as letters home, scrapbooks and diaries. We have a particularly good representation of seafarers involved in the two World Wars, and of captains and crew of famous vessels such as the *Titanic* and *Lusitania* (see Vol. II, chap. 8).

Many of the shipping company archives described fully in Volume I also contain staff records, particularly relating to officers, but also engineers, deck staff, apprentices and cadets. For example, the apprentice registers of T. & J. Brocklebank begin in 1809. Details of pilots can be found in the Liverpool Pilotage records from 1779, and information on the crew of vessels belonging to the Mersey Docks & Harbour Board may be found in the MD&HB archive (see Vol. I, chap. 2). Another possible source of information could be the records of maritime educational establishments. The Maritime Archives & Library holds the records of two of the training ships, which were moored on the Mersey in the latter half of the nineteenth century, the HMS *Conway*, which became a national institution for the training of future officers of the Merchant Navy, and the TS *Indefatigable*, founded to give sea training to poor boys. Both of these collections contain records of the cadets who trained on them (see Vol. II, chap. 4).

Records relating to the charitable relief of seafarers and their families can be found amongst the archives of Liverpool marine associations and charities like the Royal Liverpool Seamen's Orphanage, and are described in the appropriate chapter. Photographs of Merchant Navy ships on which seafarers served, can often be found amongst their personal papers, in shipping company archives and also in photographic collections, such as those held at the National Maritime Museum and at the Maritime Archives & Library (see Vol. II, chap. 9). Microfilms of the Tower Hill Memorial Registers, 1914-1918 and 1939-1945, are available in the Library (see Vol. II, chap. 10).

Although the largest section of the personal collections held by the

Maritime Archives & Library relate to seafarers, there are also a small number of collections relating to individuals connected with maritime life but based on shore. These include Henry Stripe, who was employed as a shipping clerk with J. Bibby & Sons (Bibby Line) for forty-six years from 1840-1886 and wrote of his experiences in his notebook, Sir Percy Bates, member of the shipping firm, Edward Bates & Sons, and one time Chairman of Cunard Line, and the memorandum book of Jesse Hartley, the first Dock Engineer & Surveyor of the Mersey Docks & Harbour Board.

Reference

Smith, K. and Watts, C.T. & M.J. *Records of Merchant Shipping and Seamen.* Public Record Office, Readers Guide No. 20, 1997.

Seafarers

Askew William Anderton (1878-post 1919)

Askew William Anderton was born in Liverpool in 1878. After six years apprenticeship in the Fitting and Machine Departments of W. Rowlandson & Co., Liverpool, Hydraulic and General Engineers, Iron and Brass Founders, he went to sea as a second class engineer on the *Haddon Hall*, *Newby Hall*, *Normandy*, *Highland Scot* and *Tripoli*. He was a war munitions volunteer in World War I and was also on the staff of the Liverpool City Mission. His brother, Benjamin Anderton, was a professional missionary.

Records

Letters re: employment in engineering companies and employment references, 1893-1900.
Letters re: service on the *Tripoli*, *Haddon Hall*, *Highland Scot*, *Newby Hall* and *Normandy*, 1900-1907.
Certificate of competency as second class engineer, 1903.
Discharge certificates, 1903-1923.
Letter from Alex Armstrong (Liverpool City Mission) re: Askew Anderton's appointment to the staff of the Mission, 1910.
Newspaper obituary re: death of Benjamin Anderton, Missionary, and letter from Alex Armstrong, Superintendent of Liverpool City Mission to Mrs. B. Anderton, expressing Mission's sympathy, 1911.
Certificate of enrolment as war munitions volunteer, 1915.
Certificate authorising wearing of war service badge issued through Cammell Laird & Co. (Birkenhead) by the Admiralty, 1917.
Memorandum of interview between General Manager and Engineer in Chief of

M.D.H.B. re: pay and conditions of workmen employed in the Engineer's Department, 1917.

DX/294   1892-1923   24 Items

William Archer (fl. 1883)

William Archer, from Wigton, Cumberland, kept a diary during a passage from Liverpool to Sydney, New South Wales and Portland, Oregon, U.S.A., on the iron barque *Lizzie Bell* in 1883. Although the diary does not indicate his position, he was almost certainly higher than an ordinary seaman as he writes about drinks in the captain's cabin and socialising with other captains and professional people in Portland. He also shows considerable knowledge of farming and the timber trade. The diary portrays life on board the *Lizzie Bell*, including the experience of entering the Tropics, bad weather resulting in injuries sustained to the crew, and the captain's wife giving birth on board. The diary ends with vivid daily entries describing his time ashore in Oregon including a festive day to celebrate the completion of the North Pacific Railway.

Record

Diary (with transcript), 1883.

DX/871   1883   1 Volume

William Cecil Barker (fl.1855-1878)

William Cecil Barker of London began his seafaring career as midshipman on the *Alnwick Castle* on a voyage to Australia in October 1856. After returning to England on the *European*, he sailed as third mate on the troopship *Havering* for India and witnessed a Suttee Hindu burial ceremony at Madras. He was progressively fourth to second officer on further voyages to India on the *Golden Fleece*, serving in the company of a West Indian boatswain. He later joined the Union Steamship Co. sailing on various vessels to West African ports, and on the *Teuton* to South Africa. In 1876 he visited Newcastle-upon-Tyne to superintend the building of a new steamship, the *Nubian* for the Union Steamship Co. He describes all of the above events in two volumes of a highly detailed journal, and also in the draft letters home to his parents written during his first voyage on the *Alnwick Castle*.

Records

Journal, 2 volumes, 1855-1878.
Draft letters to parents, 1857.

DX/1177   1855-1878   3 Items

William Baxter (1904-post 1969)

William Baxter, born in 1904 in Dundee, Scotland, served his apprenticeship as an engine fitter at HM Dockyard, Rosyth between 1920 and 1925. In 1926 he attended the Lauder Technical School, Dunfermline. He started his seagoing career in July 1926 with Bibby Brothers & Co. on the *Leicestershire* and continued with the company, sailing out of Liverpool until c.1936, mainly on the *Oxfordshire* (I) and the *Staffordshire* (I) as third class engineer.

Records

Apprenticeship indenture, HM Dockyard, Rosyth, 1920.
Certificate of service under the Admiralty, 1926.
Engineering certificates, 1934.
Discharge certificates, 1926-1936.
References, 1926-1936.
Testimonial re: retirement, 1969.
Trade union papers, 1920-1980.
Formula and job books, 1940-1968.
Industrial, trade union and sporting diaries, 1946-1968.
DX/1186   1920-1980   1 Box

James A. Bell (c.1880-post 1950)

James A. Bell was a member of a seafaring dynasty of three generations of chief engineers serving with the Cunard Line. His grandfather, James Bell, served on the first Cunarder, the *Britannia*, on her inaugural transatlantic steamship service in 1840, and continued to go to sea for thirty-six years. His father, Robert T. Bell, was apprenticed with the British & North American Royal Mail Steam Packet Co. Liverpool (Cunard) as engine fitter before entering sea service in 1870 as third engineer on the *Stomboli*. In a career spanning forty-one years, Robert T. Bell served as chief engineer on eight ships, including the *Bothnia*, to which he was appointed in 1880. James A. Bell followed his father and grandfather into service with Cunard as chief engineer on the *Campania* and *Aquitania*, and his brother, Robert T. Bell, was on the engine room staff of the *Queen Mary*. James A. Bell retired after forty years service, one of his notable achievements being to increase *Aquitania's* speed by almost three knots when she was already twenty-five years old.

Records

Certificate of competency as second engineer awarded to James Bell, 1863.
Letter of completion of apprenticeship of Robert T. Bell with British & North

American Royal Mail Steam Packet Co. Liverpool, as engine fitter, and sea service, 1870.

Letter of reference for service of Robert T. Bell as third engineer on the *Stromboli*, and sixth, fifth and fourth engineer on the *Cuba* and *China*, 1871, and for service as second engineer, 1875.

Certificate of competency as first-class engineer awarded to Robert T. Bell, 1875.

Certificate of competency as first-class engineer awarded to James A. Bell, 1907.

Photographs of Robert T. Bell, c.1880 on *Caronia* and *Aquitania*, James A. Bell with crew and passengers on *Aquitania* and Robert T. Bell, Jun. on the *Queen Mary*, c.1919-1939.

Cunard newsletters and newspaper articles re: James A. Bell, c.1938-1950.

"Crossing the Line" ceremony scrolls and photographs, 1938.

Book: *The Ship Beautiful: Art and the Aquitania*, by A.M. Broadley, c.1914.

D/BLL   1863-1950   1 Box

James Bigham (fl. c.1820-c.1960)

James Bigham was a shipwright from St. Woollas, Monmouthshire. He became a ship's carpenter in 1845.

Records

Apprenticeship indenture as shipwright, St. Woollas, Co. Monmouth to William Perkins, 1833.

Testimonial, 1843.

Mariner's register ticket, issued at Liverpool, as carpenter, 1845.

Discharge certificate as carpenter on *Bencoolen*, 1857.

DX/191   1808-1857   5 Items

Robert William Blythyn (1874-1915), Robert James Blythyn (1902-post 1954), William Blythyn (1905-post 1961), George Knill (1899-1931)

All members of this seafaring family were born and lived at Bootle, Merseyside, and were employed by the Cunard Steam Ship Co. R.W. Blythyn was born in 1874, and served as saloon steward on the *Lucania*, *Carmania* and *Lusitania*. He was lost at sea when the *Lusitania* was torpedoed on 7 May 1915. R.J. Blythyn, son of R.W. Blythyn, was born in 1902. He served as first-class waiter on *Aquitania*, *Mauretania* (II), *Carmania* and *Queen Mary*. William Blythyn, younger son of R.W. Blythyn, was born in 1905. He served as a saloon steward on *Ascania*, *Britannic*, *Parthia*, *Carinthia* (III) and *Media*. George Knill was born in 1899. He went to sea at the age of sixteen as a scullery boy, his first ship being the *Lusitania*. When on his second voyage, she was torpedoed, he managed to swim away and thus survived to marry Mary Blythyn, daughter of R.W. Blythyn, whom he never met. He became a ship's cook and died in 1931 aged only thirty-two, at Greenwich Seaman's Hospital in an endowed bed named after the *Lusitania*.

Records

R.W. Blythyn

Discharge certificates, 1879-1908.
Photograph of crew of *Lusitania*, 1910.
Papers relating to his death on *Lusitania*, 1915.
Widow's pension papers, scroll of honour, 1916-1955.
Complete printed index list of passengers and crew of *Lusitania*, 1916.

R.J. Blythyn

Discharge certificates, 1919-1954.
Wages and trade union papers, 1949-1954.
Photographs of work activities, 1927-1945.

W. Blythyn

Identity and service certificate, c.1920.
Discharge certificates, 1946-1961.
Photograph W. Blythyn and crew of the *Carinthia* with "boat competition" trophy, c.1957.

G. Knill

Discharge certificates, 1915-1931.
DX/1055   1879-1961   1 Box

Captain Robert Capper, DSC, RD, RNR (1872-1947)

Captain Capper was born in Kirkdale, Lancashire in 1872. In 1886 he was apprenticed for five years to William Sherwen of New Ferry, Cheshire on the barque *Primera*, sailing mostly to Australia. In 1893 he joined the barque *John O'Gaunt* for four years. In 1897 he joined the Cunard Line as junior officer on the *Aurania*, and in the same year obtained his master's certificate. He next served in the Royal Navy where he was promoted to sub-lieutenant in 1898 and lieutenant in 1903 before returning to the Cunard Line in 1903. In 1906 he was chief officer of the *Etruria* followed by the *Mauretania* in 1910. He was in command of the *Pannonia* in 1913 when she rescued one hundred and three passengers from the Spanish ship *Balmes* after it had caught fire off the coast of

Bermuda and was awarded a gold medal by the Spanish Life Saving Society. In 1918 he was awarded the DSC and made a commander, after guiding five lifeboats for eight days in mid-Atlantic after his ship, *Ausonia*, was torpedoed and shelled by enemy submarines. In 1919 he took up a shore based appointment as marine superintendent of Cunard Line in Montreal, Canada, transferring back to Liverpool in 1930. In 1921 he was placed on the Retired List, RNR with the rank of captain. Captain Capper retired in 1932 and died in 1947.

Records

Apprenticeship indenture to William Sherwen, New Ferry, 1872.
Certificate of competency as master, 1897.
Certificates of sub-lieutenant, lieutenant and commander, RNR, 1898, 1903, 1915.
Typed reports by Captain Capper re: the rescue of the *Balmes*, and the sinking of the *Ausonia*, including a report of an earlier escape from submarine attack, holograph log covering the sinking of *Ausonia*, and voyage in open lifeboats until rescue by *Zinnia*, 1913-1918.
Letters: testimonial from passengers, letters of appreciation from master of *Balmes*, Masonic letter of praise, letter of appreciation from Sir Alfred Booth, Chairman of Cunard Line re: the rescue of the *Balmes*. Award of DSC and investiture, 1913-1918.
Photographs: album of ships, officers in uniform, including Captain Capper, activities on board Cunard ships, and family. Loose photographs of similar, including the *Primera* at Tasmania, 1889-1930.
Postcards of interior views of *Aquitania*, and sinking of German armed ship *Cap Trafalgar* by the *Carmania*, 1914.
Newscuttings re: rescue of the *Balmes*, Captain Capper's appointment as marine superintendent, and transfer back to Liverpool, sport trophies, career of thirty five years at sea, and Mrs. Theresa Edgar, only female survivor of the *Ausonia*, 1913-1945.
Canadian passport of Captain and Mrs. Capper with photographs, 1922-1928.
Obituary, *The Southport Visitor*, 1947.
DX/186   1872-1947   1 Box

Lieutenant-Commander Charles C. Cartwright, OBE, RNR (1878-post 1916)

Charles Cartwright was born in Birkenhead in 1878 and educated at the Liverpool Institute. In 1894 he was apprenticed to Staveley, Taylor & Co., Liverpool, and spent the next three years aboard the barque *Craigmullen* after which he completed his apprenticeship with T. & J. Harrison, gaining his second mate's certificate in 1898. He joined the Asiatic Steam Navigation Co., and during the Boxer Uprising, was engaged in carrying troops from India to Taku. For this service he received the Transport Medal. Between 1902 and 1904 he returned to the Harrison Line, gained his master's certificate, and joined the White Star Line. In 1908 he entered the Royal Navy and served on board HMS *Essex*, after which he was appointed sub-lieutenant, and then acting-lieutenant on HMS *Argonaut*. He eventually completed his training on the cruiser HMS *Achilles* in 1909. At the end of 1909 he returned to the merchant service as chief-officer on the *Highland Brae* (Nelson Line). Two years later he was promoted to the position of captain. His next command was the *Highland Laddie* (Nelson Line), a passenger and refrigerated cargo steamer, on the London to River Plate service. In 1914 he was appointed as Board of Trade Nautical Surveyor attached to the London office, until the mobilisation of the Royal Naval Reserve in August 1914 when he was appointed to the battleship HMS *Canopus*. He was present at the battle of the Falkland Islands when the German squadron was destroyed.

Records

Hand-written log book re: *Craigmullen* (with typescript), 1894-1896.
Unofficial log book of HMS *Canopus* including Falkland Islands and Eastern Mediterranean campaign, 1914-1916.
Newscutting: *The Journal of Commerce*, "Men You Know Lieut. C.C. Cartwright, RNR," 1915.
Photographs of Commander Cartwright in Royal Naval Reserve uniform, and long whites, c.1890-post 1914.
DX/906   c.1890-1916   1 File

Captain Richard Vere Essex Case, DSC, DSO & Bar, RD & Clasp (1904-1991)

Captain Case was born in Liverpool in 1904 and educated at the Liverpool Institute. He joined the training ship HMS *Worcester* as a cadet in 1918 and served his Merchant Navy apprenticeship with the Pacific Steam Navigation Co. In 1928 he obtained his master's certificate, and in 1937 joined Coast Lines as second officer. On the first day of World War II he was called up with the rank of lieutenant-commander, RNR. His early war service was spent on anti-submarine trawlers based at HMS *Beaver* on the Humber. He was placed in charge of the 12th Anti-Submarine Striking Force in command of HMT *Stella Capella*, and he was awarded the DSC for his inspired leadership and example. He was involved in the Norwegian campaign of 1940 providing anti-submarine protection to capital ships and transport in the fjords, and was awarded a Bar to his DSC. In the same year he was commissioned to the *Flower* class corvette HMS *Campanula*. Amongst his RNVR officers was the novelist Nicholas Monsarrat, whose experiences on HMS *Campanula* during the early part of the Battle of the Atlantic, provided background material for his novel *The Cruel Sea*. He was awarded the DSO for Atlantic convoy duties in 1942 when he commissioned the first *River* class frigate *Rother*, and survived three days of intensive air attack. He returned to civilian life in 1945 as marine superintendent for Coast Lines and was promoted to chief marine superintendent in 1953. In 1954 he was promoted to captain, RNR in the New Year's Honour List. In 1958 he was appointed as the Queen's RNR Aide-de-Camp. He retired in 1969 and died in 1991. Exhibits relating to Captain Case are on display in the Battle of the Atlantic gallery.

Records

Royal Naval Reserve training certificate book, 1920-1953.
Diaries, 1938-1945.
Letters and certificates re: rank of midshipman and sub-lieutenant, 1920-1926.
Certificates of reference from HMS *Irwell*, *Royal Sovereign*, *Argus* and *Castor*, 1920-1945.
Letters re: awards and promotions, 1937-1945.
Certificate of award of DSO, 1943.
Naval messages, telegrams and instructions re: wartime ship movements, 1940-1945.
Correspondence re: purchase by Lieutenant-Commander Case of the *Rother's* ship's bell, 1949.
Letter re: termination of naval service, 1945.
Photographs of Captain Case, c.1940.
Newscuttings re: wartime activities, awards, promotions, etc., 1940-1969.
Obituary, *The Daily Telegraph*, 1991.
DX/1707   1920-1991   1 Box

Apprenticeship indenture, Pacific Steam Navigation Co., 1921.
Reference re: service on PSNC ships, *La Paz*, *Ebro*, *Orduna* and *Ortega*, 1923.
B/PSNC/38/2/2   1921-1923   2 Items

Charles Arthur Cheshire (1846-post 1879)

Charles Arthur Cheshire was born in 1846 and was apprenticed to Nathaniel Glenton, sailmaker. He was later employed as a sailmaker on board the *Somerset* in 1868.

Records

Apprenticeship indenture, 1862.
Naval certificate of character/certificate of discharge, 1868.
DX/342   1862-1879   2 Items

Captain William Cousins (1880-1940)

Captain Cousins was born in Liverpool in 1880 and saw active service in both World Wars. He was in command of the Liverpool coasting steamer, *Aysgarth Force* (West Coast Shipping Co., Ltd.) when it rescued the French schooner, *Perseverance*, after a collision in 1914. He later commanded the *Holme Force* and *Dalegarth Force*. He was killed in 1940 after a torpedo attack on the *Holme Force* eight miles off Newhaven.

Records

School certificate, 1894.
Identity and service certificate with photograph, 1918.
Letters and newscuttings re: rescue of *Perseverance* and French government's award to the crew of *Aysgarth Force*, 1914.
Empire Day certificates, 1915.
Commemorative scroll re: his death during active service, 1948.
Photograph of *Holme Force*, Captain Cousins, crew and family, c.1860-c.1940.
DX/1014   c.1860-1948   1 Box

Captain Edward John Curtis (1866-post 1924)

Captain Curtis was born in 1866 in Northamptonshire. He sailed with the Bibby Line between 1896-1900 on the *Shropshire* and *Yorkshire*. His career was principally with the Nelson Line's refrigerated cargo-passenger liners between the United Kingdom and the River Plate starting as third mate in 1901, rising to chief officer in 1904 on the *Highland Brigade*, and later as captain of the *Highland Glen*.

Records

Discharge certificates, 1896-1905.
Receipt for epaulettes, 1909.
Letter from Nelson & Wythes, agents for the Nelson Line, requesting Captain Curtis to attempt a record trip on the *Highland Glen's* voyage from Buenos Aires to London, 1911.
Letter of appreciation from passengers of the *Highland Glen*, 1911.
Programme for fancy dress ball, *Highland Glen*, 1911.
Postcards of Nelson Line steamers, 1912 and 1924.
DX/1077   1896-1924   1 File

Captain Daniel Dow (1860-post 1919)

Captain Daniel Dow was born at Castlebellingham, Co. Louth, Ireland in 1860. He was apprenticed to T. & J. Brocklebank from 1876-1887, serving on the *Baroda*, *Majestic* and *Tenasserim*. After qualifying as master in 1887, he joined the Warren Line as junior officer on the *Kansas*. In 1888 he entered Cunard Line as fourth officer on the *Catalonia*, and three years later became second officer on the *Etruria*. He was commissioned as a sub-lieutenant in the Royal Naval Reserve in 1892, and undertook twelve months foreign service in the Royal Navy as lieutenant on HMS *Porpoise* on the China Station. Upon rejoining Cunard he served on the *Sylvania*, *Ultania*, *Aurania*, *Pannania*, *Campania*, *Umbria*, *Caronia*, *Mauretania* and *Lusitania*. Under Captain Dow's command both the *Mauretania* and *Lusitania* broke the transatlantic speed record. At the outbreak of World War I, *Lusitania*, with Captain Dow in command, continued to sail through the danger zone patrolled by enemy submarines. However, he was on shore leave when she was torpedoed in May 1915. Captain Dow was appointed to HMT *Mauretania* carrying troops to the Dardenelles, and in 1917 on the HMT *Royal George* transported troops to India. He retired from active sea service in July 1919 after a career of forty-three years.

Records

File of biographical newscuttings, 1904-1919.
File of telegrams, correspondence, photographs and ephemera, including congratulatory telegrams re: taking command of the *Mauretania* and breaking the transatlantic speed record, 1910-1914.
File of newscuttings re: career on *Lusitania*, 1914.
Four scrapbooks of newscuttings and correspondence re: service with Cunard, especially *Lusitania*, war service on the *Royal George*, and Captain Dow's retirement, 1915-1919.

D/DOW   1904-1919   3 Boxes

Captain Griffith Charles Evans, OBE (1859-1944)

Captain Evans was born in Holywell, North Wales in 1859. He was apprenticed in 1875 to T. & J. Brocklebank and sailed on his first voyage to India on the *Mahanada*. In 1885 he went over to steamships and obtained his first command on the *Lake Ontario* (Beaver Line) eventually commanding all the ships belonging to the Beaver Line, including *Lake Winnipeg* and *Lake Huron*. He was responsible in 1898 for transporting 4,500 Douklobors from the Baltic Sea direct to Canada on *Lake Huron*. During World War I he conveyed 71,000 Canadian and United States troops including Canada's first Expeditionary Force. In 1918 he was in command of the *Missanabie* when she was torpedoed and sunk off Co. Cork, Ireland. He was awarded the OBE for his war service. In 1922 he was the first captain to command the *Empress of Scotland* after her re-fit and oil conversion. In 1923 he was awarded a pair of engraved binoculars from the Newfoundland Government for rescuing the crew of the schooner *Ida M Cunningham* when in command of the *Metagama*. Captain Evans retired from the sea in 1923 and died at Rhuddlan, North Wales in 1944.

Records

Certificate of competency as master, 1885.
Certificate of election as a member of Trinity House, 1904.
Identity and service certificate (with photograph), 1918.
Commemorative scroll issued by Canadian Pacific Railway for services during World War I, 1918.
Personal log book of voyages on barques *Blackwell* and *Annie McNairn*, and ships *Lake Superior*, *Lake Huron*, *Lake Ontario*, *Lake Champlain*, *Montrose*, *Montreal*, *Manitoba*, *Metagama*, *Minnedosa* and *Empress of Scotland*, 1881-1923.
Abstract of logs for *Lake Manitoba* and *Montreal*, 1906-1913.
Copy letter books, 1912-1913.
Letters: Trinity House confirming admittance as a "Younger Brother," Ministry of Shipping and St. James's Palace re: OBE award; Mercantile Marine Service and Canadian Pacific re: award of binoculars, 1904-1923.
Photographs: *Missanabie* sinking after torpedo attack, Captain Evans and Staff Captain Aikman in uniform, receiving retirement wishes on *Metagama* during last command and in Egypt, 1918-1923.
Newscuttings: passenger account describing the *Missanabie* passing the site of the *Lusitania* twenty four hours after her sinking, *Missanabie* and Captain Evans bringing passengers and military personnel safely into port after passing through submarine waters, award of binoculars and the rescue of the crew of *Ida M Cunningham*, Allan Line merger with Canadian Pacific Line and retirement, 1915-1923.
Obituary, *The Rhyl Journal*, 1944.
D/EV   1885-1944   3 Boxes

Captain Thomas Gary Fraser (1850-1934)

Captain Fraser was born in Harrington, Cumberland in 1850, went to sea in 1865 as an apprentice on the ship *Corea* (Bushby & Edwards, Liverpool), and gained his master's certificate in 1874. He sailed on five ships, the *Corea*, *Doriga* (Johnston, Churchill & Co., Liverpool) and *Alpheta*, *Larnaca* and *Maxwell* (Johnston, Sproule & Co., Liverpool). He was captain of the *Doriga* when it sank in the Bay of Biscay in 1879. His last voyage was on the *Maxwell* which in July 1892, on route to San Francisco, was wrecked in a gale on the Liverpool Bar and eventually sank. The crew were rescued by the New Brighton lifeboat. He compiled his journals in 1915. They cover all of his twenty five voyages between 1865-1892 to South America, Australia, New York, San Francisco and Dunkirk. They are some of the most interesting examples of such journals to survive and have been published in full.

Records

Journals, 1865-1892.
DX/1210/R   1865-1892   4 Volumes

Reference

Gee, M. *Captain Fraser's Voyages*. London, 1978.

Edward Gee (1895-1983)

Edward Gee was born in 1895 in Sunderland and served as chief officer on the *Oak Branch* (Nautilus Steamship Co., Ltd., Sunderland). While chief officer, he lost an arm as a result of an accident. In 1924 he was appointed assistant cargo superintendent at Liverpool, and in 1930 cargo superintendent. He died in 1983.

Records

Discharge certificates, 1911-1915.
Certificate of competency as master, 1921.
References and testimonials including Canadian Pacific, Nautilus Steamship Co., Ltd., 1912-1933.
Letters re: loading of cargo, 1930-1943.
Photographs including Edward Gee in uniform, c.1920-1930s.
Written examination papers, 1929-1930.
Obituary, *Crosby Herald*, 1983.
SAS/23A/3/4   1911-1983   1 File

William Gerrard (1888-post 1929)

William Gerrard of Bootle, Liverpool, was a fireman on many liners including *Mauretania (I)*, *Aquitania*, *Orita*, *La Negra*, *Otaki* and *Carpathia* from 1914-1929, sailing to the USA, the River Plate and Australia. He was awarded the British War Medal and Mercantile Marine Medal, and was later employed by the British & Argentine Steam Navigation Co., Ltd., and Lamport & Holt Ltd., sailing on *La Rosarina*, *El Uruguayo* and *Biela*.

Records

Discharge certificate, 1914-1929.
Argentine immigration regulations booklet, with photograph, 1927-1929.
Note of authorisation to wear war medals, 1927-1928.
DX/274   1914-1919   3 Items

Captain James Goffey (1807-post 1855)

James Goffey was born in 1807, into a family which is believed to have been in Liverpool since 1775. He began his career as a mate on board the brig *Jane*, sailing for Africa in 1826, and his navigation exercise books survive in the collection. He undertook his first voyage as master on board the brig *Gannet* to Bonny, Africa in 1839. He obtained his master's certificate in 1851 and continued to sail to Africa until at least 1857, the date of his last document in the collection. James, in partnership with his brother William, a joiner, formed the firm J. & W. Goffey, which continued to trade with Africa well into the twentieth century, under the control of his sons Thomas and William, until the decline of sail after World War I.

Despite the records of the partnership not surviving, the records of Captain James Goffey are an important and rare record of Liverpool's trade with Africa in the early to mid-nineteenth century. The collection is rich in working documents of the trade, including voyage accounts, and cargo and provision books, which include detailed accounts of oil taken on board and the names of native dealers.

Records

Accounts of voyages, 1843-1855.
Navigation and course notes, 1826-1852.
Personal papers and correspondence, 1839-1855.
Cargo and provision books, etc., 1836-1857.
Business correspondence (including bills of lading), 1840-1855.
Accounts and general finance, 1841-1855.
Miscellaneous correspondence and papers, 1840-1850.
Note of interview with W. Goffey, 1972.
B/GOF   1826-1972   2 Boxes

Richard Arthur Hammond (1920-post 1980)

Richard Hammond was born at Sutton Coldfield, Warwickshire in 1920. He became a cadet on HMS *Conway* in 1935 and his letters home to his parents provide a fascinating record of life as a cadet. After an unsuccessful application to Blue Funnel, he was accepted by Ellerman Hall Line as a cadet and sailed on his first voyage on board the *City of Bedford* to Bombay in May 1937. He served on a number of Ellerman ships throughout the World War II, obtaining his second mate's certificate in 1946. In 1959 he joined Shell oil tankers with which he served for the rest of his career, obtaining the position of master on the MV *Falmouth* in 1975. He retired from his last vessel, the *Shell Supplier*, in 1980.

Records

Letters home written from HMS *Conway*, 1935-1937.
Letters home from Ellerman Line ships, 1937-1943.
Correspondence with Hall Line Ltd., Mercantile Marine Service Association and Liverpool Sailor's Home outfitting department, 1939-1940.
Photographs of R.A. Hammond in *Conway* uniform, c.1935.
Discharge certificates, 1940-1980.
Scrapbook of wireless reports of Ellerman Hall Line ships, 1937-1939.
Newscuttings re: *Conway* Cadets and School Cadet Corps, n.d. c.1935.
D/HAM   1935-1980   1 Box

George Hugh Haram (1823-post 1837)

George Haram kept a diary at the age of thirteen when he became apprenticed to John Strancham on the barque *Jane* of Liverpool in 1836. For nine months the *Jane* traded along the coasts of Chile and Peru and his diary records details of the weather and sail settings, incidents on board, ships sighted, cargoes, passengers and ports of call. At the front of the journal are listed the contents of his chest, which are noted as identical to those of his grandfather during his apprenticeship. The journal ends in December 1837 en route from Callao to Liverpool.

Record

Journal, 1836-1837.
DX/1135/R   1836-1837   1 Volume

William Harvey (c.1880-post 1900)

William Harvey was employed as a greaser by the Anglo-Australian Steam Ship Co. and sailed to Canada, Australia, USA, Penang and Las Palmas.

Records

Discharge certificates, 1893-1900.
Handwritten testimonial from chief engineer, *Port Adelaide*, Anglo-Australian Steam Ship Co., London, 1898.
DX/336   1893-1900   24 Items

Captain Henry Hatchwell (1854-post 1893)

Captain Hatchwell was born in Devon in 1854 and was apprenticed at the age of fourteen to Captain William Whiteway on the barque *Anne Cheshyre* of Liverpool (Brundit & Co.). He also served on the *Frankby*, *Lady Bird*, *Letterewe* and *Pavonia*. He was the first captain of the barque *Thorne*, built in 1878, and remained captain when she was sold to James Dowie & Co., Liverpool, six years later. He commanded her until 1893.

Records

Apprenticeship indenture, 1867.
Discharge certificates, 1873-1890.
References re: ships *Anne Cheshyre*, *Frankby*, *Lady Bird*, *Letterewe* and *Thorne*, 1873-1890.
Letter of exoneration from any accident occurring to the *Thorne* while he was captain, 1893.
Statement of account for *Thorne*, 1890.
Copy photograph of the *Thorne*, c.1890.
DX/1158   1867-1890   1 File

Captain Eric Hewitt RD, RNR (1904-1995)

Captain Eric Hewitt RD, RNR was born in 1904 in Fenton, Staffordshire. He joined the training ship HMS *Conway* as a cadet in 1919. When he left the *Conway* in 1921 he received a Double Extra Conway Certificate, and joined the Royal Naval Reserve where he was appointed a probationary midshipman. After his RNR training he served with the Glen Line, and in June 1924 passed his 2nd Mate's Certificate and joined the Royal Mail Line. He was promoted to Lieutenant RNR in 1927. He completed a Submarine Qualifying Course and served a year in submarines until he was promoted a lieutenant commander in 1936 when he returned to surface craft. In January 1942 he was promoted to commander, and was attached to Captain Walker's Liverpool-based anti-submarine flotilla. After VE day in 1945 Captain Hewitt joined the staff of the Supreme Commander South East Asia Command (SEAC), Admiral Lord Louis Mountbatten, and in 1947 joined the staff of Lord Mountbatten after his appointment as Viceroy of India.

Captain Hewitt joined the training ship HMS *Conway* as staff captain in April 1948, and upon the retirement of *Conway*'s captain superintendent, Captain Goddard in August 1949, became captain superintendent. In 1953 the *Conway* ran ashore in the Menai Straits on a voyage to Birkenhead for a re-fit, and was written off as a "Constructive Total Loss." Captain Hewitt successfully managed the re-location of the school from a training ship afloat to a shore establishment based at Plas Newydd, Anglesey. In June 1956 Hewitt was appointed ADC to the Queen until June 1958. Although he should have retired in 1955 he was kept on the active list until 1959 by which time he was the most senior captain on the Navy List. On 1 May 1968 the management of the *Conway* was taken over by the Cheshire Education Committee and Captain Hewitt was replaced with an academic Headmaster. In retirement Captain Hewitt became a part time coastguard at Penmon at the eastern end of the Menai Strait, and was appointed the High Sheriff of Anglesey in 1971. Captain Hewitt died on 13 December 1995.

Records

Family papers, 1904-1984.
"Reflections" - Life on the *Conway,* 1917.
Career papers, 1921-1949.
Photographs and album, 1921-1961.
Personal papers including letters, 1931-1984.
Papers relating to HMS *Conway,* 1951-1975.
Articles written about Captain Hewitt by Captain McManus, 1996-1997.
Press cuttings, programmes for opening of new shore establishment at Plas Newydd c.1961.
D/HEW   1917-1997   2 Boxes

Walter George Hiscock (1895-1966)

Walter George Hiscock was born in Oxford in 1895. In 1909 he joined the training ship HMS *Conway*, and on graduation in 1911, was recommended for an appointment as midshipman in the Royal Naval Reserve. In 1912 he was apprenticed with Thos. Law & Co., Glasgow, and sailed for the next two years on the barque *Inverness-shire*. His reserve commission was activated in 1914 when he was assigned to the armed-merchant cruiser, HMS *Macedonia*, and was present at the Battles of Coronel and the Falkland Islands. Next came a shore appointment planning secret mine-laying operations, followed by an appointment as assistant signal officer two months before the end of World War I on the armed merchant cruiser, HMS *Otranto*. He was amongst those rescued after a disastrous collision with the merchant trooper *Kashmir* in 1918. His last sea appointment in 1918 was as a member of the clerical staff of Admiral Browning on HMS *Hercules*. He spent the rest of his working life as a librarian at Oxford University. He died in 1966.

Records

Certificate of examination as second mate and nomination as midshipman, RNR, HMS *Conway*, 1911.
Apprenticeship indenture to Thos. Law & Co., 1912.
Certificate for assistant paymaster in the Royal Naval Volunteer Reserve, 1916.
References from Captain H. Brabender, *Inverness-shire* and Admiralty re: mine-laying operations, 1914, 1924.
Letters from Government House, Falkland Islands re: *Inverness-shire*, Captain E.C. Goldworthy, survivor of HMS *Otranto*, Ministry of Defence and Admiralty Registry re: HMS *Otranto*, 1935-1964.
Voyage narratives: *Inverness-shire* including his first voyage, as midshipman on armed merchant ship HMS *Macedonia* and the voyage and sinking of the HMS *Otranto*, 1910-1918.
Photographs of W.G. Hiscock as a HMS *Conway* cadet and senior cadet of the *Inverness-shire* at Liverpool, apprentices including himself on the *Inverness-shire*, as assistant paymaster sub-lieutenant, RNVR and of the surrender of the German Navy at Kiel, Germany, 1918.
Newscuttings re: court inquiry into the collision between HMS *Otranto* and the *Kashmir*, 1920 and obituary, *The Oxford Magazine*, 1966.
Admiralty chart of the Falkland Islands with pencilled marks presumed to be positions of the *Inverness-shire* in abandonment, 1883.
DX/1705   1909-1966   1 Box

Thomas Holding (fl.1795)

Thomas Holding was born in Ramsey, Isle of Man in 1749, and served at sea during the early years of the Napoleonic Wars. His medical certificate stated that he was unfit for sea service and was rejected as a volunteer for the Navy owing to deafness from an abscess in the right ear. The certificate is signed by the "surgeon for sick and wounded seamen and prisoners of war at this port" (Liverpool). This was intended to grant him immunity from imprisonment.

Records

Medical certificate, 1795.
DX/991   1795   1 Item

Daniel Horrigan (1896-post 1959)

Daniel Horrigan was born in Liverpool in 1896. He served his apprenticeship with Ismay, Imrie & Co., managers of White Star Line from 1911 until 1913 when all White Star Line engineering apprentices were transferred to Harland &

Wolff Ltd., after they opened their new establishment in Bootle, Merseyside. In 1916 he was called up for active service with HM Forces. After the First World War he was employed as a ship's engineer with China Mutual Steam Navigation Co., Ocean Steam Ship Co. and Straits Steam Ship Co., Ltd. (all part of the Ocean Group). He retired in 1959.

Records

Apprenticeship indentures to Ismay, Imrie & Co., Liverpool, 1911 and 1913.
Discharge certificates with photograph, 1920-1945.
References from Harland & Wolff, Junior Technical School, Bootle, and ships *Orestes*, *Rhesus*, *Cyclops*, *Antilochus* and *Titan*, 1916-1959.
Certificate of service with Ocean Steam Ship Co. and the China Mutual Steam Navigation Co., Ltd., 1923.
Certificate of competency as first class engineer, 1945.
National registration identity card and British seaman's identity book with photograph, 1945.
Photograph of the football team of the crew of the *Ningchow*, 1926.
SAS/23A/2/4   1911-1959   1 File

James Howard (fl.1815)

James Howard was an enrolled rigger at the Port of Liverpool, No. 13 in John Smith's Company, who was protected from being pressed into the Royal Navy as riggers were essential occupations of a busy port.

Records

Certificate of protection from impressment for three months (framed), 1815.
DX/102   1815   1 Item

William Frank Jefferies (1903-post 1945)

William Frank Jefferies was discharged from the Lancashire Navy League in 1922, served on numerous merchant ships, including the *Ceramic*, *Aurania* and *Samaria* and was serving on the *Laurentic* when she was sunk by enemy action. In 1940 he served in the Royal Naval Reserve during World War II. W.F. Jefferies was awarded a silver medal by the Liverpool Shipwreck and Humane Society for the rescue of a woman from the Mersey in July 1937. The collection also contains items belonging to fellow old boys of the Navy League, Alfred John Bellis who lost his life on the *Laurentic* in 1935, and Michael Reilly, AB, on the *Brazil*, who was awarded a certificate by the Liverpool Shipwreck and Humane Society in 1933, for rescuing people from a capsized sailing vessel at Tutoya Bay, Brazil.

Records

Discharge certificate from the Lancashire Navy League, 1922.
Discharge certificates, 1920-1939.
Identity and service certificate, c.1930.
Call up paper, Royal Navy, 1938.
Discharge certificate from Royal Navy, 1944.
Photographs of crew on various (unknown) ships, c.1930.
Memorial card and programme of service for A.J. Bellis, 1935.
Framed certificates from the Liverpool Shipwreck and Humane Society awarded
to W.F. Jefferies and Michael Reilly, 1933, 1937.
D/JEF   1920-1944   1 Box

Frank Leslie Jordan (1878-post 1916)

Frank Leslie Jordan was born in Yorkshire and worked as a ship's carpenter and
boatswain in Liverpool and Hull between 1894 and 1916. He was employed by
Houlder Line, Wilson Line and Rover Steamers. From his first voyage in 1894
on the *Cambrian Prince* until 1903 on the ship *Mastells*, he kept a personal log.

Records

Apprenticeship indenture to Thomas Williams & Co., Liverpool, 1894.
Personal log book, 1894-1903.
Discharge certificates, 1899-1914.
References from ships *Cambrian Prince*, *Milton*, *Beacon Grange*, 1896-1916.
Miscellaneous career papers, 1905-1914.
DX/1178   1894-1916   1 File

Lt. Cdr. R.W. Keymer, RN (1901-1957)

Lt. Cdr. Ronald W. Keymer was born in 1901 at Flockton, near Huddersfield and
educated at King's College, Canterbury. The archives relate to his Royal Naval
service from 1939-1944. He was made a lieutenant commander on the 19 January
1939 "for service in connection with submarines." Upon taking a position with Sea
Command on the 9 April 1940, Lt. Cdr. Keymer was sent to Norway to obtain naval
intelligence on the Norwegian Coast for the Admiralty. In 1940 he was given
command of a French vessel, the English-built corvette *La Malouine*, as part of the
Western Approaches Escort Force, controlled from Derby House, Liverpool. In
August 1941, he took command of the HMS *Gorleston*, and undertook numerous
convoy escort duties until 1943. By June 1944 Lt. Cdr. Keymer was in command of
HMS *Hind*, and was serving as senior officer of the 112th Escort Group. In addition
to convoy escort duties, the *Hind* took part in the Normandy Landings of Operation
Neptune, 5-6 June 1944.

Records

Files of correspondence and other papers re:
Norway, April-July 1940.
Report of proceedings, *La Malouine*, 1939-1941.
Attack on Convoy HX72, 1940.
Report of proceedings, Convoy OS4, HMS *Gorleston*, 1941.
Report of proceedings, Convoy SL87, 1941-1942.
Chase and attack on U-boat shadowing Convoy OS10, 1941.
Chart showing *Gorleston's* movements during Operation Raspberry, 1942.
Chart showing *Gorleston's* attacks on U-boat whilst escorting Convoy OS28, 1942.
Report of proceedings, Convoy OS34, 1942-1943.
Convoy SL118, 1942.
Convoy KMF3 and Algiers, 1942.
Escort of floating dock to Mediterranean, 1943.
HMS *Hind*, Normandy, 1944.
Captain's file: *Hind's* U-boat, 1941-1944.
D/KEY   1939-1944   2 Boxes

Joseph Lesley (1901-post 1979) and Hannah Lesley (1912-post 1979)

Joseph was an AB seaman on the *Empress of Britain* and Cunard ships *Carmania*, *Carinthia*, *Franconia*, and Hannah (née Carter), a ship's laundress, served on the *Antonia* and *Franconia*. After World War II Joseph was employed by the Mersey Docks & Harbour Co. as a dock gateman.

Records

Career certificates, 1914-1952.
Discharge certificates, 1921-1936.
Miscellaneous career and personal documents, 1921-1970.
Postcards of Cunard White Star's, *Antonia*, 1936.
National registration identity card, 1943.
DX/384   1921-1970   27 Items

Carl Liddy (1887-post 1914)

Carl Liddy was born and lived at Liverpool, and was employed as a waiter on board the *Campania*, *Lusitania* and *Carmania*.

Records

Discharge certificate, 1911-1914.
Oil painting of ferry *Egremont* by Carl Liddy, c.1914.
DX/232 1911-1914 2 Items

Captain Cecil Frederick Lock (1903-post 1965)

Captain Cecil Frederick Lock was born in 1903 in Bristol, and served during World War II, having gained proficiency in Merchant Navy defence courses. He was a survivor of the *Chilean Reefer* which was sunk in 1941, and was awarded many medals and emblems, including the Atlantic Star and Burma Star.

Records

Apprenticeship indenture, 1918.
Testimonials from Rowland & Marwood's Steam Ship Co., Whitby, for service on the *Erlsbrough*, *Brunholme*, *Scoresby*, *Sandsend*, *Stakesby*, *Larpool*, and *Alouette* (originals and typed copies), 1922-1942.
Discharge certificate, 1922-1945.
Certificate of competency as master, 1927.
Telegram offering position of chief officer, 1928.
Certificate of efficiency as lifeboatman, 1933.
Certificate of attendance Merchant Navy defence course, 1938.
Certificate of registration (armed forces), 1939.
Description of war medals, 1939-1945.
Certificate of proficiency Merchant Navy A/A gunnery course, 1942.
Certificate of proficiency Merchant Navy defence course, 1942.
Certificate of completion of course in depth charges, 1942.
Account of wages, 1944 (Liberation of Europe).
Letters enclosing campaign stars, emblems and ribbons, 1945 and 1949.
Medical book issued by Alfred Holt, 1953-1961.
Certificate for completion of radar course, 1960.
Passport, 1965.
DX/259 1918-1945 36 Items

Alexander Mann (1873-post 1927)

Alexander Mann was born in 1873 in Wallsend on Tyne and became a carpenter, but was discharged for slackness from the Iron and Steel Ship Building Yard at Wallsend near Newcastle-on-Tyne in 1890. He later served in World War I and was awarded the British War Medal Ribbon and Mercantile Marine Medal Ribbons, and the British War and Mercantile Marine Medals.

Records

Reference from Iron and Steel Ship Building Yard, Wallsend, 1890.
Photographs of Alexander Mann aged twenty-five years, 1899 and his father, Joseph Mann from Wallsend-on-Tyne, n.d.
Certificate and account of wages, *Kumaral*, 1909.
Discharge certificate, 1915-1927.
Authority to wear war medals for Mercantile Marine, 1919-1921.
Documents (photocopies) relating to Alexander Mann: marriage certificate, family papers, 1869-1980.
DX/223   1890-1980   17 Items

Agnes McCann (1896-post 1954)

Agnes McCann was born in 1896 in Liverpool and qualified as a nurse in 1941. She was employed as a stewardess on board several ships, including *Britannic*, *St. Seriol*, *Tilapa*, *Samaria* and *Dorsetshire*.

Records

Letter listing nursing qualifications, 1943.
Reference from Ministry of Pensions Hospital, Liverpool, 1946.
Discharge certificate, 1946-1951.
British seaman's identity card, 1946-1954.
General Nursing Council certificate of enrolment, 1946.
National Union of Seamen, members contribution book, 1946-1951.
Card relating to emergency signals, rules for safety and security, *Britannic*, c.1944.
Card giving details of fire stations, boat station, etc. (*St. Seriol*), 1947.
Shipping company ephemera including *Elizabethan News*, 1942 and menus from *Erria*, *Empire Bure*, *Samaria* and *Dorsetshire*, 1942-1951.
DX/279   1943-1951   18 Items

Herbert Gresford Moss (1903-post 1940)

Herbert Gresford Moss was a second-class engineer who served his apprenticeship as a fitter with Cammell Laird & Co., Birkenhead, after which he served on the *Northumberland*. He was later employed by Chadburn's (Ship) Telegraph Co., Ltd.

Records

Apprenticeship indenture, 1919.
Discharge certificate, 1933-1935.

Certificate of competency as second class engineer, 1935.
Naval dockyard pass issued by Chadburn's (Ship) Telegraph Co., Ltd., c.1940.
DX/530　　　　　　1919-c.1940　　　　　　　4 Items

Basil Mylrea (1863-post 1931)

Basil Mylrea was born in Peel, Isle of Man in 1863 and was an AB (Shoregang) rating, travelling to U.S.A., Mexico, West Indies, South Africa, etc.

Records

Discharge certificates, 1891-1931.
National Sailors and Fireman's Union membership contribution book, 1914-1917.
Notice re: conditions of the Royal Seamen's Pension Fund, c.1919.
National Union of Seamen membership contribution books, 1928-1929.
Correspondence with Ministry of Health re: pensions, 1929-1930.
DX/257　　　　　　1863-1930　　　　　　　44 Items

Eusebis Olarra (1889-post 1956)

Eusebis Olarra was born in Spain in 1889 but lived in Salford for most of his working life. He was employed as chief steward with the Larrinaga Steamship Co., Ltd.

Records

Discharge certificate (Spanish) with photograph, 1915.
Discharge certificates (British), 1915-1952.
Immigration discharge certificate (Argentine) with photographs, 1948.
Letters: Larrinaga Steamship Co., Ltd. re: cash award for service on *Minnie de Larrinaga* after attack in 1917 by submarine, 1920; to Mrs. Olarra re: arrival of *Maria de Larrinaga* at London docks, 1947.
Receipts for ships provisions, 1945.
National Union of Seamen contribution book, 1952-1956.
DX/1441　　　　　　1915-1956　　　　　　　1 File

Captain James Cope Page (1856-post 1897)

Captain James Cope Page was born in 1856 in Liverpool and was apprenticed in 1871. He became a master mariner in 1879, and obtained his pilotage certificate in 1883 in Sydney, Australia. He was highly commended in 1886 for his bravery whilst captain of the *Prince Louis*, for successfully navigating his ship to port after a collision with a sunken vessel. His daughters were both born at sea and were called Leeuwin and Ildefonso after the islands the ships were passing at the time of their births. Captain Cope Page's gold watch, which was presented to him by the owners of the *Prince Louis* (Moran, Galloway & Co.) for efforts in saving the *Prince Louis*, and a painting of the *Prince Louis* are held by the Maritime History department.

Records

Apprenticeship indenture, 1871.
Discharge certificate from *Black Prince*, 1877-1878.
Certificate of competency as master, 1879.
Marine Board of New South Wales (Australia) pilotage certificate, 1883.
Certificates re: membership of the Freemasons, Master Mason in the St. George (Bermuda) Lodge, 1879 and the Grand Lodge of Scotland, 1879.
References from Moran, Galloway & Co., owners of the *Black Prince*, 1876-1883, and the masters of the *Black Prince*, 1878-1879.
Newspaper reports re: involvement in Marine Court of Enquiry into the recovery of the abandoned ship *L'Avvenire*, 1879 and presentation of a gold watch, c.1888.
DX/302   1871-1973   9 Items

Captain Walter Paton (1825-1884)

Captain Walter Paton was born at Leith in 1825 and gained his master's certificate in 1847. He commanded several vessels and his knowledge of steam engines and high speed navigation, among other important accomplishments, led to his appointment as captain of the *Great Eastern*. His father, also Walter, was a surveyor for Lloyd's Register and died in 1873. His elder son, Walter, was drowned trying to rescue a shipmate whilst serving on the *Rokeby Hall* in 1877. His younger son, James, was born on board the *Great Eastern* at New York and embarked on a career at sea, before cancelling his indentures after the death of his brother, Walter. Captain Walter Paton died in 1884, and James started his own business. His invention, Patons Cleanall Powder, was an immediate success with ships masters, and encouraged him to produce Matchless Metal Polish, which further contributed to the success of the business which became known as Paton Calvert & Company.

Records

Letters of appreciation to Captain W. Paton from the passengers of the *Charity*, *Genova* and *Cleopatra*, 1853-1856.
Letters re: Captain Paton's command of the *Great Eastern*, 1862-1863.
Family letters, 1867-1892.
Letters of condolence re: death of Walter Paton on vessel *Rokeby Hall*, with copy of the ship's log describing the incident, 1877.

Report re: the appointment of Captain W. Paton to the post of surveyor at Liverpool for the Record of American and Foreign Shipping, 1878.

Testimonials relating to the application of Captain W. Paton for the post of principal officer to the Liverpool Board of Trade, 1881.

Statistics of the journeys made, and the goods carried, by the *Cleopatra* and *Ottawa*, during the Crimean War, 1856.

Photograph album which includes personnel, machinery, etc. at Paton Calvert factory and an album of a visit to Germany and family photographs.

Loose photographs of groups, probably Paton Calvert employees outside the factory, and a bust of Sir James Paton.

The First Fifty Years, 1887-1937, a History of Paton Calvert.

Miscellaneous memorial cards, telegrams, a Daguerreotype portrait probably of James Paton, and a wooden penholder inscribed "used by Admiral Beatty at the Town Hall," 1919.

D/PAT	1847-1894	1 Box

Captain T. Powles (fl. c.1880-1903)

Captain Powles, from Runcorn, Cheshire, was captain of the barque *James Kerr* (W. Thomas & Co., Liverpool). He kept three notebooks written in diary form, during voyages from Buenos Aires, Argentina to Port Natal, South Africa and from Durban, South Africa to Newcastle, New South Wales, Australia, between 1902 and June 1903. In the notebooks he refers to the *James Kerr* as the "Old Jim" and gives many descriptive details of life on board and ports of call. The notebooks also contain very interesting photographs of himself, shipboard activities and ports of call.

Records

Notebooks (with transcript), 1902-1903.

SAS/23A/8/4	1878-c.1918	1 File

William Henry Puxley (1881-post 1939)

William Henry Puxley was born at Harwich in 1881. He became a first-class engineer serving on a number of ships, including *Albanian*, *Alexandria*, *Tagus*, *Oporto*, *Flaminian*, *Castilian*, *Falernian*, *City of Oxford*, *Andalusian* and *Belgravian*, in the early years of the twentieth century prior to World War II.

Records

Discharge certificates, 1900-1939.

Certificate of competency as first class engineer, 1904.

Photograph in uniform, c.1904.

DX/367	1900-1939	11 Items

Thomas William Quirk (1826-post 1891)

Thomas William Quirk lived in Everton, Liverpool, and was employed by the Mersey Docks & Harbour Board as a pilot from 1856.

Records

License to be a pilot into/out of Port of Liverpool, Chester Water, Pile of Foudrey and Isle of Man, 1856.
Photograph of pilot boat No. 4, *Auspicious*, c.1860.
Liverpool pilotage certificate (blank), c.1860.
Diary (monthly) and tide table, 1865.
Bills of sale for 1/64th shares in *Auspicious*, *Leader*, *Criterion*, 1865-1878.
Memorandums re: sickness grant and superannuation, 1869-1871.
Marriage certificate, 1873.
Sundry receipts, c.1878.
Licence No. 288 (pilotage), Mersey Docks & Harbour Board, 1882.
Newspaper cuttings: *Liverpool Daily Post* on Liverpool pilotage service, 1950 and new shore based pilot station at Point Lynas, Anglesey, c.1975.
DX/372   1856-c.1975   17 Items

Samuel Rattle (1870-post 1921)

Samuel Rattle was born at Greenwich in 1870. He served his apprenticeship with Mathew Little and became a seaman and cook. He served in World War I and was awarded numerous war medals.

Records

Birth certificate, 1870.
Apprenticeship indenture, 1889.
Discharge certificate, 1907-1910.
Photographs (photocopies) of S. Rattle and his wife, c.1910.
Instructions for wearing British War Medal, c.1918.
Medals: British War Medals, Mercantile Marine War Medal, 1914-1918.
Certificate of authorisation to wear medals, 1921.
Letter re: award of medal by Marine Department of Board of Trade, 1921.
DX/337   1870-1921   11 Items

Alexander Rintoul (1827-post 1862)

Alexander Rintoul was born at Alloa, Scotland in 1827, and was employed as a ship's carpenter.

Records

Discharge certificates, 1845-1862.
Mariner's register ticket, 1845.
Account of wages, 1859.
DX/407   1845-1862   29 Items

Captain William Robinson (1817-1872)

Captain Robinson was born in London in 1817. His father, once a wealthy slave owner in the USA, sold his estate out of moral conviction and returned to Britain. His son chose a seafaring career and was apprenticed in 1829. In 1835 he made his first trip to Africa and underwent a conversion experience. In 1846 he obtained his first command. From about 1861 Captain Robinson combined his seafaring career with involvement in missionary work as a Primitive Methodist. He died at sea in 1872.

Records

Printed biography: Reverend John Hall, *Life on the Ocean; or Memorials of Captain Wm. Robinson*, London, 1874.
Magazine: *Christian Herald and Signs of Our Times*, contains a biographical article and line drawings, including a portrait of Captain Robinson, 1884.
Personal letters from Captain Robinson to his daughter from barques *Huddersfield*, *Dee* and *Ant*, 1869-1872.
Certificate of gift forms for small specimens: birds, fish and insects, presented to Liverpool Public Museum, 1867-1870.
Photographs of Captain Robinson and possibly his son, n.d., c.1870.
Memorial card, 1872.
SAS/23A/9/4   1867-1884   1 File

Captain Henry Richard Saalmans, OBE (1894-1954)

Captain Saalmans was born in Liverpool in 1894. He served in the Royal Navy in World War I and was present at the Battle of Jutland, and afterwards transferred to the Merchant Service as an officer cadet. He obtained his master's certificate in 1925. He served between the wars on Elder Dempster ships including the *Accra II* and *Mary Kingsley*. He was awarded the OBE and Lloyds War Medal for bravery at sea, as a result of his service on the *Empire Bard* during a convoy to Russia. He was later attached to the fleet auxiliary and was master of the *Sea Valour* between 1943 and 1946. He died in 1954. Captain Saalman's OBE decoration and Lloyds War Medal are on display in the Battle of the Atlantic Gallery at the Merseyside Maritime Museum.

Records

Identity and service certificate with photograph, 1918.
Discharge certificates, 1926-1941.
Certificate of competency as master, 1925.
Merchant Navy personnel forms, 1943-1946.
Letters re: OBE award and Lloyds War Medal, 1936-1942.
Photographs of Captain Saalmans and ships *Mary Kingsley*, *Sea Valour*, *Accra II* and HM Hospital ship No. 5, 1915-1942.
Newscuttings re: OBE award, his brother receiving the MBE, *Mary Kingsley*, *Empire Bard* at Murmansk port and his death, 1935-1954.
DX/1642   1918-1954   1 Box

Captain Joseph Harold Salt (1902-post 1964)

Joseph Harold Salt was born at Caernarvon on 15 January 1902. His first appointment was as sixth engineer on the Royal Mail Line vessel *Araby*, for three months. On 14 October 1924 he joined the Cunard vessel *Antonia* as fifth engineer, and was to stay with the company for the rest of his working life. He served at Suez and Tobruk during World War II on the *Bantria* and his photographs are a unique personal record of his war at sea. He continued his service with Cunard and by August 1952 was serving as third engineer on the *Queen Mary*. He stayed with her until December 1960, when he was appointed chief engineer on the *Mauretania*. The last certificate of discharge in his collection shows that he was still serving on the *Mauretania* in 1964.

Records

Professional certificates, 1917 and 1926.
Discharge certificates, 1923-1964.
Letters and ephemera relating to career, 1917-1964.
Photographs taken whilst serving in Suez and Tobruk during World War II, and photographs of passengers and crew members on board *Queen Mary* and *Mauretania*, 1942-1963.
D/SALT   1917-1964   1 Box

Mary Scott (1920-post 1966)

Mary Scott was born in Liverpool in 1920, and was employed by Cunard Line for 21 years, first as a bath attendant and later as a stewardess.

Records

Wage slips, *Samaria*, *Ascania*, *Scythia*, *Georgic*, *Queen Mary*, *Saxonia* and *Carinthia*, 1947-1964.
Merchant Navy clothing book, 1949.
Cunard Line contract for bath attendant, 1955-1957.
Certificate of efficiency as lifeboatman, 1966.
Taped interview re: career, c.1985.
DX/1231   1947-1967   1 File

Alfred Douglas Shepherd (1875-post 1904)

Alfred Douglas Shepherd was born in Liverpool in 1875. At twelve years old he was apprenticed on the training ship *Indefatigable*. In 1890 he was apprenticed to W.H. Ross & Co., and spent five years as third mate with the *Scottish Hills* (Windram & Co., Liverpool) and later as second mate on the *Riverside* (T.C. & H.C. Jones, Liverpool) and *Ellisland* (J. Houston & Co., Liverpool).

Records

Apprenticeship indenture to the *Indefatigable*, 1887.
Apprenticeship indenture to W.H. Ross & Co., Liverpool, 1890.
Discharge certificates, 1890-1899.
Certificate of competency as master, 1902.
References, 1895-1902.
Photographs including crew of the *Scottish Hills*, passengers on deck of the *Riverside* and Shepherd as third mate and fourth officer, 1899-1904.
SAS/23A/10/4   1887-1904   1 File

Stephen Slinger (1869-post 1941)

Stephen Slinger was born in Birkenhead in 1869 and became a steward on the *Eskdale* (J.D. Newton & Co., Liverpool), the *Ajax* (Inman & International Steam Ship Co., Liverpool) and other ships.

Record

Bible containing notes of voyages, nostalgic comments and family details c.1885-1941. Contains the wing of a flying fish caught at the Equator, mounted on the back cover. Printed in 1885.
DX/1170   1885-1941   1 Volume

John Stevens (c.1913-1982)

John (Joannes) Stevens, a Belgian national, was serving on the Belgian merchant vessel *Princes Maria Pia*, sailing between London and Antwerp, when war with Germany was declared in 1939. The crew were given the choice of returning to Belgium or joining the Allies and becoming part of the exiled Belgian Navy. The home port for the Belgian Navy became Liverpool, with its headquarters in Water Street. After undergoing training as a gunner, Stevens rejoined the *Princes Maria Pia* on convoy escort duties. He was discharged at Port Talbot in 1941 and served on various vessels from Liverpool. In 1944, on the *Belgique*, he took part in the D-Day invasion, and in 1946 he returned to Belgium for repatriation. Upon his return to Liverpool, he worked as an engineer at Grayson Rollo Engineers Ltd. and later at Alexandra Towing Co. Ltd.

Records

Discharge certificates, 1937-1946.
"Crossing the Line" certificate, 1937.
Shore leave certificates, 1939-1940.
Certificate of proficiency at Merchant Navy gunnery course, 1942.
Certificate of registration under Aliens Order, 1920.
Identification cards, port of New York, Belgium, Alexandra Towing Co. Ltd., 1943-1971.
Album of photographs of family life and Merchant Navy career, 1913-1946.
Photographs of John Stevens in Belgian Merchant Navy uniform, c.1939, and in civilian clothes in Belgium during his repatriation, c.1946.
D/STE   c.1913-1971   1 Box

Thomas Sumner (1838-c.1920)

Thomas Sumner was born in Warrington in 1838 and later lived in Bootle, Merseyside. In 1862 he spent a month as a boilermaker on the paddle steamer *Great Eastern* (Eastern Steam Navigation Co., London). After leaving the *Great Eastern*, he joined David Rollo Ltd., Sandhills Lane, Liverpool, as ships manager, subsequently establishing his own business, Thomas Sumner Ltd. (Liverpool) as engineers, boilermakers and shipbuilders.

Records

Discharge certificate from *Great Eastern*, 1862.
Abstract of log of the *Great Eastern*, New York to Liverpool, 1863.
Framed photographs of the engine room staff of the *Great Eastern*, 1862.
DX/1236   1862-1863   1 Box

Reference

Dugan, J. *The Great Iron Ship*. London, 1953.

Gordon Lindstrom Sykes-Little (1935-post 1978)

Gordon Lindstrom Sykes-Little was born in 1935 and lived at Southport, Lancashire. He joined the Palm Line briefly in 1952, but was chiefly employed with the company as purser between 1955-1957. He joined the Pacific Steam Navigation Co. in 1957 as senior purser. He was on board the *Reina del Pacifico* when she went aground for two days on Devil's Flat, Bermuda in 1957, and his collection includes photographs taken of the grounding and his summary of the incident. He joined Shaw, Saville & Albion in c.1966, then served with Ellerman City Lines from 1976-1979. The collection also comprises of the uniform jacket of purser and senior purser, waistcoat, raincoat and tropical shorts and socks, worn by Gordon Sykes-Little during his career. These items are held with the Maritime History Department.

Records

Correspondence re: employment between G. Sykes-Little with the Palm Line, Pacific Steam Navigation Co. and Ellerman City Lines, ,1952-1979.
Wage slips, *Lagos Palm* and *Delphic*, 1956 and 1966.
Files of official ship papers re: pursers duties, including contract of service for *Kroo* labour, staff wages, movements of ships, cargo manifests, cash books, receipts, and work list and report on black Asian crew, 1951-1978.
Photographs of G. Sykes-Little in purser's uniform on board various Palm Line ships, passport photograph, passenger activities, *Kroo* boys and *Reina del Pacifico* aground at Bermuda, 1953-1957.
Postcards of *Reina del Pacifico*, *Santander*, *Northern Star*, *Gothic*, *Icenic*, *Megantic* and *Southern Cross*; interior views of ships *Flamenco*, *Kenuta*, *Cuzo* and *Cotopaxi*. Also passenger ferries, c.1950-1960.
Family letters, telegrams and greetings cards, 1956-1978.
Newspapers: *The Bermuda Mid Ocean News*, *The Royal Gazette*, 1957.
Tourist ephemera: maps, brochures, cards, leaflets and guidebooks, 1950-1959.
D/LIT   1950-1979   5 Boxes

Captain Robert Thomas (c.1845-1903)

Captain Robert Thomas was master of various vessels owned by Hughes & Co. of Menai Bridge, Anglesey, involved in the coastal trade and also the transatlantic and South American trade. Ships commanded by Captain Thomas included the *Etta*, *British Princess*, *Merioneth* and the *Afon Alaw*. Captain Thomas was master of the *Afon Alaw* from its launch in 1891 until his death at San Francisco in 1903. The collection does not contain any personal career papers belonging to Captain Thomas, but consists mainly of letters of instructions from the owners and other ships papers, and photographs of Captain Thomas and crew aboard the *Afon Alaw* and *Merioneth*.

Records

Letters of instructions to Captain Thomas, 1876-1879.
Discharge certificates for foreign seamen, engaged at Antwerp and Cardiff for the *Etta* and other vessels, 1876-1877.
Disbursements at Rio de Janeiro of the *Etta*, 1876, and the *British Princess* at Hamburg and South America, 1876-1878.
Certificates of authority to assist Captain Thomas in Peruvian waters, 1877-1879.
Dispute of claims of demurrage of *British Princess* at Guano Loading Co., deposits, Peru, 1878.
Quarantine certificate issued to the *British Princess* at Falmouth, 1880.
Newscuttings re: the *Merioneth's* record passage to San Francisco, 1888.
Specification for steel sailing ship (*Afon Alaw*) to be built by Alexander Stephen, Glasgow, 1891.
Specification for iron sailing ship to be built for Messrs. L.H. MacIntyre & Co., Liverpool by Sunderland Shipbuilding Co., n.d., c.1891.
Notebook containing notes on draught, list of crew, etc., c.1890.
Photograph of Captain Thomas and crew of the *Merioneth*, 1875.
Photographs of the *Afon Alaw*, and Captain Thomas, crew and owners of the *Afon Alaw* on board at San Francisco, c.1891-1903.
Note: His diary and other papers are deposited at Gwynedd Archives Service.
D/THOMAS   1876-1903   1 Box

Reference

Eames, A.*Shipmaster*, Gwynedd Archives Service, 1980

Charles Thompson (c.1870-1943)

Charles Thompson was born in Gloucester and educated at Bristol Seamen's Orphanage. He spent his whole career on sailing ships, retiring from the sea c.1900. In 1905 he came to Liverpool and became a butcher and later a janitor at Liverpool College. He died in 1943 in Crosby.

Records

Diary as able seaman on barque *St. Mary's Bay* of Glasgow, carrying coal on a voyage from Cardiff to Algoa Bay, South Africa, Burma and Holland, includes full crew list and course details, 1889-1890.
Diary as second mate on barque *Rising Star* of Maryport, Cumberland, carrying dynamite from New York to Valparaiso, Callao, Talcahuano (Chile) and Falmouth, includes crew list and course details, 1896-1897.
SAS/23A/11/4   1889-1897   1 Box

Captain Alfred William Trant, OBE (1867-1934)

Captain Trant was born in Bootle, Merseyside in 1867. At the age of seventeen he was third mate on the *Drumpark* (Gillison & Chadwick, Liverpool). He passed his extra master's certificate in sail in 1891 and became a master in steam in 1892. He joined F. Leyland & Co., Ltd., Liverpool, and commanded several of their ships, principally the *Devonian* (I) on the Liverpool to Boston route. After the *Devonian* (I) was torpedoed in 1917 he became employed as liaison officer between the Royal Navy and the Merchant Navy on convoys. For this service he was awarded the OBE in 1919. He continued on the Liverpool to Boston route on the *Devonian* (II), and later commanded the Red Star Line's ship *Westernland*, before retiring in 1932. Captain Trant took part in rescue work several times in the North Atlantic, chiefly in the *Volturno* disaster and in the towing of the *Mexico* to Halifax, Nova Scotia in 1913. He died in 1934.

Records

Apprenticeship indenture to James Gillison, Liverpool, 1882.
Certificate of competency as extra master, 1891.
References from master of the *Drumpark*, 1886 and master of the *Palm*, 1888.
Typed description by Captain Trant as commander of the *Devonian* (I) of the towing of the *Mexico*, 1914.
Hand-written account of the loss of the *Devonian* (I) by torpedo, c.1917.
SAS/23A/11/6   1882-1914   1 File

Captain John Henry Trinick (1868-post 1940)

Captain Trinick was born at Salcombe, Devon in 1868. He first went to sea at the age of ten on the brigantine *Netherton*, commanded by P. Trinick (possibly his uncle). During his sea going career, he was employed by the Furness Withy Line, c.1888, by James R. De Wolf & Son, 1891-1897, and between 1898-1903 by the Chesapeake & Ohio Steamship Co. as chief officer, and later as captain of the *Shenandoah*. He later returned to Furness Withy and retired in 1940 after many years service.

Records

Father's master's certificate (John Trinick), 1865.
Discharge certificates, 1878-1893.
Apprenticeship indenture to Benjamin Balkwill, Devon, 1882.
Testimonials and references, Chesapeake & Ohio Steamship Co., James R. De Wolf & Son, and various ship captains, 1887-1905.
Letter re: retirement, 1940.
Photographs of passengers and crew, and ships in ice at St. John's, Newfoundland, 1914-c.1937.
SAS/23A/11/9   1865-1940   1 File

F.W. Tritton (fl. c.1890-post 1892)

F.W. Tritton was a steward on the tramp steamer *Ghazee* (Mogul Steamship Co.), sailing to the Far East and New York, 1890-1892. His journal reveals the harshness of life on board, and the brutality of the officers to the crew during the three voyages made. The narratives describe the long tramp voyages in great detail, and are also an important survival since the records of the Mogul Steamship Company were totally destroyed during World War II.

Records

Journal in three volumes:
Vol. 1 – Voyage Birkenhead to Hull via China, Japan and Odessa (Russia), 1890-1891.
Vol. 2 – Voyage Birkenhead to Hull including list of ports of call with dates, crew lists and comments on disciplinary measures, 1891.
Vol. 3 – Voyage Liverpool to Hull via China, Japan and New York, 1891-1892.
DX/684   1890-1892   3 Volumes

Lieutenant Commander O.N. Tugwell, RNR (1892-post 1832)

Oliver Norman Tugwell joined the White Star Line training vessel *Mersey* in 1908, when aged sixteen. The collection includes the diary of his first voyage on the vessel from Liverpool to Sydney, Australia, and provides a detailed record of life on board as seen through the eyes of a young cadet. He describes all aspects of the cadet's education and their life at sea. From 1919 Lieutenant Tugwell served on numerous White Star vessels including the *Tropic*, *Canopic* and *Ionic* on the New York to Bremerhaven service. He also served with the Royal Naval Reserve during World War I and took part in the peace celebration march in 1919. He appears to have continued service with Cunard-White Star Line in the

1930s, possibly aboard the *Franconia*, and to have travelled extensively in Indonesia and the Far East.

Records

Log of voyage on *Mersey*, 1908-1909.
Papers and newscuttings re: *Mersey*, 1908-1910.
Papers re: World War I and RNR service, 1914-1921.
Arrangements for peace celebration march, 1919.
Excursion programme for the *Franconia* world cruise, 1935.
Miscellaneous papers, 1920-1932.
Photographs and postcards ethnological, personnel, ships and travel, c.1920.
D/TUG   1908-c.1932   1 Box

Edward John Walsh (1878-post 1928)

Edward John Walsh was born in Dublin and served on the *Lusitania*, *Mauretania*, *Cymric*, *Laertes* and *Persic*. The documents and ephemera relate to his life and career.

Records

Certificate of service in Royal Navy, 1895-1917.
Discharge certificates, 1908-1914.
Photograph album containing photographs including HMS *Triumph* and crew of the *Sandpiper*, *Minerva* and *Arabic*, c.1895-1928.
Postcards including *Eumaes*, c.1895-1928.
DX/286   1895-1928   43 Items

Lt. Samuel Walters R.N. (b. 1778)

Lt. Samuel Walters was born at Ilfracombe, Devon in 1778. After serving his apprenticeship as a shipwright, he went to sea in 1796 as a carpenter's mate on the *Ocean*, sailing from London to India. In 1798 he joined the Royal Navy as a midshipman on the HMS *Argo*, and in 1805 was appointed a lieutenant on HMS *Raisonable*. From 1805-1810 he recorded his experiences in a diary, describing the events of naval warfare and including watercolours and drawings of naval ships, including the *Raisonable* and *Courageux*.

Record

Manuscript diary, illustrated.
DX/1146/a   1805-1810   1 Volume

Captain Charles Walker Webster (1901-post 1971)

Captain Webster was born in 1901 in Wallasey, Cheshire. He saw action when serving on HMS *Asturias*, a converted cruiser liner during World War II. He worked for "K" Steamship Co., then the Blue Star Line until his retirement from sea service in 1966. He then became a harbour master for Blue Star until 1971.

Records

Discharge certificates, 1929-1962.
Certificates as temporary lieutenant, RNR, HMS *Asturia*, 1940-1941.
References: Royal Mail Lines; master of the *Avonmoor*, Liverpool; Kaye & Sons; New Egypt & Levant Shipping Co., 1945-1954.
Photographs: officers of HMS *Asturia* at Greenock and a convoy, 1940-1942.
Medals: the 1939-1945 medal; the Pacific, Italy and Atlantic star medals and George VI medal, c.1939-1945.
DX/1189   1929-1962   1 File

Individuals

Anonymous Passenger

Journal of a voyage to Europe by an American china buyer who sailed on the *Asia* from New York for Liverpool on the 26 February 1862. After travelling around the Potteries, Stoke-on-Trent on business, he departed on the *Europa* arriving back at New York on the 31 May 1862.

Record

Journal of a voyage to Europe (microfiche available).
DX/1425   1862   1 Volume

Sir Percy E. Bates (1879-1946)

Sir Percy E. Bates was born in Liverpool in 1879 and was educated at Winchester College. In 1899 he joined the firm of Wm. Johnston & Co., Ltd., shipowners in the Baltimore and Mediterranean trades. Following the death of his father in 1900, he joined his elder brother, Bertie, in the family firm of Edward Bates & Sons. His brother's untimely death in 1903 left Percy, aged twenty-four, as

Principal of Edward Bates & Sons, and he also became a Director of the Pacific Steam Navigation Co., Ltd. and a member of the Mersey Docks & Harbour Board. He was elected Chairman of the Liverpool Steam Ship Owners Association in 1911 and 1945.

During World War I Percy Bates was Director of Commercial Services at the Ministry of Shipping in London and in 1920 he was created a Knight Grand Cross of the Order of the British Empire. In 1922 he became Deputy Chairman of Cunard Steam Ship Co., Ltd., and later succeeded Sir Thomas Royden as Chairman in 1930. He was responsible for the idea of using two ships instead of three for the North Atlantic weekly passenger service, and the construction of the liners *Queen Mary* and *Queen Elizabeth*. He was also Deputy Chairman of T. & J. Brocklebank, a Director of Port Line and other Cunard subsidiaries, and also of the Great Western Railway. During World War II he was made a member of the Advisory Council of the Ministry of War Transport in London. He died on the 16 October 1946, the same day that the *Queen Elizabeth* sailed on her inaugural voyage.

Records

Booklets re: T. & J. Brocklebank sailings, etc., 1904-1921, 1939 and 1964.
Souvenir brochures for the *Aquitania*, *Queen Mary*, *Mauretania* (II) and *Queen Elizabeth*, 1913-c.1950.
Maiden voyage certificates for the *Mauretania* (II) and *Queen Elizabeth*, 1936-1939.
Launch card for the *Queen Elizabeth*, 1938.
Memorandum and articles of association of the Cunard Steam Ship Co., 1949 and 1969.
Miscellaneous ephemera re: Cunard liners, etc., c.1930-1973.
D/BAT   1880-1973   1 Box

Reference

Bates, P.E. *Bates of Bellefield, Gyrn Castle and Manydown*. Privately published, 1994.

Miss Ida Foster Botham (fl. 1894)

Miss Ida Foster Botham accompanied her uncle on a business trip to India, sailing from Liverpool on board the *Clan Macintosh* in 1894. In her journal she describes the voyage and their transfer to another vessel after the *Clan Macintosh* broke a propeller shaft and had to be towed into Aden, and visits to Delhi and the Taj Mahal.

Record

Journal of voyage from Liverpool to India.
DX/652/1   1894-1895   1 Item

Dockers' Records

Few records of dockers working in the port of Liverpool survive in written form. Some taped interviews can be found in the oral history collections (see Vol. II chap. 9).

A synopsis of an anonymous docker's diary written during the depression, which shows the difficulty of finding work on the docks during the early part of 1923, and describes working conditions and the hiring process under the "pen" system. Transcript available.
DX/833   1923   1 File

An autobiography of a "rogue docker" at Birkenhead Docks.
DX/1164   1963-1976   1 Item

Diary of a Liverpool Dock Worker: The Memoirs of Mr Pridgeon, who was a master stevedore and later ships' foreman for Alfred Holt & Co.
OA/1695   1883-1940   1 Item

Jesse Hartley (1780-1860)

Jesse Hartley was born at Pontefract, Yorkshire, in 1780. His father was a stone mason, architect and bridgemaster, and Jesse's earliest professional works were undertaken in West Riding under his father's direction. In 1824 he was appointed to the post of Dock Surveyor and Engineer by the Trustees of Liverpool Docks, and during a career of thirty-six years he constructed and altered every dock in the city, adding 140 acres of wet docks and some ten miles of quay space. Perhaps his most famous monument are the Albert Dock warehouses, which were unique at their time of opening for their hydraulic handling equipment and dock machinery, and today are the home of the Merseyside Maritime Museum.

Record

Memorandum book containing sketches and notes re: projects in West Riding, Yorkshire. N.B. Records relating to his work in Liverpool can be found in the Mersey Docks & Harbour Board archive (see Vol. I, chap. 2).
DX/86   1797   1 Volume

Reference

Ritchie-Noakes, N. *Jesse Hartley: Dock Engineer to the Port of Liverpool 1824-1860*. Liverpool, 1980.

Alfred Holt (1829-1911)

Alfred Holt was born in Rake Lane, Liverpool in 1829. He was apprenticed as an engineer to the Liverpool and Manchester Railway, and in 1852 set up business as a consulting marine engineer in India Buildings, Liverpool. In 1865 Alfred, in partnership with his brother Philip Holt, formed the Ocean Steam Ship Co. (Blue Funnel Line) to run steamers equipped with compound engines, designed by Alfred, to China. (For further details, see Vol. I, chap. 4.) In 1872 Alfred visited America, sailing from Southampton on the *Tagus* on the 2 April 1872 and returned to Liverpool on the 29 July 1872, and recorded details of the voyage and his visits to US cities in a journal.

Record

Journal of a visit to the USA
DX/1464   1872   1 Volume

William Midgley (b. 1881)

William Midgley of Keighley, West Yorkshire, suffered from chest problems and was sent on a sea voyage by his father, W. Midgley (Sr.) for the sake of his health. He departed from Liverpool on board the clipper *Grasmere* for a passage to Melbourne, Australia in 1899, and describes the voyage in a fifteen-page narrative letter.

Records

Memorandum to William Midgley (Snr.), Fleece & Dalton Mill, Keighley, from Gracie, Beazley & Co., Water Street, Liverpool, re: prices of berths and sailing opportunities, 1899.
Narrative in letter form, written by William Midgley, describing voyage to Melbourne, 27 August - 6 December 1899.
Sailing card for the *Grasmere*, Liverpool to Melbourne and Victoria, July 1899.
Photographs of the *Grasmere* in Canning Dock, Liverpool, and William Midgley on board, c.August 1899.
Receipt for Quoy Kee & Co., Chinese Store, Brewarina, Victoria, Australia, October 1900.
DX/1097   1899-1900   8 Items

Christopher Pike (fl. c.1853)

Christopher Pike of London, travelled to Birkenhead on the 1 September 1853 and after a week looking around Liverpool, embarked on the barque *Electric* for a voyage to Cadiz. He describes life on board, the time spent in quarantine at Cadiz, and the rest of their holiday in Cadiz. He departed Cadiz on the 23 November 1853 and arrived at Dartmouth on the 14 December 1853.

Record

Manuscript journal of voyage and three month sojourn in Cadiz.
DX/1067   1853   1 Volume

Janet Smith (1863-1940)

Janet Smith was a lady's maid accompanying her employer on a voyage to New York in 1896. They sailed from Liverpool on the *Umbria* on the 5 September 1896 and returned on the *Campania* on the 17 October 1896. She describes life on board, her duties and social activities. She also describes their journey to and time spent in Montreal, Canada.

Record

Diary kept by Janet Smith during a visit to Canada (transcript available).
DX/1093   1896   1 Volume

Annie Stephens (fl.1909)

Annie Stephens accompanied her husband, Captain T. Stephens, on board his ship the *Anselma de Larrinaga* for a voyage from Eastham, Cheshire to Buenos Aires, Argentina, from 24 April to the 4 September 1909. In two notebooks she wrote of life on board, in particular her seasickness and the many hardships she endured during the voyage. These are a rare record of the experiences of a captain's wife at sea.

Records

Notebooks kept by Mrs. Annie Stephens (transcript available).
DX/1128   1909   2 Volumes

H.E. Stripe (1813-post 1886)

H.E. Stripe was born in London in 1813 and came to Liverpool in 1832. He was employed as a clerk at the Liverpool ship owning firm of J. Bibby & Sons (now Bibby Line Ltd.) for forty-six years from 1840-1886. In his notebook entitled "Sketch of the Commercial Life of H.E. Stripe," he gives a vivid and detailed description of his journey to Liverpool and his various employments, especially his career with Bibby's. His diary includes details of the staff and captains employed at Bibby's, particularly the rise of Frederick Leyland in the company. He also includes much contemporary information on the topography and social life of Liverpool during the mid-nineteenth century.

Record

Manuscript notebook, "Sketch of the Commercial Life of H.E. Stripe"
DX/1477   1886   1 Volume

Joseph H. Worthington (fl. 1836-1911)

Joseph H. Worthington was a prominent Liverpool shipowner and sometime chairman of the Liverpool Shipowners Association. His fifteen volumes of diaries are an extremely useful source of information regarding the social life of a Victorian Evangelical Lay Anglican and leading commercial figure. However, references to his work are limited and confined to brief notes of trips to London, visits from businessmen and meetings, for example, of the Committee of Lloyd's Register. The diaries illustrate the way in which positions were gained and careers advanced in the mercantile world. Joseph H. Worthington lived in Oxton, now part of Birkenhead, and commuted across the Mersey to his office in Liverpool.

Records

Diaries (fifteen volumes), contents predominantly of a personal nature, visits to shipbuilding yards, family and relations' situations in business, visit to USA and Canada, charity services and social functions, 1836-1891.
Sketchbook initialled A.H.W., 1911.
DX/308   1836-1911   16 Items

Individual Vessels

The Maritime Archives & Library holds many documents relating to individual vessels hidden amongst the shipping company, seafarers, slavery and family collections. These relate mainly to the age of steam, and usually to vessels that were part of a fleet, and very rarely include examples of everyday working documents such as bills of lading and receipts for stores, etc. It is even more unusual for such documents to survive for a sailing vessel in great quantity. However, the Maritime Archives & Library holds two collections of working documents relating to individual sailing ships, which are a rare survival of documents of this nature.

Warlock

The barque *Warlock* was built at Whitehaven in 1840 and was owned by Dixon & Co., Ltd. of Liverpool. The archive includes over 100 bills and receipts regarding the fitting out of the vessel in Liverpool after a voyage to Valparaiso, Chile under the command of Captain J. Pagen in 1853 (uncatalogued).

DX/1149   1852-1853   1 Box

Albion

The barque *Albion*, was owned by Dr. William Harland (father of Sir E. Harland, shipbuilder) of Scarborough. She sailed between Liverpool and Canada from 1838 until her shipwreck in the Gulf of St. Lawrence on 25 June 1849. The archive of over 800 documents comprises letters to the owner from ship's captains and agents in Liverpool, receipts for purchase of provisions, insurance papers, crew lists and documents relating to the sale of the materials following her shipwreck. The collection is currently being listed.

D/ALB   1838-1847   1 Box

Compiled by E. Edwards, M. Evans, A. Glynn, D. Littler and H. Threlfall.

CHAPTER 8

SPECIAL COLLECTIONS:
TITANIC AND LUSITANIA

This chapter has been compiled in response to the continuing popular fascination with the history of two famous Liverpool-registered ships, the *Titanic* and the *Lusitania*. Much of the fascination arises from the fact that the sinking of both of these ships remains shrouded in mystery. The White Star liner *Titanic*, the largest ship of her time at 46,329 gross tonnes, sank with the loss of over 1,500 lives after striking an iceberg in mid-Atlantic on the 14 April 1912. The *Lusitania* was the first British passenger ship to be built with four funnels, and was one of two super liners built by Cunard with the intention of taking back the coveted Blue Riband for the fastest Atlantic crossing. She won the Blue Riband on her second voyage on the 11 October 1907, crossing the Atlantic in 4 days, 19 hours and 52 minutes. However, on her return voyage from New York in May 1915, she was torpedoed off the coast of Ireland, a victim of World War I, and sank with the loss of 1,198 lives.

Whilst the majority of White Star Line records have not survived, the Maritime Archives & Library has made a particular point of collecting original documents relating to these two famous ships, and has been fortunate to have acquired a small number of important collections. These include the research collection of the late Leslie Harrison, former secretary of the Mercantile Marine Service Association, who spent much of his life attempting to clear the name of Captain Stanley Lord of the *Californian*, who was accused of failing to go to the *Titanic's* aid. Another significant collection is the *Titanic* Signals Archive, the original telegrams sent from on board the rescue ship *Carpathia*, including ones from J.B. Ismay, informing the *Titanic's* owners in New York of the tragedy.

Many individual, and more poignant personal items have also been donated, including the telegram sent by Esther Hart, informing her family of her own and her daughter Eva's survival, and the loss of her husband. There is also an unused first-class ticket which belonged to a clergyman whose wife fell ill the night before the *Titanic* was due to sail. Photographs of the *Titanic* and *Lusitania* and other famous liners can be found in the McRoberts photographic collection (see Vol. II, chap. 9), and the Mersey Docks & Harbour Board photographic collection includes photographs of the *Lusitania* at Liverpool. It is important to note that the *Titanic*, although registered at Liverpool, never actually visited the port during her brief existence. The archive material is complemented by the Merseyside Maritime Museum's gallery, *Floating Palaces of the Edwardian Age*, which includes many objects from the Maritime History Department's collection, including the 5.93m long builder's model of *Titanic* and a survivor's life-jacket.

References

Ballard, R.D. *The Discovery of the Titanic*. London, 1987.

Booth, J.R. and Coughlan, S. *Titanic; Signals of Disaster*. Westbury, Wiltshire, 1993.

Eaton, J.P. and Hass, C.A. *Titanic, Triumph & Tragedy*. Wellingborough, 1986.

Harrison, W.L. *A Titanic Myth - The Californian Incident*. Hanley Swain, Worcestershire, 1992.

Hickey, D. and Smith, G. *Seven Days to Disaster! The Sinking of the Lusitania*. Glasgow, 1981.

Hoehling, A. and Hoehling, M. *The Last Voyage Of The Lusitania*. London, 1957.

Lord, W. *A Night to Remember*. London, 1956, repr. 1976.

Warren, M.D. *The Cunard Turbine-Driven Quadruple-Screw Atlantic Liner: Lusitania*. Wellingborough, 1986.

Loss of the SS Titanic - Court of Inquiry, Report, Evidence, &c. Public Record Office reprint of the British Inquiry of 1912, 1997. (Copy available on microfilm with US Inquiry, 1912.)

Records

Titanic

Photographs of the *Titanic* and other White Star Line ships can be found in the McRoberts photographic collection, which includes ones of *Titanic* and her sister ship *Olympic* being fitted out at Belfast, and *Titanic* leaving Southampton on her maiden voyage.

McRoberts Collection,   1911-1912   1 Volume   Vol. 82

A number of general arrangement plans etc., of the *Titanic/Olympic* including a plan of the lifeboats, can be found in the Cunard plan collection.

B/CUN (Plan Collection)   1911   8 Bundles

Photograph of the centre anchor for *Titanic* being dispatched by railroad from N. Hingley & Sons Ltd., Ships' Anchor-makers, Dudley.

DX/1291   1911   1 Item

Souvenir issue of the *Shipbuilder* devoted to the *Titanic* and *Olympic*.

DX/1745   1911   1 Item

A first-class passenger ticket for the *Titanic* belonging to Reverend Stuart Holden, a clergyman, whose wife became ill the day before the *Titanic* sailed, forcing him to cancel his voyage, 10 April 1912 (see figure 4).

DX/1063/R   1912   1 Item

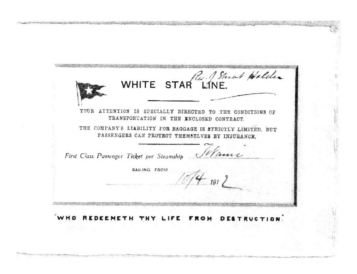

Figure 4:   First-Class ticket for the maiden, and only voyage of the White Star liner *Titanic*, belonging to the Reverend Stuart Holden, whose wife fell ill the day before the *Titanic* was to sail from Southampton, forcing him to cancel his voyage. The ticket retains its original mount.

Source: Merseyside Maritime Museum, DX/1063/R.

The *Titanic* signals archive comprising of two albums of telegraphic messages sent from the *Carpathia*, including ones sent by J.B. Ismay, announcing the news of the tragedy.
D/TSA   1912   1 Box

A telegram sent by survivor Esther Hart to relatives, informing them of the loss of her husband and the return of herself and her daughter, Eva, on *Celtic*, 20 April 1912. Also two xeroxes of letters home describing the disaster.
DX/1549/R   1912   3 Items

Archives of Miss Mildred Brown, survivor (n.b. not the unsinkable Mrs. Molly Brown!). Includes a letter giving a description of the disaster and its aftermath, written aboard the *Carpathia*, 1912, and a volume re: the formal investigation into the loss of the *Titanic* and *Lusitania*, 1915.

D/BRW   1912-1916   1 Box

Memorial service programme to commemorate the sinking of the *Titanic*, with local list of crew (Liverpool and Birkenhead), and King's sympathy message.

DX/1193   c.1912   1 Item

Transcripts of survivor Hon. Gladys Cherry's three letters home, written on board the rescue ship, *Carpathia*, describing the events of the sinking in graphic detail, 17-19 April 1912. Also two issues of the *Daily Mail*, 16 and 22 April 1912.

DX/1522   1912   1 File

Newscutting of a chart of the site of the sinking and the first official list of survivors, from the *Liverpool Echo*, 15-16 April 1912, and a supplement to *The Sphere* with an artist's impressions of the interior of the vessel and iceberg, 25 May 1912.

DX/873 and DX/919   1912   1 File

A collection of books, newscuttings, pamphlets and magazines, compiled by Teresa Beddoes.

D/Ti   1912-1980   2 Boxes

Research collection of Leslie Harrison, relating to the case of Captain Stanley Lord, of the *Californian*, many collected at the time of the disaster with the intention that they would be used to clear his name. They include an affidavit of Captain Lord, telegrams, statements of evidence, press reports, correspondence with survivors and crew, etc., and the official reports of the Inquiry, of the British and American courts (currently being catalogued).

D/LO   1912-1996   17 Boxes

Lusitania

A number of general arrangement plans and associated papers can be found in the Cunard archive.

B/CUN   c.1907   2 Bundles

Papers of R.W. Blythyn, steward on the *Lusitania*, which includes a list of passengers and crew for the last voyage, photograph of crew and also newscuttings, memorial napkins, etc. (see Vol. II, chap. 7).

DX/1055a   1897-1955   1 Envelope

Career papers of Captain Daniel Dow, who served on both the *Lusitania* and *Mauretania* during his career with Cunard, 1907-1920 (see Vol. II, chap. 7).

| D/DOW | 1905-1920 | 3 Boxes |

Brochure "Luxury and Comfort on board *Lusitania* and *Mauretania*," and a letter from Swan Hunter re: speed of the *Lusitania*.

| DX/1412a | 1908 | 2 Items |

Handwritten account of Anne Richardson, survivor of *Lusitania* sinking and other wartime experiences.

| DX/1729 | 1915 | 1 Item |

Correspondence re: victims, life jackets, the survivors' relief fund and a change of route for Cunard vessels.

| D/LUS | c.1915-1918 | 1 Box |

Discharge book, stamped "vessel sunk off Kinsale," belonging to George Knill, a fifteen-year-old scullery boy, who swam away from the sinking vessel (see Vol. II chap. 7).

| DX/1055e | 1915-1931 | 1 Item |

Career papers of Frederick Rowan, alias Grant, a fireman on board *Lusitania* at the time of the sinking. Includes letter re: money paid for personal loss in *Lusitania* sinking, 1915-1946.

| DX/1237 | 1915-1946 | 1 Envelope |

Telegram and newspapers re: the sinking of the *Lusitania* and Inquiry. Includes testimonial and photograph of an American passenger who was saved by *Lusitania's* carpenter, Neil Robertson.

| DX/1478 | c.1915-1994 | 1 Envelope |

Book issued by the Cunard Line re: the sinking of the *Lusitania*. The first section lists all crew and passengers aboard the ship. The second section lists all crew and passengers lost or saved.

| DX/1055b | 1916 | 1 Item |

Compiled by D. Littler.

CHAPTER 9

PICTORIAL AND AUDIO

The Merseyside Maritime Museum holds a wide range of pictorial and audio records, and these can be divided into the following categories: maps, charts, dock plans and drawings, ship's plans, photographic records, postcards, film, video and audio tapes. Much of the material is embedded in larger collections, notably that of the Mersey Docks and Harbour Board. This chapter is a brief summary of the scale and content of these records and at the time of writing, we have to admit that not all of this material has been listed in full. Given the size of many of these collections, their locations and varied degree of cataloguing, it is advisable to check availability before your visit.

There are also other sources of pictorial material in the Museum's collections. These are the oil paintings, watercolours, drawings, posters and prints curated by the Maritime History Department. The paintings have been collected to represent the work of the Liverpool marine painters of the late eighteenth and nineteenth centuries. The ship portraits provide detailed information about the individual appearance of ships before photography and as many of the backgrounds are of Liverpool and the Mersey, provide detailed topographical evidence. Other works include views of Liverpool which show how the town and port developed from the late seventeenth century. They include the first authentic view of Liverpool painted in 1682 and the Buck brothers' engraving of 1728 which shows all the new developments including the first dock opened in 1715. Much of the best of this collection is on show in the Art and the Sea gallery and there is a catalogue of the oil paintings. There are also a notable collection of ship bows, early nineteenth century prints and a growing collection of passenger liner posters. In addition, the collections of the Museum of Liverpool Life contains pictorial material on life inland of the port and the City Record Office has a major collection which covers all aspects of the city.

Maps

The MDHB collection contains the widest selection of Ordnance Survey maps because as a port authority, it had an interest in the coastal and estuarial margins, which stretched from the upper Mersey to Anglesey. The collection is not comprehensive. Its main value lies in the large number of the two largest scales: 1/2500 and 1/1250. The 1/2500 (twenty-five inches to one mile) covers areas outside Liverpool and Birkenhead, and shows areas in considerable detail including railway tracks true to scale. The 1/1250 (fifty inches to one mile) was used for urban areas and provides even more detail; but coverage is restricted to the dock areas of Liverpool and Birkenhead. Many have been annotated for the Board's own purposes. Other areas within Liverpool can be supplemented by the Liverpool Hydraulic Power Company's collection of Ordnance Survey maps which were used to map their hydraulic mains and the addresses to which they supplied power, and a number of small-scale nineteenth-century maps at six inches to one mile and one inch are available.

There are also a number of town maps or plans, but this is not a fully comprehensive collection. There are other good collections of maps and town plans held by the Liverpool City Record Office.

Charts

The earliest navigational chart in the collection is a portalan on parchment showing the Mediterranean and the eastern Atlantic dating from the sixteenth century. At present, it is on show in the Transatlantic Slavery gallery. Chartmaking developed rapidly in northern Europe in the late sixteenth century, which saw Ortelius' first significant world map of 1570, Mercator's projection and sea charts and sailing directions by Wagenhaer. These were used by English hydrographers and mariners.

The first comprehensive survey of British coastal waters was that of Captain Greenville Collins published as *Great Britain's Coasting Pilot* in 1693. This included a chart of the Mersey and Dee estuaries with directions on negotiating the mass of treacherous sandbanks, notable landmarks, etc. His work remained current for many years after and the collection contains a 1756 edition of his work.

The first charts produced by the British Admiralty from its surveys was published in 1801 and there is a world-wide collection of about 1810 to 1940 bound in volumes in the records of the Liverpool Underwriters Association (see Vol. I chap. 3) and also a selection of unbound miscellaneous Admiralty charts. The growing number and size of ships called for more detailed local hydrographic work along with an improved system of sea marks, buoys and lighthouses. Denham's survey of the Mersey and Dee published in 1840 (and available in the Maritime Archives & Library) was a notable contribution. The MDHB from 1858 maintained a detailed programme of surveys of Liverpool Bay and the Mersey as far inland as a line between Garston and Eastham. The Board's collection contains many detailed surveys especially of entrances together with their own published charts.

Dock Plans and Drawings

This is a sub-section of the MDHB collection, ranging from Timothy Lightoller's plan of 1765 to drawings of the building of Royal Seaforth Dock opened in 1974. Liverpool and Birkenhead docks and river frontages, together with all their buildings, bridges, locks, cranes, railway tracks and other equipment, are covered in greater or lesser extent with much detail on proposals and implementations in the mid to late nineteenth century. There are also some plans from other ports.

The collection is still being sorted. The situation has advanced from the summary in the first volume of this *Guide* (see Vol. I, chap. 2) in as far as most of the north Liverpool docks and Birkenhead dock folios have been identified but their individual contents remain to be listed. The same applies to the rolled plans. (It is important to note that the reference numbers Drawers A-I cited in Vol. I, chap. 2, pp. 41-42 are incorrect and were only used for descriptive purposes, bearing no relation to the storage reference numbers). Please consult the existing catalogues for the South Docks plans in the Library. Please telephone in advance of a personal visit to check availability and access arrangements.

Ship's Plans

Merchant ships and small craft were usually built without plans until the late eighteenth century. There were various methods of determining the shape such as the use of moulds or half models. The Brocklebank collection (see Vol. I chap. 4) contains one of the earliest and finest collections of liner and sail plans of merchant ships in the country. Starting with the *Nestor* of 1792 and finishing with the *Everest* of 1863, they chart the rapid progress in design of wooden sailing ships built in their shipyard at Whitehaven.

The Cunard Line technical collection (see Vol. I, chap. 4) is the other main source of detailed plans. These originated in Cunard's Naval Architects' department whose records were separated from the main body of the company's records, which were deposited with the University of Liverpool. They contain a good selection of general arrangements for most classes of vessel built since 1900, plus plans for some of the White Star liners taken over in the merger of 1934. There is also a very large boxed collection of "as built" drawings for the accommodation and fittings for the *Queen Mary*, 1934, *Mauretania* (2), 1938 and *Caronia*, 1948 and to a lesser extent for the *Queen Elizabeth* (2), 1969. The latter are a recent addition and require sorting and listing.

The Ocean collection (see Vol. I, chap. 4) also contains a good selection of general arrangements for twentieth century vessels, which indicate cargo capacities. There are also diagrams of passenger accommodation and storage of actual cargoes on specific voyages in the section for Elder Dempster, T. & J. Harrison and the PSNC (see Vol. I, chap. 4).

The Maritime Archives & Library's plan collection also includes plans of smaller craft. Mersey flats (the local sailing barge) are well covered in the Frank Howard collection with detailed plans recovered from a contemporary model and abandoned hulks. Lancashire nobbies, the local type of inshore sailing fishing boat, have a similar comprehensive coverage in the plans drawn up by Len Lloyd. Steam yachts and launches are covered in the Wynn collection (D/WYN).

This ancient family of landowners in North Wales built a series of yachts starting with the screw propelled auxiliary schooner *Vesta* of 1848. The Hon. Frederick Wynn was a great boating enthusiast and conducted an extensive correspondence with yacht builders, some of which is in the Merseyside Maritime Museum's collection and some in the Newborough archive at the Gwynedd Record Office, Caernarfon.

There is also a loose miscellaneous ship plan collection compiled by the old Liverpool Museum shipping department. This is classified under the following headings:

> Ocean-going powered merchant ships
> Ocean-going sailing merchant ships
> Coastal – powered merchant ships
> Coastal – sailing and oared ships and boats
> Warships – both powered and sail
> Miscellaneous

It is of variable quality. Some are no more than photographs of plans in other collections or accommodation diagrams. But there are some important individual items such as the original sail plans of important ships like the four-masted barque *Holt Hill*, or the steam coasters of the Zillah Shipping Co., Ltd. A database of this ship plan collection is available, but it is wise to telephone in advance to check availability as access to the ship plan collection is limited.

Photographic Records

Although a number of pioneer photographers worked in Liverpool, images of the port and its ships are rare before the 1890s. The two earliest in the collection are a view of the Mersey off the Pier Head about 1855-1865 in the MDHB collection and Georges Dock in about 1863 in the Chapman collection of lantern slides.

The photographic collection can be divided into negatives, prints and slides. There are two major collections of negatives: the MDHB which also includes prints (see Vol. I, chap. 2) and the Stewart-Bale collection (see separate entry). In addition, there are smaller collections of negatives including I. Pimblott & Sons Ltd., covering the machinery and products of their shipyard at Northwich between 1906 and the 1940s, the Joe Williams collection of people and ships from the 1930s to the 1950s (with some earlier photographers' work) and the David E. Smith collection (part of the Liverpool Nautical Research Society collection) of the last sailing schooners on the Mersey in the 1920s (see separate entry).

The negatives from fieldwork projects such as the hulk surveys conducted in the Falkland Islands between 1987 and 1990 are also held (D/JHE). The Photographic Department of NMGM also holds negatives of ships and the port of Liverpool, including copy negatives of historic material and large format transparencies of objects and archives in the Merseyside Maritime Museum's collections.

The McRoberts collection is the most important of the collections of photographic prints, and is described in detail later. Coverage of modern shipping (or at least until the early 1980s) is provided in the collection of the *Journal of Commerce*, the now defunct Liverpool daily shipping newspaper. The *Journal* obtained prints from a number of existing photographic firms which are subject to copyright and therefore copies cannot be supplied.

Photographic prints can also be found among the shipping company collections, notably in Brocklebank and Ocean, and PSNC. A large number of prints of ships owned by John Holt & Co. (Liverpool) Ltd., including launches, voyages and port scenes, are described in a separate entry.

Glass lantern slides are relatively few in number, but preserve images from the past that have not survived as negatives and prints. The two most important collections are E.C. Woods, which contains slides used for his lectures, for example on lighthouses and the Chapman collection. The latter were taken for, and by, an unknown yachtsman associated with the Tranmere Sailing Club or the Royal Mersey Yacht Club. It contains images of local yachts, traditional boats and life on the river, as well as the early view of Georges Dock crammed with small sailing ships in about 1863. There is also a quantity of 35 mm colour slides, most of which are concerned with scenes in and around the Merseyside Maritime Museum from 1980 onwards. These collections are at present uncatalogued.

Photographs

John Holt (Liverpool) Ltd.

John Holt (Liverpool) Ltd. began in 1867 as a mercantile firm involved in the West African trade. It bought its first steamer, the *Balmore*, in 1907 and from that time onwards built up a fleet of vessels operating a successful UK – West Africa service until 1965 when it sold its fleet to Elder Dempster.

The collection covers a wide range of subjects including ships, staff, events, port operations, ethnic scenes and crafts, salvage and property. The earliest ship photograph is a copy of an artist's impression of the sailing vessel *Maria* of 1852.

All of the ships of the John Holt ocean-going and river fleet are featured, many of them providing views of the launch, together with interior and exterior images. For example, the *John Holt* (1946) has shots of her launch, a comprehensive series of photographs beginning with her loading, duties while underway, and ending with her arrival at Lagos. Of particular importance is the collection of 111 staff portraits, all named, and many captioned with the staff member's position.

The property section includes photographs of John Holt's residential and commercial properties wherever the company traded along the West African coast. The collection has been sorted by category, and is listed on database. (For information on the archives of John Holt (Liverpool) Ltd., see Vol. I, chap. 4 and Vol. II, chap. 12.)

B/JHPHO   1852-1964   13 Boxes

Journal of Commerce **Photographic Collection**

The *Journal of Commerce* newspaper was instituted in 1861, and was published monthly until c.1985, when the paper closed, and NMGM acquired the photographic collection.

HMS *Mary Rose* of 1509 and HMS *Victory* of 1765, are the earliest images, and the small number of nineteenth century vessels include Cunard's paddle steamer *Britannia* of 1840, and Bank Line's steel barque *Olivebank* of 1892. The rest of the collection covers twentieth century vessels of many categories, which include naval vessels, tugs, container ships, tankers and roll on-roll off ferries, passenger liners, trawlers, dock ships and bulk carriers.

There are several sets of photographs which picture interior and exterior views, for example, *Brighton*, a British Transport Commission vessel of 1950, *Bretagne*, a Soc: Generale de Transport passenger line of 1952, the Cunard passenger liner *Franconia* of 1955 and *Act 1*, an Associated Containers' container ship of 1969.

Due to copyright restrictions, this collection can only be used for research and we are unable to provide reproductions of the images.

JOCPHO   1861-1992   18 Boxes   3,261 Images

McRoberts Collection

John McRoberts' interest in maritime matters was fostered by his father, a Chief Engineer with the Belfast Steamship Co., who took John on voyages across the Irish Sea during his childhood. After leaving school, he took up a post with the Cotton Exchange, but with the outbreak of World War II, he left to join the RAF. At the end of the war he returned briefly to the Cotton Exchange, but in 1945 he joined the *Journal of Commerce*, where he was employed in the shipping movements department. He remained there for twenty-one years until his retirement in 1966.

He amassed a vast collection of nautical photographs and ephemera, and his collection of ship photographs alone is estimated at 25,000. Although he purchased and exchanged photographs with other enthusiasts world-wide, from 1927 he took photographs of vessels on the Mersey himself. On his death in 1982, his collections of prints were received by the Merseyside Maritime Museum by bequest. Arranged in albums, his black and white photographs include most British companies from c.1850. There is also an album of Royal Navy vessels and one of sailing vessels. Important Commonwealth and Foreign companies, lightships, lighthouses and local views are also included. Phases one and two of the computerisation of the original card index are complete and 13,579 images are available on database so far. The collection is currently being re-housed in new albums.

Records

101 albums of black and white photographs, c.1850-1982.
8 boxes of marine newscuttings, 1927-1970.
40 miniature waterline models are held by the Maritime History department.
McR   c.1850-1982   120 Boxes

David E. Smith Collection

David E. Smith, ARPS, a member of the Liverpool Nautical Research Society, took photographs of sailing vessels, mostly schooners, which traded on the Mersey, Isle of Man and some of the South Coast ports, from the 1920s. His collection was bequeathed to the Society upon his death in 1990. Many of the photographs were reproduced in the book, *Tall Ships on Camera*, in 1992.

Records

Photographs of vessels filed alphabetically, many comprehensively captioned, c.1923-1966.
Indexed negatives captioned with the name and type of vessel, place and date of photograph, c.1923-1926.
Large format photographs, including the schooner *M A James* on the Mersey, 1927, and the five-masted barque *Kobenhavn* docking at Birkenhead, 1927.
Photographs of the Tall Ships Race, 1966.
D/SMITH   c.1923-1966   5 Boxes

Reference

Williams, D. *Tall Ships on Camera* Liverpool, 1992.

Stewart Bale Collection

Stewart Bale Ltd. was a commercial photographic company that was in business from about 1911 until the early 1980s. Born in the 1890s, Edward Stewart Bale was still a child when he and his parents emigrated from Australia to Britain. Edward's father ran an advertising agency, however, he had difficulty in finding illustrative work of a sufficiently high standard, and consequently Edward trained as a photographer. Additional employees were taken on as the photographic side of the business expanded, and Stewart Bale Ltd. began to earn a reputation as specialists in the field of commercial photography.

       Based in Liverpool at a time of considerable social, industrial and commercial development, Stewart Bale received commissions from all over the UK. The main strengths of the archive are merchant shipping, civil engineering, architecture and commerce. Examples are wide ranging and include the construction, launch and fitting out of passenger liners, cinemas and dance halls, the building of the two Liverpool Cathedrals, the two Mersey Tunnels and the devastation inflicted on British cities during World War II. The company also opened an office in London. The bulk of the archive survives in negative format and dates mainly from the 1950s and 1960s, although a few examples from the earlier period have survived.

The work of Stewart Bale has been recognised nationally as being of outstanding quality. Containing probably over 200,000 items in total, the collection was in urgent need of bringing into public custody and was purchased by NMGM in 1986.

On acquisition no subject index existed for the collection, however, other supporting documentation in the form of company day books and a client index is largely intact. A curatorial and conservation programme is in place to facilitate wider access to the collection. To date, 46,000 images are listed with 7000 entries available on computer database. Access to this collection is *strictly by appointment only*.

Records

Estimated 135,000 large format dry gelatine glass plate negatives (mostly 305 mm x 204 mm).
Estimated 70,000 large format cellulose triacetate film sheet negatives (mostly 254 mm x 203 mm).
Estimated 300 prints.
SB   c.1920-1960   c.200,000 Items

Postcards

The postcard in the form of a stamp pre-paid card issued by the Post Office, was introduced in Britain in 1870. In 1894, the Post Office abolished its monopoly and allowed the sale of privately published picture postcards. They proved enormously popular and by 1910 it was estimated that the British sent 800 million picture postcards every year. They provided a cheap and easy means of communication at a time when telephones were scarce. Attractive, often coloured images, made them highly collectable, and it is not surprising many featured ships and shipping scenes. Some illustrations were commissioned from marine artists, others were black and white photographs. The latter became important to ship enthusiasts intent on building up a collection of images of their favourite ships or shipping companies, and specialised companies such as the Nautical Photo Agency (which concentrated on sailing ships) or B. & A. Fieldon of Blundellsands, Liverpool. Shipping companies used them extensively to promote their passenger services and coloured cards were usually available free on board.

There is a large collection of postcards mainly of merchant shipping in the Stern collection and the E.C. Woods collection has some naval material and good coverage of the training ships in the Mersey. Numerous examples of postcards can be found in the miscellaneous DX collection, being mostly collected by passengers and crew. A notable exception being a selection designed by the artist, Odin Rosinvinge, and donated by his family (DX/1061/R).

Film and Video Tapes

The Maritime Archives & Library holds a small quantity of 16-mm film. The Ocean archive contains a number of promotional and training 16-mm films made between 1950 and 1970 (see Vol. I chap. 4). There is 16-mm "home movie" footage of cruising on Cunard liners in the Mediterranean in the 1930s and film by the Museum photographers taken between 1960 and 1980, including the last departure of the White Star liner *Britannic* in 1960 and the building of a Dee salmon boat at Jones' Yard, Chester in 1980.

In addition, there is video footage of Liverpool port scenes in the 1980s including the docking of a container ship at Royal Seaforth Dock and the launch of HMS *Campbelltown* from Cammell Laird's Yard in 1987. The hulks in the Falkland Islands are covered in the fieldwork of 1987 (D/JHE). A number of video tapes of commercially produced shipping films are available in the Library collection. Viewing of films and videos is *strictly by appointment only*. The film collection is currently being catalogued.

Audio Tapes

The oral history of seafaring and the port has proved a useful additional source of evidence, especially for social history and as an ingredient to enhance the exhibitions. The oral history collection is on various formats from reel to reel tapes, to digital audio tapes, and ranges in date from the mid-1960s to the present. The quality of recording and information is variable and little of the material has been transcribed, or catalogued.

Among the most important are the series recorded by the late Norman Morrison about the Pilotage Service in 1973, Philip Donnellan (BBC) with the members of the Cape Horner's Association in Bournemouth in 1971, M.K. Stammers with various retired Mersey flatmen in 1971-1975, the South Docks Survey with MDHB employees in 1981-1983 and Professor Tony Lane with retired seafarers for his research on seafarers (Liverpool University Docklands History Project). There are also interviews with the former residents of the Merseyside Maritime Museum's Piermaster's House in 1982-1983, coopers, sailing ship apprentices, veterans of the Battle of the Atlantic and employees of the Ocean Steamship Co. in the Ocean Archive. Listening facilities are limited, and an advance appointment is essential.

Compiled by E. Edwards, K. Howard and M. Stammers.

CHAPTER 10

MARITIME LIBRARY

The reference library of the Merseyside Maritime Museum covers all aspects of maritime history, focussing particularly on that of the port of Liverpool. It contains many important and rare materials which are all available for consultation. The collections consist of printed books, pamphlets and substantial runs of periodicals.

Classification Scheme

The books in the library are classified using an in-house classification scheme. Books are classified alphabetically by author/book title. The classification number appears on the book spine, followed by the first three letters of the author/title. **The 540 shipping companies class, however, has its own unique number arranged alphabetically by company name followed by author (enabling grouping of shipping companies).**

Due to the size of some volumes, it has necessitated two additional sequences. The oversize sequence is denoted by /OS immediately following the catalogue number. The pamphlet sequence (any item without a spine or less than fifty pages) is denoted by /PM immediately following the catalogue number. The pamphlet collection is not stored in the searchroom, but is available upon request.

Main Headings

000	Reference
200	Maritime Technology
300	Ships and Boats
400	Seafarers
500	Maritime Commerce (includes slave trade/emigration/maritime law)
600	Port Services
700	Maritime History - ports, areas, countries
800	Naval History
900	Maritime Art

Indexes

Subject index (arranged numerically by subject number).
Author index (arranged alphabetically by author).
These are available in computer print-out format in the searchroom.

Rare Books

Rare books are available on request and are identified by /R immediately following the catalogue number. Some important rare books include:

Anon. *The Young Emigrants*. London, 1826.
514.YOU/R

Clarkson, T. *The History of the Rise, Progress and Accomplishment of the Abolition of the Slave Trade*. London, 1808.
512.CLA/R

Hutchinson, W. *A Treatise Upon Practical Seamanship*. Liverpool, 1791.
410.HUT/R

Instructions to Surgeons Superintendents of Government Emigrant Ships. London, 1866.
514.INS/R

Lever, D. *The Young Sea Officer's Anchor, or A Key to the Leading of Rigging and to Practical Seamanship*. London, 1811 (an important rigging and seamanship manual of the early nineteenth century).
410.LEV/R

Liverpool Directories, 1766-1979 (gaps).

Robertson, M. *Futility or the Wreck of the Titan*. London, 1912.
340.ROB/R

Periodicals

Current periodicals are available on open access in the searchroom, back runs are stored in the stack and are available upon request. A wide selection of periodicals are available:

American Neptune, 1943 to date
International Journal of Nautical Archaeology, 1974 to date
International Journal of Maritime History, 1989 to date

Mariners Mirror, 1911-1914 (complete), 1919 to date
Nautical Magazine, 1979 to date
Naval Chronicle, 1799-1818 (complete)
Northern Mariner (Canadian), 1991 to date
Sea Breezes, 1920 to date
Shipbuilding and Shipping Record, 1919-1973
Ships Monthly, 1971 to date

Please note that access to the periodicals listed below is *strictly by appointment only*.

Engineering, 1876-1952
Fairplay, 1963-1987
Motor Ship, 1937-1989
Sea Trade, 1973-1984 (complete)
Shipbuilding & Marine Engineer Builder, 1925-1964
War Illustrated, 1939-1947 (complete)
Neptune, 1941-1944

House Magazines/Newsletters

A selection of shipbuilding and shipping companies publications are available, including:

Associated Tugs Social & Welfare Club – *The Gog*, 1952-1955.
Blue Star Line, Lamport & Holt Line, Booth Line & Associated Companies – *Blue Star News*, 1973-1974, *Gangway*, 1976-1997 (gaps).
British & Commonwealth Group – *Clansman*, 1975-1987.
Cammell Laird – *The Cammell Laird Magazine*, 1957-1964, 1965.
Coast Lines – *Argonaut/Log Lines*, 1946-1969.
Cunard Line – *Cunard Magazine*, 1920-1926 (complete), *Cunard News*, 1950-1957, *Leisure News*, 1990-1992.
Elder Dempster, Guinea Gulf & Henderson Lines – *Sea*, 1954-1986.
Elder Dempster Pensioners Association – *Elders of Elders News*, 1986 to date.
Furness Withy Group – *The Log*, 1967-1990.
Harrison Line – *Harrison Line Newsletter*, 1988-1990.
I.O.M. Steam Packet Co. – *Seawatch*, 1991 to date.
Mersey Docks & Harbour Co. – *Mersey*, 1924-1935, *Port News*, 1979 to date, *Port of Liverpool Handbook*, 1983 to date.
Ocean Transport & Trading Ltd. – *Ocean*, 1978-1979, *Ocean Mail*, 1978-1979, *Ocean News*, 1990 to date, *Ocean Newsletter*, 1988-1990.
Association of Ocean Group Pensioners – *The Nestorian Association*, 1984 to date.

Royal Mail Line & Pacific Steam Navigation Co. – *Pacific Breezes*, 1949-1958, *Atlantic & Pacific Breezes*, 1919-1966, *Pacific & Atlantic Breezes*, 1972, *The Piper*, 1974-1978.
Vickers Group – *Vickers News*, 1959-1964.
VSEL – *Link*, 1986 to date.

Reference Sources

Guides

A selection of guides to archive repositories in the UK, USA and Canada.
Class No. 080

Dictionaries

Ansted, A. *Dictionary of Sea Terms*. Glasgow, 1933.
030.ANS

Blanckly, T.R. *A Naval Expositor*. (limited edition reprint), East Sussex, 1988.
030.BLA

Paasch, H. *From Keel to Truck: A Marine Dictionary in English, French and German*. Antwerp, 1885.
030.PAA/R

Biographical Dictionaries

Jeremy, D.J. & Shaw, C. *Dictionary of Business Biography*. 5 vols., London, 1986.
030.JER

Bibliographies

Albion, G.R. *Naval & Maritime History: An Annotated Bibliography*. Mystic, Connecticut, 1963.
020.ALB

Millar, W.C. *A Comprehensive Bibliography for the Study of American Minorities*. 2 vols., New York, 1976.
020.MIL

Obin, A. (ed.). *Bibliography of Nautical Books*. Southampton, 1997.
020. BI

Encyclopaedias

Paasch, H. *Illustrated Marine Encyclopaedia.* Antwerp, 1890.
040.PAA/R

Kemp, P. *Oxford Companion to the Sea.* Oxford, 1976.
090.KEM

Other Useful Works

Bonsor, N.R.P. *North Atlantic Seaway.* 5 vols., Jersey, 1979.
311.BON

Conway's All The World's Fighting Ships. 5 vols., London, various.
801.CON

Fairburn, W.A. *Merchant Sail.* 6 Vols., Bath, Maine, 1945 (indispensable for information concerning merchant sailing ships in the USA).
312.FAI

Jane's Fighting Ships. London, various.
801.JAN

Lloyd's War Losses 1st World War – Casualties to Shipping Through Enemy Causes. London, 1990 (A facsimile reprint of Lloyd's war loss books held at the Guildhall Library).
821.LLO

Lloyd's War Losses 2nd World War, Vol. 1 – British, Allied & Neutral Merchant Vessels Sunk or Destroyed by War Causes. A facsimile reprint of London, 1989 (Lloyd's war loss books held at the Guildhall Library).
822.LLO

Various US Publications of Passenger/Emigrant Lists, c.1600-1851.

Theses

Bee, J. "A Worthwhile Venture? The Transatlantic Experience of a Teesdale Family in the Nineteenth Century." BA Thesis, Durham University, 1994.
Bridgeman, I.R. "History of Yeoward Line." Unspecified Thesis, Liverpool University, 1983.
Chatterton, L.P. "Irish Emigration to America During the Great Famine." Unspecified Thesis, Keele University, 1996.

Forshaw, D.M. "An Economic and Social History of Liverpool, 1540-1680." BA (Hons.) Thesis, Nottingham University, 1953.

Foster, K.J. "The Search for Speed Under Steam: The Design of Blockade Running Steamships, 1861-1865." MA Thesis, Carolina, 1991.

Frost, D. "The Kru in Freetown and Liverpool: A Study of Maritime Work and Community During the 19th and 20th Centuries." PhD Thesis, Liverpool University, 1992.

Geddes, D.C. "George Geddes and the New Brunswick Timber Trade, 1809-1812." PhD Thesis, London University, 1988.

Keeley, P. "The History and Major Influences of the Liverpool Underwriters Association, 1802-1996." BSc Thesis (Hons.), Liverpool University, 1996.

Kennerley, A. "The Education of the Merchant Seaman in the 19th Century Sailor's Homes, 1815-1970 – Voluntary Welfare Provision for Serving Seafarers." DPhil Thesis, Exeter University, 1989.

Kinsella, M.M. "The Defence of Liverpool During the Wars with France, 1793-1815." MA Thesis, Liverpool University, 1989.

Poole, B. "Liverpool's Trade in the Reign of Queen Anne." MA Thesis, Liverpool University, 1961.

Simmons, D. "Liverpool and the Formation of the North Atlantic Shipping Combination." MSc Thesis, London University, 1985.

Tanner, M. "Registration & Control of Fishing Boats in the Nineteenth Century." MPhil Thesis, St. Andrews University, 1993.

Conference Proceedings

International Congress of Maritime Museums – Paris, 1981; Rotterdam, 1987.

Symposium – The Shipowner in History (held at National Maritime Museum, 1984).

Society for Nautical Research Conference – Battle of the Atlantic (held at Merseyside Maritime Museum, May 1993).

Information Files

A collection of articles on maritime history, particularly Liverpool, grouped by subject. They are a useful introduction to any researcher unfamiliar with the subjects. Subjects covered are: American Civil War, Boatbuilding, Cammell Lairds, Dock Labour, Emigration, Family History, Fishing (Mersey & North West), History of Albert Dock, Life at Sea, Lifeboats & Safety at Sea, Liverpool Shipping & World Trade, Liverpool & The Slave Trade, Merseyside Maritime Museum History, Mersey Ferries, Other Mersey & Local Ports, Pilotage, Port Industries, Port of Liverpool, Port of Liverpool at War, Port Services, Shipbuilding (Mersey & Other Local Ports), Shipping Companies, Ship Models, Shipwrecks, *Titanic*, Training Ships on the Mersey, Tugs & Towage, Women at Sea.

Research Collections

Captain Beard Collection

Alphabetical compilation by name of sailing ship histories compiled by Captain Jack Beard, DSC. (See Vol. II chap. 11, Liverpool Nautical Research Society).

Cochrane Collection

Alphabetical compilation by name of steamship histories compiled by Douglas B. Cochrane. Available on microfiche in the Search Room.

Lloyd's Publications

Lloyd's Registers, 1764 to date

An annual alphabetical list of vessels giving details current at the time of publication. A dispute within the shipping community led to the publication of two separate registers. One, known as the Red Book, was published by a group, most of which were shipowners, while the other, known as the Green Book, was published by a group of underwriters. The content was somewhat similar. However, the same vessels did not always appear in both registers.

Lloyd's Registers until 1890, were almost exclusively limited to British registered vessels, although some foreign vessels which regularly traded with the United Kingdom, were included. For a short period from 1834-1837, all British vessels of fifty tons and over were included. This practice became the norm in 1875 when all vessels which had not been surveyed and classed at Lloyd's, were included. Since 1890 all British and foreign sea-going merchant vessels over 100 tons have been added.

The information contained in the registers varied according to the year. The main categories and years they were published in the registers are:

Name of vessel	1764 to date
Previous names (if any)	1764 to date
Official number	1872/3 to date
Signal code	1874/5 to date
Rig/description	1768 to date
Tonnage	1764 to date
Gross, net & under-deck dimensions:	
load-draught	1775-1833
length, breadth & depth	1863 to date
Description of engines	1874/5 to date

Date of build	1764 to date
Green Book gives age	1800-1833
Place of build	1764 to date
Builder	1860 to date
Owner	1764 to date
Master	1764-1920/1
Dates of service: owner/vessel	1887-1920/1
Number of crew	1764-1771
Port of registry	1834 to date
Port of survey	1764 to date
Class	1764 to date
Casualties, etc.	1775-1954/5

Lloyd's Lists 1741-1826 (reprints), 1827-1974 (microfilm)

Originally twice weekly, now a daily newspaper containing shipping movements and casualties. The movements are arranged geographically by port, listing arrivals and departures.

Lloyd's Lists Indexes 1838-1927

They cover the shipping movements and casualties section of Lloyd's Lists. Each index covers one year and is arranged alphabetically by name of the vessel. Steamers and sailing vessels are distinguished. Ship's masters are given if known and in later indexes other information is given, particularly where it is necessary to distinguish between different ships bearing the same name, such as vessel's net registered tonnage, port of registry, nationality, type or owners.

Lloyd's Shipping Index

A summary of information contained in Lloyd's Lists. Divided into two sections, sailing vessels and steamers, alphabetically listed by ship's name within each section. Recording the movements and latest reports at Lloyd's.

Lloyd's Weekly Shipping Index, 1880-1913.
Lloyd's Weekly Index, 1914-April 1917.
Lloyd's Confidential Daily List, 1917-1918.
Lloyd's Daily Index, 1919-1935.
Lloyd's Shipping Index, 1936-1980.
Lloyd's Weekly Casualty Reports, 1920-1980.
Lloyd's Confidential Index, 1959-1990 (gaps). These records are available *strictly by appointment only*.
Lloyd's Confidential Index (foreign), 1959-1965 (gaps). These records are available *strictly by appointment only*.

Lloyd's Register of Yachts 1878-1990 (gaps)

The register is complementary to Lloyd's Register and the arrangement similar. It covers yachts of all nationalities except those covered by Lloyd's Register of American Yachts. Entries under name give owner, builder and designer.

Lloyd's Voyage Supplements 1946-1973

The voyage supplements list the movements of ocean-going vessels on their current voyages, giving dates of arrival and sailing at all ports visited. These records are available *strictly by appointment only*.

Lloyd's Captain's Register 1869-1887 (gaps)

Details the service of masters and mates who held masters' certificates. Contains details of masters and mates of merchant ships and their certificate number. A summary is given of service.

Lloyd's List Law Reports, 1951-1963. These records are available *strictly by appointment only*.

Lloyd's Reports of Prize Cases, Vols. I-VI, 1912-1920.

Law Reports

Maritime Law Reports, 1860-1920.
Admiralty and Ecclesiastical, 1865-1875.
Spinks Ecclesiastical and Admiralty Reports, 1853-1854.
Swabeys' Admiralty Reports, 1855-1859.
Lushingtons' Admiralty Cases, 1859-1862.
Prichards' Digest of Admiralty and Maritime Law, 1887.
English Admiralty Reports, 1798-1850.

Maritime Registers

Liverpool Registers

Liverpool Register of Shipping, 1835.
Liverpool National Registry Book of Shipping, 1845.
Marwood's Shipping Register, 1854.

Other Printed Registers - Merchant Navy

Registry of Iron Vessels, 1862-1885.

Mercantile Navy List and Maritime Directory, 1872-1957 (gaps), monthly supplements (part I, sail and steam, 1959 and part II, motor, 1964). Official list of British-registered merchant vessels (published for the Register General of Shipping and Seamen) giving the following information: name of vessel, official number, signal code, rig, tonnage, dimensions, construction, materials, horsepower, description of propeller, date of build, place of build and owner.

Merchant Vessels of the United States 1879-1918.

American equivalent to Mercantile Navy Lists. Useful for tracing American vessels which are too small to be included in Lloyd's Register.

Mitchell's Maritime Register, 1872-1882 (gaps).

Bureau Veritas, 1877-1955. The French equivalent to Lloyd's Register. These records are available *strictly by appointment only*.

Det Norske Veritas, 1921-1966 (gaps). The Norwegian equivalent to Lloyd's Register. These records are available *strictly by appointment only*.

Turnbull's Steamship Insurance Register, 1890-1910. These records are available *strictly by appointment only*.

Printed Registers - Royal Navy

Navy Lists, 1822-1977 (gaps).

Brassey's Naval Annual, 1886-1926. Give details of British and foreign navies.

The Customs Bills of Entry

The Bills of Entry series for the major ports of Great Britain and Ireland have long been recognised as a major source for maritime ports, economic and commercial history. The Maritime Archives & Library holds the master set from H.M. Customs & Excise Library, originally at King's Beam House in London.

They were published daily by the Customs Authorities for the convenience of the merchant community. Each bill contains what is termed "ships reports" which are of great value in the study of merchanting. They contain details of all ships arriving in port and particulars of the port registration, the tonnage, master, dock, ship's agent and last port of clearance, together with a full account of all merchandise carried and to whom it was consigned. Summaries of imports, exports and articles entering and released from the bonded warehouses appeared in every issue, as did information regarding ships entered outwards, ships cleared outwards and ships loading.

Liverpool

1820			
1825-1832			
1834-1835			
1837			
1847			
1852-1855			
1856-1897	A and B Bills		
1898	B Bills only		
1899-1937	A and B Bills		
1939	A and B Bills		
C/BE/1		1820-1939	187 Volumes

Bristol

1832-1833		
1835-1837		
1840		
1843		
1845-1849		
1851-1870		
1872-1879		
1881-1903		
1905-1917		
C/BE/2	1832-1917	73 Volumes

Clyde

1841
1843-1939

Clyde and Forth

1919-1937		
C/BE/3	1841-1939	98 Volumes

Dublin

1850		
1860		
1863		
1865-1866		
1884		
1889-1923		
C/BE/4	1850-1923	41 Volumes

Hull

1831		
1835		
1837		
1863		
1884-1937		
1938		
1939 (to 4 September)		
C/BE/5	1831-1939	60 Volumes

Tyne

1875-1880		
1883		
1885-1927		
C/BE/6	1875-1927	50 Volumes

London

1779-1781	
1783	
1817-1818	B Bills only
1819	A and B Bills
1820	A Bills only
1821-1823	A and B Bills
1824-1832	B Bills only
1834	B Bills only
1836	B Bills only
1838	B Bills only
1839-1840	A and B Bills
1841	B Bills only
1842-1845	A and B Bills
1846-1847	A Bills only

1847-1853	A and B Bills	
1854	A Bills only	
1855-1856	A and B Bills	
1857-1859	A Bills only	
1860-1924	A and B Bills	
1927-1933	A and B Bills	
1934 (January-June)	A and B Bills	
1934 (July-December)	A Bills only	
1935-1937	A Bills only	
1939 (to 4 September)	A Bills only	
C/BE/7	1779-1939	214 Volumes

Weekly Trade Lists

1822-1823		
1845-1846		
1850		
C/BE/8	1822-1850	4 Volumes

References

Carson, E. Customs Bills of Entry, *Sources for Maritime History*. (I), 176-189.
Williams, D.M. "Merchanting in the First Half of the Nineteenth Century: The Liverpool Timber Trade." *Business History*. Vol. 8 (1966), 103-117.
Williams, D.M. "Liverpool Merchants and the Cotton Trade 1820-1850." In Harris, J.R. (ed.). *Liverpool and Merseyside: Essays in the Economic and Social History of the Port and its Hinterland*. Frank Cass, 1969.

Microform Collections

The microform collections consist of copies of original documents held at the Maritime Archives & Library and elsewhere. The Maritime Archives & Library reference number or location for the original documents, are given at the end of each entry.

Microfiche

Instructions to Surgeons, Superintendents of Government Emigrant Ships, 1866.
Journal of Surgeon on board the *Kingston*, off West Africa, 1832-1833 (see Vol. II, chap. 2, DX/1175).
The Development of the Liverpool Corporation Estate, 1760-1835 (British Library).
Log of the *Unity*, 1769 (see Vol. II, chap. 2, D/Earle/1/4).

Benezet, A. *Historical Account of Guinea*, 1772 (see Vol. II, chap. 2, DX/1624/R).

Journal of a China Buyer, 1862 (see Vol. II, chap. 7, DX/1425).

Index to Liverpool Statutory Register of British Merchant Ships, 1855-1908, 1948-1972 (see Vol. I, chap. 1, C/EX/L1).

Training ship *Indefatigable*, 1865-1881 Annual Reports (see Vol. II, chap. 7, D/B/115N).

Mayor Boat Yard, Tarleton, Station Account of Permits, 1870-1880 and Ledger of Work, 1902. (Private)

MDHB Contract Book (see Vol. I, chap. 2, MDHB/ENG/3-12).

MDHB Engineers Reports, 1825-1915 (see Vol. I, chap. 2, MDHB/ ENG/3-12).

Microfilm

Exchequer Port Books for Liverpool, 1681-1682 (Public Record Office).

American Papers from the House of Lords Record Office, 1808-1819 (House of Lords Record Office).

Register of Merchant Ships, Board of Trade Transcripts, 1855-1889 (Public Record Office) (see Vol. I, chap. 1, C/EX/L1).

Colonial Office Papers re: emigration including Liverpool Emigrant Officers Reports, 1833, 1834 (Public Record Office) (see Vol. II, chap. 3).

Liverpool Plantation Registers, 1743-1773, 1779-1784 (see Vol. I, chap. 1, C/EX/L/3/1-4).

South Docks Plans, c.1820-1970 (see Vol. I, chap. 2, MDHB/M/D).

Journal of W. Amphlett to USA, 1818 (British Library).

Liverpool Trade Lists, 1798, 1800 (British Library).

Lloyd's Lists, 1827-1974 (British Library).

Lloyd's Lists Indexes, 1838-1927 (Lloyd's of London).

Lloyd's Captains Register, 1874-1887 (Guildhall Library).

Conway Cadet, 1889-1966 (see Vol. II, chap. 4, D/CON/14).

Memorial Registers 22, 39, The War Dead of the Commonwealth, The Tower Hill Memorial, 1914-1918, 1939-1945 (Commonwealth War Graves Commission)

Liverpool Steamship Owners Association Minutes, 1858-1952 (see Vol. I, chap. 3, D/SS).

Customs Bills of Entry, 1820-1908. (see separate entry, C/BE)

Jefferson Collection Receipt Book, 1722-1771.

Morecambe Bay Fishing Boat Mutual Insurance Co., Ltd. Policies, 1894-1956,

Liverpool Directories, 1766-1796, 1800-1813 (Liverpool City Library).

Passenger List of early Cunard Fleet, 1840-1853 (Liverpool University Archives) (see Vol. II, chap. 3).

Gregory, A.T., The Emigrant or Life in Canada (Ontario Archives) (see Vol. II, chap. 3).

Diary of G. Holbrook's voyage from Liverpool to Philadelphia, 1789-1790 (New York Public Library) (see Vol. II, chap. 3).

Diary of C. Cooper, MRCSE, Surgeon on board Emigrant Ship, 1853 (New York Public Library) (see Vol. II, chap. 3).

Journal of Captain B. Blundell (1687-1756), founder of Liverpool Blue Coat School (Lancashire Record Office) (see Vol. II, chap. 1).

Liverpool Shipowners of the 19th Century (compiled by Liverpool Nautical Research Society) (see Vol. II, chap. 11).

US and British Enquiry Reports on *Titanic*, 1912 (US National Archives) (see Vol. II, chap. 8).

Laird Family Papers, 1830-1860 (originals in private hands) (see Vol. II, chap. 6).

Aperture Cards

T. & J. Brocklebank, ships' plans, 1792-1863 (see Vol. I, chap. 4, B/BROC).

Fraser Trenholme, letter book, 1862-1865 (see Vol. II, chap. 1, B/FT).

South Docks Project, selected MDHS archives and plans, c.1800-1900 (see Vol. I, chap. 11).

Ships' Plans, c.1800-1950 (selected) (see Vol. I, chap. 2, MDHB/ENG).

Grayson's of Liverpool, Shipbuilding Book, 1850 (original in private hands) (see Vol. II, chap. 5).

Compiled by H. Threlfall.

CHAPTER 11

RESEARCH, MISCELLANEOUS AND NON-MARITIME

This chapter describes the small number of collections which do not belong in the preceding chapters, namely, the research collections, miscellaneous accumulations and non-maritime records.

The non-maritime collections range from the business records of local manufacturers to local societies, and includes our parent organisation, the National Museums & Galleries on Merseyside. These collections have been given detailed treatment where it was considered there might be an interest for maritime historians. Vulcan Foundry Co., Ltd., for example, exported many of the locomotives it produced through the port of Liverpool, and was a shipbuilder for a short period in the 1850s. All of the non-maritime and business records described in the following chapter are stored at the reserve store and are available *strictly by appointment only*.

Two of the largest research collections held at the Maritime Archives & Library are described in this chapter. These are the records compiled by members of the Liverpool Nautical Research Society, which are an invaluable source of information of Liverpool's maritime history, particularly eighteenth and nineteenth century shipowners and shipbuilders, and the Merseyside Docklands History Survey, a study undertaken on Liverpool's South Docks in the early 1980s.

Miscellaneous collections have only been included in this *Guide* where there is a distinct maritime connection. The two collections described in this chapter are those of the Liverpool solicitors, Alsop, Wilkinson, who specialised in maritime affairs, and the Bryson Collection of business and family ephemera, much of which originated from the rubbish bins of solicitors offices. Many of the smaller collections of miscellaneous items are held in the DX collection (and its predecessor, the SAS collection). The series DX/1 to DX/600 covers the period between 1974 and 1986, and DX/700 and all succeeding numbers cover items acquired since the inception of National Museums & Galleries on Merseyside. All of the maritime items from this series, relating to subjects covered earlier in the *Guide*, such as slavery and emigration, are described in the appropriate chapters. Although most of the non-maritime items of the DX/1 to 600 series have been transferred to the Merseyside Record Office and the Liverpool City Record Office, many of the collections relating to NMGM's areas of interest have been retained, and are held at the reserve store, available *strictly by appointment only*.

Research Collections

The Liverpool Nautical Research Society

The Liverpool Nautical Research Society was established in 1938 to encourage public interest in Liverpool's maritime past and to collect and disseminate information about its ships and seafarers. It continues to discharge these tasks today and is based at the Maritime Archives & Library. The core of its records are the personal research papers of members A.C. Wardle, W.S. and J.S. Rees, C. Woods, and Captains E.A. Woods and J. Beard. Captain Beard's list of late nineteenth century British deep sea sailing ships is an invaluable collation of information from newspapers, Lloyd's Registers and other sources; while the other members have compiled authoritative lists of Liverpool fleets and shipbuilders. The Society has also published its researches since 1946 and compiled useful indexes of articles on shipping companies published in *Sea Breezes*, etc., which are available in the Library (along with a copy of Captain Beard's list which is also available on microfilm). The records fall into two distinct categories:

1.   Research files, essays, etc., compiled by members of the Society.
2.   Original records donated to the Society.

The collection is currently being re-catalogued.

Records

Research

Detailed notes on shipbuilders on the Mersey, Dee, and at the Isle of Man, London, Belfast, and elsewhere in the UK between the eighteenth to nineteenth centuries.
Detailed genealogies and biographical notes on some Liverpool shipowners and some shipbuilders, eighteenth to nineteenth centuries.
Handwritten volume of notes re: nineteenth century Liverpool shipping companies with fleet lists (available on microfilm).
Fleet lists of shipping companies, Liverpool and elsewhere (including Canada and USA).
Notes on shipping lines, 1790-1871.
American ships bought by Liverpool shipowners, 1852-1871.
List of pilot boats, 1766 onwards.
Notes on Blockade runners (American Civil War).

Original records

The *Engineers' Ledger* by J. Jordan, 1848, contains engineering notes on various ships including the *Albert* of Dublin and an iron ship for Edward Bates.

Log of barque *Lancashire Witch* (London to Rio), 1865.

Liverpool Customs letter re: loss of the *Montezuma*, 1847.

Registry certificate for *Chieftan*, 1825.

Bills of sale, *Roscote*, 1873 and *Stav*, 1921.

Notes on ferries and Sir Thomas Johnson, Fortunatus Wright and William Hutchinson.

Liverpool Shipbuilding Enquiry, 1850 (hand-written copy by W.H. Wakefield).

Notes on Liverpool Pilotage Service by J.S. Rees, 1761-1887.

Photographs of sailing and other ships and shipwrecks from c.1938.

Numerous abstracts of logs, menus, postcards and brochures, c.1880-1950.

Captain Beard's original card files and personal correspondence, c.1960.

(Note: Captain Beard was born in Queensland in 1888. He began his seafaring life in sail in 1903. Having served in both World Wars, on his retirement he joined the Royal Navy Minewatching Service in Liverpool. He ended his days in small-scale commercial fishing off the Isle of Man, c.1950-1960.)

LNRS   1865-c.1970   27 Boxes

Merseyside Docklands History Survey

This collection was compiled between 1981-1983 by Nancy Ritchie Noakes and a team of researchers. It relates to the South Docks which stretch from George's Dock, via Canning, Albert, Salthouse and the Old Dock Site to Herculaneum Dock, all of which are no longer functioning as commercial docks. A selection of the material was edited and published in 1984 by HMSO as volume 7 of the Royal Commission on Historic Monuments supplementary services, entitled *Liverpool's Historic Waterfront*. The material consists of copies and extracts from original records held by the Maritime Archives and elsewhere, essays and analyses based on these sources and an industrial archaeological survey. Survey drawings of the docks, buildings and fixtures provided material for a booklet entitled *Quayside and Warehouse Fixtures in Liverpool's South Docks* (Merseyside County Museums, 1983). *Discovering Dockland*, an education pack aimed at twelve to sixteen year olds, was produced to explain the functions of the docks from a vessel's first contact with a pilot to the final stage when her cargo is ready for delivery (a copy is available in the Library but is no longer in print). A brief illustrated monograph on the dock engineer Jesse Hartley who was largely responsible for the development of the south docks, was also written and is still available.

The MDHS research collection occupies three filing cabinets and researchers who are interested in matters relating to the south docks, should make maximum use of this material before turning to the original Dock Board archives.

Records

Approximately 4300 black and white prints of general interior and exterior views and details of building structures and machinery, c.1981-1983.
Slides of dockside faces of dock walls in the south docks, c.1981-1983.
Council for British Archaeology report cards for all superficial features and buildings, arranged by dock name, with brief description and a 3½" x 5" photographic print on the reverse, c.1981-1983.
Oral history tape recordings, with transcripts, summaries and index, c.1981-1983.
A number of re-drawn plans and microfilms of dock company records, c.1981-1983.

MDHS   1981-1983   c.7000 Items

Other Research Collections

Note: Research collections relevant to specific subjects covered in previous chapters, have been described in the appropriate chapter. These include:

1.   Dr. D.P. Birch's and J. Gordon Read's research collections on emigration (see Vol. I chap. 3).

2.   Michael K. Stammers' research files re: his printed works, *The Passage Makers* (a history of the Black Ball Line), 1978 and *Mersey Flats & Flatmen*, 1993 (D/MKS). M.K. Stammers has also researched the Liverpool sailing ship, *Jhelum*, which survives as a hulk at the Falkland Islands (see Vol. II, chap. 5 – D/JHE).

3.   William McQuie Mather's ship model-making research collection (see Vol. II, chap. 6).

4.   Leslie Harrison's research on the case of Captain Stanley Lord and the *Titanic* (see Vol. II, chap. 8).

5.   Maurice Rigby's research on the Confederate Navy's *Alabama* (D/RIG).

Miscellaneous Records

Alsop, Wilkinson

This firm of Alsop, Wilkinson, solicitors, was founded in 1798 by Thomas Harvey. Alsop, Wilkinson has specialised in maritime cases for well over a century. James Alsop joined the firm in 1871 and built on the contacts of his predecessor, Thomas Jevons who, through the network of Unitarians, had connections with the great shipping names of Holt, Rathbone, Booth and Bowring. In 1928 a merger with Batesons strengthened the maritime and commercial side of the business.

The records briefly described below illustrate the many useful maritime documents often held by legal firms.

Records

Papers relating to the estate of Alexander Elder, founder of Elder, Dempster & Co., 1897-1930.
African Association agreement, 1894.
African Oil Mills papers re: salvage off coast of Africa, 1891-1898.
Papayanni Line agreement, 1890.
Bottomry bond, 1886.
R.W. Leyland agreement, articles of partnership, etc., 1893.
Great Eastern mortgage, agreements, etc., 1887-1888.
City of Liverpool Steam Navigation Co. mortgages and deed, 1892.
British & African Steam Navigation Co. prospectus, agreement and letters, 1900 and 1902.
PSNC decree, etc., 1863 and 1871.
Miller & Mossman, commission merchants and shipowners, deed of arrangement, 1866.
William Pirrie & Co., shipowners, deed of arrangement, etc., 1866.
Hodgson & Blain, iron shipbuilders, lease for 14 years of land by Brunswick Dock, 1845.
Papers re: collision of *Wien Hohenfelde* of Rostock, with *Magnet*, 1875.
Seacombe Forge & Rivet Co. lease and mortgage of land near docks, 1866-1872.
Booth Steamship Co., valuations and agreements, 1901.
Wakefield Nash & Co., statement of affairs, etc. (including grants of land in Texas signed by Sam Houston), 1859-1879.
Imperial Direct West Indies Mail Service agreement and deed, 1902-1911.
Powell & Hough, shipowners (coastal), articles of partnership and agreements, 1890.
Stoddart Brothers, ship brokers, articles of partnership and agreement, etc., 1886-1889.

Papers re: prize cases in World War I, 1915.
Papers re: case of the steamer *Pearl* (cotton seized in American Civil War in Alabama), 1861-1872.

B/AW	1845-1915	7 Boxes

The Bryson Collection

The Bryson collection of business ephemera was compiled by Joe Bryson, who had a varied career as a soldier, fairground artist and angler, and also collected old documents, a hobby he pursued for over twenty years until the 1970s when he returned to his native Cumbria. The collection was purchased from him as a whole, and although it was recognised that a large proportion of the collection would probably not be relevant, it was believed that the maritime content would make the acquisition worthwhile. This has indeed proved to be the case, although the sorting of the collection has been impeded by the shortage of staff time and the size of the collection itself, at some 1,400 boxes. A proportion of the non-local material has been transferred to other repositories. Unless otherwise stated, items from this collection are available *strictly by appointment only*.

Records

The collections falls into a number of categories:

200 boxes of maritime material, eg papers relating to ships' cargoes, average adjustment records, bills of exchange, log books and emigrant papers, and the records of the Union Marine Insurance Co. The majority of the maritime items are available at the Maritime Archives & Library, and are described in the appropriate chapters of this *Guide*. Some interesting maritime documents not described so far include:

Epitome of accounts of Edward Oliver, shipowner.

DB/115	1858	1 Item

Partnership agreement of William Gregson & Co., ropemakers of Liverpool.

DC/115CC	1753	1 Item

Documents relating to the building of the *Banshee*, an American Civil War blockade runner.

DB/115S	1862	3 Items

Agreement for building vessels at Woodside.

DB/115S	1852	1 Item

Agreement for cargo rates on Mersey & Irwell Navigation.
DB/115S   1797   1 Item

Ship underwriter's account book, 1846-1847, for Eyre Evans & Co. of Liverpool.
DC/109C   1846-1847   1 Item

MSS memoir of "Mrs. Parry" married to a "drunken sailor."
DB/105C   c.1865   1 Item

Files of correspondence re: R.A. Watson, Timber Merchant of Liverpool.
DB/108E   c.1869   1 Item

Cotton Porters Employers Committee minute book (covering the period of the General Strike).
DB/111M   1917-1931   1 Item

Documents re: Fund for the Advancement of Officers Children (signed by J.B. Ismay).
DB/115AA and BB   1920-1928   2 Items

Some 400 boxes of non-maritime material have been sorted and a card index produced, and sorting is nearing completion of 400 boxes of unsorted material relating to Merseyside and elsewhere in the U.K.
DB   1753-c.1960   c.1,400 Boxes

Turner & Dunnett

Turner & Dunnett were a leading firm of printers of commercial stationery in Liverpool in the late nineteenth century. They produced stationery, such as bills of lading, passenger tickets and receipts for all of the leading Liverpool shipping companies, including the White Star Line, Inman Line, Cunard Steamship Co. and African Steamship Co., and many smaller companies, for which few records have survived, such as George Peplow, Forwood & Sons, Atlas Steamship Co. and the MacIver Line.

Records

Two volumes of blank stationery samples.
SAS/31B/3/1-2   c.1895   2 Volumes

Non-Maritime Business and Other Records

The non-maritime business and other collections form an interesting and varied group of archives. Many collections were acquired to accompany the object collections of the Liverpool Museum and the Department of Regional History. Two of the largest and most important are the Vulcan Foundry engineering records and those of BICC (British Insulated Callenders Cables Ltd.). Other local firms represented in the collection are the toy manufacturers, Meccano, the Liverpool Hydraulic Power Co. and the electrical engineers, Wingrove & Rodgers.

Many of the non-business records, such as the Liverpool Geological Society and the Liverpool Naturalists Field Club, reflect the important natural history collections held by the Liverpool Museum, which includes the natural history correspondence of the 13th Earl of Derby, 1799-1850. Other non-business records include the Merseyside Unity Theatre, and the correspondence files of Ben Shaw, the former County and City Councillor, who was a Trustee of the National Museums & Galleries on Merseyside. The records of the National Museums & Galleries on Merseyside are also held under the Public Records Acts, 1958.

The military records of the King's Liverpool Regiment collection have been transferred to the Archives Department by the Department of Regional History. The World War I battalion war diaries and basic reference books are available at the Maritime Archives & Library, but the bulk of the collection is available *strictly by appointment only*.

A number of the most important non-maritime collections are described in the following section, and a list of other collections held, but not described, can be found at the end. It is important to note that unless otherwise stated, all of the non-maritime records described in this section are available *strictly by appointment only*.

Ayrton Saunders & Co., Ltd.

Ayrton Saunders & Co., Ltd., was founded as manufacturing chemists in 1868 in Hanover Street, Liverpool. These premises, together with three depots on Park Lane, Liverpool, Prenton, Birkenhead and Burslem, were sold in 1989 and the company was taken over by A.A.H. Pharmaceuticals. In 1990 the firm moved into new premises on Spindus Road at the Speke Hall Industrial Estate. The firm was run by A.A.H. from its premises on West Lane, Runcorn. In 1997 Mr. G.F. O'Brien of Liverpool, owner of a chain of retail chemist shops, purchased the name and now runs the expanded business from Spindus Road.

Records

Cash and bank ledgers, 1934-1973.

Directors minute books, 1903-1973.
Reports and accounts, 1940-1986.
Shareholders registers, 1909-1986.
Price lists, 1885-1968.
Catalogues, 1905-1960.
Correspondence, 1947-1973.
House magazines, 1925-1967.
Photographs, 1920-1921.
B/AS   1885-1986   50 Boxes   2 Parcels

BICC (British Insulated Callenders Cables plc)

British Insulated Callenders Cables plc originated from the merger of two nineteenth century pioneer electric cable companies, Callenders of Erith, formed in 1882, and British Insulated Wire Co., formed in Prescot in 1890. In 1902 British Insulated Wire Co. merged with the Telegraph Manufacturing Co. of Helsby, and they became British Insulated & Helsby Cables Ltd. In 1925 the firm was re-named British Insulated Cables Ltd. In 1945 British Insulated Cables merged with Callenders to form British Insulated Callenders Cables Ltd., which subsequently became known as BICC plc.

Other companies merged or taken over include Anchor Cable Co. of Leigh, Telegraph Construction & Maintenance Co., Ltd., the company formed to lay the first cable across the Atlantic in 1864, and Balfour Beatty, Civil Engineers.

BICC plc is now an international group, with world-wide interests especially in Asia and North America, and Balfour Beatty, the Civil Engineering and Construction division, is heavily involved in the UK railway infrastructure maintenance sector.

Records

Minute books, 1856-1977.
Management records, 1900-1934.
Historical material, 1847-1986.
Photographs, c.1895-1978.
Films, c.1940-1980.
Reference books, 1932-1982.
BICC   1856-1997   655 Boxes   7 Packets

Joseph Heap & Sons Ltd.

The firm of Joseph Heap & Sons Ltd., rice millers, was founded in Liverpool in 1778. The company continues to mill at the same premises in Pownall Street,

Liverpool, which it has occupied for over 200 years. The firm has consistently imported through Liverpool and at one time operated its own ships. In the 1960s it was sold to the East India Trading Co., who sold it to Steel Brothers. Later it became part of a Dutch firm called Euryza. The present firm of Joseph Heap & Sons Ltd. was the result of a management buy-out in the 1980s.

Records

Minute books, 1900-1973.
Directors' meetings, 1946-1974.
Share register, 1967.
B/JHP   1900-1974   6 Volumes

Liverpool Geological Society

Liverpool Geological Society was founded in 1859. The archive of the Society also includes the records of the Liverpool Geological Association, founded in 1880, which was incorporated into the Liverpool Geological Society in 1910.

Records

Minute books, 1859-1965.
Membership records, 1859-1957.
Correspondence, etc., c.1890-1974.
Photographs and maps, 1863-1965.
Liverpool Geological Association minute books and annual reports, 1880-1910.
NH/LGS   1859-1990   18 Boxes

Liverpool Hydraulic Power Co.

The Liverpool Hydraulic Power Co. was established in 1884. Its hydraulic mains served the whole of the business centre of the city of Liverpool, covering thirty miles in all. The central pumping station was in Athol Street. The power it produced was used for lifts, cranes, capstans, machinery and fire protection.

Records

Inspector's reports on machinery, 1887-1964.
Mains books, 1887-1954.
Service pipe books, 1887-1957.
Mains sheets, 1932-1944.
Particulars of trenches and mains, 1936-1970.
Cost book, 1922-1938.
Publicity booklet, c.1952.

There are 3 drawers of O.S. 10 ft. plans in the Maritime Archives & Library which show the routes for the mains.

B/LHPC   1887-1970   6 Boxes and Drawings

Liverpool Naturalists' Field Club

The Liverpool Naturalists' Field Club was founded in 1860. Its object being "the study of natural history in all its branches." The prime mover in those early days was the well-known cleric, the Reverend H.H. Higgins. The club was dissolved in 1980.

Records

Minute books, 1864-1980.
Proceedings, 1870-1978.
Accounts, 1947-1964, 1975.
Leaflets and newsletters, c.1957-1982.
Magazines and booklets, 1861-1981.
NH/LN   1864-1982   27 Boxes

Meccano Ltd.

Meccano Ltd., was established in 1908 by Frank Hornby, a Liverpool businessman, in order to commercially manufacture a new construction toy, "Meccano." By the late 1920s model railway engines were produced to replace the German imports which had stopped during the war, and in the 1930s diecast toys known as "Dinky" toys, were manufactured. The firm continued into the 1970s, until its collapse in 1979. The Regional History Department have some construction kits and a selection of Dinky toys and a train set.

Records

Minute books, 1944-1953.
Articles of association, deeds and agreements, 1908-1974.
Reports and accounts, 1949-1970.
Sales reports, 1963-1977.
Meccano magazines, 1925-1966.
Balance sheets, 1903-1976.
B/ME   1908-1980   50 Boxes and 5 Packets

References

Brown, K.D. "Death of a Dinosaur, Meccano of Liverpool 1908-1979." *Business Archives*, No. 66, November 1993.
Brown, K.D. *The British Toy Business, A History Since 1700*. London, 1996.

Merseyside Left/Unity Theatre

The theatre was established in 1937 and continued until 1987. The records were acquired in 1987 by the Regional History Department and subsequently transferred to the Archives Department in 1992.

Records

Committee meetings, 1937-1987.
General meetings, 1937-1987.
Accounts and balance sheets, 1945-1987.
Membership records, 1937-1946.
Scripts by L. Peck and T. Willis, c.1930-1980.
Papers re: relationship with the Labour and Communist Parties, 1946.
RH4   1937-1987   82 Boxes and 3 Packets

Reference

Lambert, A.E. "Power to the People, the Work of the Unity Theatre, 1929-1945." Unpublished thesis.

National Museums & Galleries on Merseyside (NMGM)

The records of NMGM go back to 1849 before Liverpool Museum was founded. They grew out of two generous donations. First, in 1851 the 13th Earl of Derby gave his Natural History collection, and its associated correspondence, and in 1867, Joseph Mayer gave his collection of archaeological, ethnological and decorative art material. The two sections were known as the Derby and Mayer Museums, each with its own curator, which continued until the 1920s when the titles were dropped.

Local government reorganisation in 1974 resulted in the new Merseyside County Council taking control of the Museum and in 1986, when the County Council was abolished, the Museums and Galleries were given national status as the National Museums & Galleries on Merseyside.

Records

Daily reports and committee minutes, 1849-1986.
Trustee minutes, 1986 - to date. *Prior permission from the Secretary of the Trustees of NMGM is required before consulting these records.*
Deeds, 1939-1999.
Departmental records, 1939-1998.
Publicity material, 1898-1999.
Publications, 1932-1999.
The Walker Art Gallery has retained its own archives and it is *necessary to request permission from the Walker Art Gallery before consulting these records.*
MM   1849-1999   523 Boxes, 27 Packets and 5 Rolls

Ben Shaw (1907-1986)

Ben Shaw was born in Russia in 1907 and came to England with his parents. In 1957 he was elected to Liverpool City Council and in 1974 he was elected to Merseyside County Council, becoming in due course, chairman of the Arts and Culture Committee. It was due to his interest and concern that the Merseyside Maritime Museum was established in 1984, with the Museum of Labour History following in 1986. In that year he was elected a Trustee of NMGM, but was only able to serve for a short time up to his death later that year. His collection consists of correspondence files which require further cataloguing and arrangement.

Records

File of papers re: councillor, Liverpool City Council, 1957-1965.
Files re: NMGM, Tate Gallery, etc., 1960-1986.
Files re: Merseyside County Council, Israel, Royal visits, etc., 1972-1986.
Files re: the Labour Party, Liverpool theatres, etc., 1975-1984.
D/SH   1957-1986   13 Boxes

Tate & Lyle Co., Ltd.

In 1870 Henry Tate & Sons built a sugar refinery in Love Lane, Liverpool, which opened in 1872. In 1929, as Tate & Lyle Co., Ltd., the company amalgamated with Fairries, a refinery founded by J.A. and T. Fairrie in 1847 at Vauxhall Road, Liverpool. Geoffrey Fairrie joined the board and led the reconstruction and extension of the Love Lane premises in 1936-1937. In 1981 the Love Lane refinery was closed down as part of Tate & Lyle's rationalisation scheme. The majority of the records relating to the Love Lane premises were transferred by the company to its London offices, and the records described below are a small random sample rescued from the Love Lane site prior to its demolition in 1982.

Records

Folders of correspondence, memos, etc., re: staff, machinery and insurance, 1932-1934.
Wages ledger, 1920-1922.
Payroll and time sheets, 1943-1959.
B/TL   1920-1959   2 Boxes

Reference

Hugill, A. *Sugar and All That: A History of Tate & Lyle*. London, 1978.

Vulcan Foundry Co., Ltd.

Charles Tayleur, a Liverpool engineer, founded the Vulcan Foundry at Newton-le-Willows in 1830. In 1832 Robert Stephenson, the railway engineer, joined him in partnership. In 1847 they took over the Bank Quay Foundry in Warrington and in 1852 built their first sea-going iron vessel, the clipper *Tayleur,* which was tragically wrecked off Dublin in 1854 en route to Australia. The partnership was incorporated as a private company in 1864 as the Vulcan Foundry Co., Ltd.

Vulcan locomotives were exported all over the world, with the first locomotives for Russia and Japan supplied in 1837 and 1871 respectively. During World War II the factory built the "Waltzing Matilda" tank and in 1944 Vulcan acquired another locomotive business, Robert Stephenson & Hawthorns Ltd., based in Newcastle-upon-Tyne.

With the demise of steam, Vulcan turned to diesel and electric locomotives, in conjunction with the English Electric Co., Ltd., becoming full members of that group of companies in 1955. The English Electric Co., Ltd., became part of the G.E.C. group in 1968. In 1970 Rushton Paxton Diesels Ltd. became the manager of G.E.C. Diesels Ltd., and today occupies the Vulcan works.

Records

Minute books, 1864-1924.
Annual reports, 1865-1968.
Letter books, 1901-1905.
Ledgers and journals, 1864-1921.
Drawings and photographs of locomotives built 1833-c.1950.
B/VF   1837-1995   176 Boxes, 18 Plan Boxes, 5 Packets and
                                 25 Portfolios of Drawings

Wingrove & Rogers Ltd.

Wingrove & Rogers Ltd. was founded in 1919, as electrical engineers producing control gear for another local firm, British Electric Vehicles Ltd. of Southport, who manufactured electric industrial trucks and mining locomotives. In the early 1920s with the advent of broadcasting, the firm made coils for radio equipment. In 1924 they moved to premises in Old Swan, Liverpool, and made a wide range of electro-mechanical devices. In 1926 British Electric Vehicles Ltd. was acquired, transferred to Liverpool and became known as the BEV division. The firm continued producing fork lift trucks and electric vehicles until the 1980s when it ceased trading.

Records

Administration, 1919-1984.
Legal, 1920-1979.
Financial, 1920-1987.
Investment, 1977-c.1980.
Operational, 1917-1986 (including photographs).
Staff and wages, 1930-1980.
Miscellaneous correspondence, etc., 1919-1977.
B/WR   1915-1986   64 Boxes and 3 Packets

List of Non-Maritime Collections also held at the Archives Reserve Store, and available *strictly by appointment only*.

E.H. Baker & Sons, Handcart Builders, 1931-1983.
A.W. Boyd, Local Naturalist, 1825-1972.
The Braby Group, Drum Manufacturers, 1934-1978.
E.N. Clay, Goldbeater, 1707-1970.
M. Henderson, Naturalist, 1936-1968.
Hill Dickinson, Solicitors, 1925-1967.
Hygena Ltd., Kitchen Designers, 1960-1978.
W. Johansen, Wheelwright & Blacksmith, c.1950-c.1980.
Liverpool University School of Hygiene, Department Records, 1851-1972.
Radcliffe Evans, Local Businessman, 1884-1935.
Railway Signal Co., Ltd., Signal Makers, 1886-1950.
W.E. Shepherd, Pharmacist, 1869-1968.
Various Trade Union Records, 1872-1986.
T.W. Williams, Naturalist, 1892-1976.

Compiled by D. Le Mare, D. Littler and M. Stammers.

CHAPTER 12

ADDENDA TO GUIDE, VOLUME I

This final chapter describes collections which have been acquired since the publication of the first volume of this *Guide* in 1995, and which belong to sections of the collection already described in chapters two to four of that volume, the Official Organisations, Shipping and Trade Associations and Shipping Company collections. No guide can ever be taken to be exhaustive, least of all this one, for it is the very nature of archive collections that they grow and increase with the addition and discovery of further records. Recent additions to the Maritime Archives & Library have included the records of the Liverpool Shipping Staffs' Association, and London & Overseas Freighters Ltd., and also over a hundred volumes of Merchant Navy Radio Officers examination results. We have also taken the opportunity of including an enhanced entry for one of the shipping company collections, John Holt & Co. (Liverpool) Ltd., which has been the subject of further work since it was described in the first volume of this publication. Similarly, further cataloguing of the Mersey Docks & Harbour Board early miscellaneous documents has allowed us to revise that entry with new information.

New Acquisitions

Radio Officers Marconi Examination Results

The Wireless Telegraph & Signal Co., was formed in 1897 by Guglielmo Marconi, the pioneer of the system of radio telegraphy. Premises were acquired in Chelmsford, and in 1900 the company's name was changed to Marconi's Wireless Telegraph Co., and in 1963 changed to The Marconi Co. In 1900 Marconi International Marine Communication Co., Ltd. was formed with the sole purpose of working an exclusive licence for all maritime purposes. However, there was a problem with finding suitable staff as no colleges or schools existed which covered the subject of wireless, so in 1900 the company opened the world's first wireless school at Frinton. Under the Merchant Shipping (Wireless Telegraphy) Shipping Act of 1919, all persons operating radio telegraph apparatus on board ships registered in Britain, were required to hold either 1st or 2nd class certificates of proficiency issued by the Board of Trade's Wireless Telegraphy Service. The examinations for the certificates were taken at various technical colleges and wireless telegraphy schools across the British Isles and also at the Ship Inspection Depots at Liverpool, Cardiff and Newcastle. The volumes of examination results were transferred by the Radio Communications Agency Records Office in 1999.

Records

Radio officers examination results.
D/ROE   1910-1974   118 Volumes

Reference

Reynolds, P. *Guglielmo Marconi*. London, 1978.

Liverpool Shipping Staffs' Association

The Liverpool Shipping Staffs' Association originated from the idea of a number of chartering clerks, who believed that a more friendly relationship between the staff of shipping offices might be established if they were to meet at an annual social gathering. A committee was formed under the chairmanship of J.M. Modrel (Honorary Treasurer of the Liverpool Shipbrokers' Benevolent Society), which decided that the gathering should take the form of a dinner to be designated "The Liverpool Shipbroker's Staffs Annual Dinner." The first dinner was held on the 11 January 1902 at the Falcon Restaurant, Lord Street, Liverpool. At the third dinner on the 9 January 1904, the chairman announced the decision to form "The Liverpool Shipping Staffs' Association," and a general meeting was held later that month.

In addition to the Annual Dinner, the other aims of the Association were to organise lectures and conferences for its members and also social excursions. One of the first excursions was made in June 1904, to the Baron Quay Mine at Northwich, via the Manchester Ship Canal, where the party dined down the mine. In 1907 a Benefit Fund was established to grant monetary relief to members. The Liverpool Shipping Staffs' Association continues today and its records were donated in 1998.

Records

Minute books, 1901-1993.
Trust deeds, 1914-1963.
Rule books, c.1954-1988.
Hand books, 1951-1982.
Balance sheets, 1968.
Syllabus cards (lectures, events, etc.), 1951-1969.
Annual dinner menus and programmes, 1949-1992.
Photographs of members, meetings and social events, c.1930-1950.
Newscutting album, 1906-1922.
D/SSA   1901-1993   3 Boxes

Pamphlet celebrating fifty years of the Association, 1904-1954.
SAS/23C/1/4   1954   1 Item

London & Overseas Freighters Ltd.

London & Overseas Freighters Ltd. was formed in London by two long-standing
and British-based Greek shipping families, the Kulukundis and the Mavroleons
on 8 April 1948. Originally the company operated nine second-hand dry cargo
vessels. The prefix "London" was adopted in the names of "L.O.F." ships and
the City's coat of arms was displayed on the bridge of each vessel. The early
1950s saw the acquisition of several new tankers, heralding the move towards the
transportation of bulk liquids. By 1956, a new subsidiary company had been
formed, called "London Overseas Tankers." The company experienced poor
financial returns as a result of the global oil crisis of the early 1970s with most
of the fleet being laid up in Greek waters. A similar "oil" recession followed
during the early 1980s, but the company survived to increase its "tanker tonnage"
during the 1990s and is now successfully trading from its Bermuda headquarters.

Records

Minutes, 1948-1992.
Ship's ledgers, 1972-1985.
Voyage accounts (various vessels), 1950-1988.
Vessels performance data, 1952-1961.
Charter party books, 1964-1995.
Management department transfer binders, 1952-1985.
Accounts, 1959-1962.
Shipping journals (various), 1979-1989.
Plans, c.1960-1970.
B/LOF   1948-1992   53 Volumes and 2 Boxes

Amended Entries

Early MDHB Miscellaneous Papers

This section contains a wealth of early documents relating to the development of
the port of Liverpool from c.1790 to 1890, collected by the Assistant Secretary's
office. Listing of the first thirteen boxes has now been completed and this has
improved, and in many cases extended the original description (in Vol. I chap.
2).

1. Committee reports, etc., re: improvements and dock extensions, c.1839-1844; reports re: position of gunpowder magazines, 1881-1890.

2. Committee reports, notes and evidence re: provision of new docks and piers, Liverpool Docks Bill, etc. Includes opinion of John Rennie, Engineer re: the need for extra dock accommodation, 1761-1875.

3. Parliamentary statements, correspondence, accounts and petitions re: Dock Bills and Dock Acts, 1799-1828.

4. Parliamentary papers re: Dock Bill 1865; minutes and correspondence of various mercantile associations including American Chamber of Commerce, West Indian Association, Brazilian Association, Mediterranean & Levant Association, Liverpool East India Association, British North American Association, Liverpool Shipowners Association, 1836; appointments of deputations for dock improvements, 1841; dock estate revenue, dock rates, etc., 1857-1867; town dues correspondence, 1861-1863; bye-laws for regulation of railways for Birkenhead Docks, 1863; railway arbitration, costs, correspondence, 1864; telegraphic rates correspondence, 1866; MDHB Bill for tonnage and cargo dues, 1752-1866; affidavits, summons, 1866; application to Parliament for Bill to authorise MDHB to construct new docks and landing stage, 1872.

5. Papers re: Pilotage Committee, pilotage annuity fund including Liverpool Steamship Owners Association, 1883-1971; gatekeepers re: customs in suppression of smuggling, 1864-1906; instruction book to masters of pilot boats, 1956; nomination and election of pilots, 1889.

6. Reports and proceedings of enquiries, 1833, 1854 and evidence on Parliamentary Bills re: limits of the port of Liverpool and town dues, etc., 1857, 1860; includes list of Acts of Parliament re: Liverpool by L.P. Stubbs, 1863; book on *Corporate Tradition and National Rights*, by Harriet Martineau, c.1857; reports on sanitation of dock offices, 1888.

7. Report of proceedings of the Associated Merchants of Liverpool re: abolition of town dues, 1835; proceedings in the Bill for the abolition of passing tolls, 1856; plan of Liverpool Docks re: proposed alterations for accommodation for largest vessels, 1891-1898; brochure: *The Mersey Dock Estate: Its Management and Principal Trades*, c.1950.

8. Legal Department papers re: Birkenhead Docks, includes receipts for work completed, statement of accounts, 1847-1852; notes on pilotage by J.T. Danson, 1871; proceedings in House of Lords, MDHB v Pilots re: pilotage rates, 1890; abstracts of special agreements with seamen, c.1912; abstracts

of returns for UK pilotage, 1932-1938; correspondence re: fires, lights, docks and quays bye-laws, 1937; wrecks in Garston Channel, 1919-1940; National Association of Port Employers proposals for post-war decasualisation and reorganisation, etc., 1945; dock workers, regulation of employment scheme, 1947-1951.

9. Minutes of Dock Committee proceedings, 1760-1839; resolutions, statements, reports and proceedings of special and common council, etc., 1790-1839; correspondence with Jesse Hartley re: stages at various docks, 1840-1844; correspondence to Dock Committee, 1836-1844; management of telegraph stations, 1839; heads of inquiry re: loading and discharging ships, 1839; correspondence re: attendance at sub-committee and evidence re: dock extension, 1843-1844.

10. Memorandums, notes, letters, etc., re: legal cases, eg Birkenhead Dock Co. v Sanderson, Liverpool Dock Co. v Gladstone, 1806-1865; notes, correspondence, minutes re: establishment of Dock Police Force, 1807-1836; papers re: Bill to extend Dock Committee powers, 1809-1836; account of fines, 1811-1813; dock charitable fund, 1811-1814; penalties for misdemeanours under Dock Act, 1812-1814; prisoners convicted under Dock Act 1814-1815; general administration, staff, wages and dock rate collection, expenses, etc., 1811-1866; imports and exports, 1825; correspondence re: Acts of Parliament re: warehouses, various docks, 1831-1838; statements re: tonnages, 1842-1843; Minutes of Parliamentary Sub-Committee re: new Birkenhead Docks bill, 1844; reports on salaries and Civil Service enquiry, 1863-1874.

11. Estimates, accounts re: expenses for Liverpool Docks improvements, 1785-1823, includes Charles Eyes' estimate for erecting West Docks and a basin, 1785; minutes of Dock Committee meetings, 1796; correspondence from Jesse Hartley re: estimate for Salthouse Dock warehouses, 1838; correspondence re: proposals for excavating south end Queen's Dock, Princes Dock, 1811-1818; from Mark Isambard Brunel re: footbridge over Old Dock entrance, 1822; dock improvement plans of M. Gage, 1841; opinion of Thomas Telford, correspondence, etc., re: new Graving Dock, 1821-1822.

(N.B. The box numbered 12 in Vol. I, chap. 2, has been removed from the collection).

13. Legal documents, plans for Lancashire and Cheshire, 1681-1878; Liverpool Pilot Act, 1824; bonds and sureties payable to the Dock Trustees, 1840-1878; correspondence re: Birkenhead Docks transfer to Liverpool Docks

Trustees, 1844-1848; plans of property belonging to Birkenhead Dock Co. and proposed warehouses, 1844; apprenticeship indentures, memorandums, correspondence, etc., 1856-1878; bye-laws, agreements, telegraph, 1857-1881; guarantee agreements, insurance policies, etc., 1870-1881; steam winch owners, etc., 1876-1878.

MDHB/MISC   1681-c.1850   12 Boxes

John Holt & Co. (Liverpool) Ltd.

John Holt & Co. (Liverpool) Ltd., is a successful West African merchant business founded by John Holt, who was assistant to the British Consul, Mr. Lynslager, at the Spanish Island of Fernando Po in 1862. After Mr. Lynslager's death, he continued to work for his widow until 1867 when he purchased Lynslager's merchant business from her. In that year he was joined by his brothers, Jonathan and Thomas Holt, and they expanded the business from Fernando Po to the mainland of West Africa. In 1884 the business was made into a partnership of the three brothers, and in 1897 it became a limited company, John Holt & Co. (Liverpool) Ltd.

The company bought its first steamer, the *Balmore* in 1907, and in 1909 ordered two new ships to carry its own cargoes on what became a profitable, regular UK-West African service. By John Holt's death in 1915 the company had developed into a flourishing private company with branches in all the main centres of the West African trade. From 1950 the firm was re-named John Holt Line Ltd., and changed to Guinea Gulf Line Ltd., in 1954. In 1965 the fleet was sold to Elder Dempster (Liner Holdings Ltd.).

By the 1960s John Holt & Co. (Liverpool) Ltd., was providing a wide range of exporting and importing services to Nigeria, which included river transport, storage, cargo handling, insurance, shipping agency and engineering. By this time the firm also had a building division for distributing supplies, a leather and rubber division, a motor division with a network of garages, and a pharmaceutical division, operating through the West African Drug Co., Ltd. It was involved in the trade of a wide range of export and import commodities in Nigeria from agricultural machinery to wines and spirits.

Today the John Holt Group Ltd., continues to flourish operating in the UK, Malawi and Nigeria, engaged in the manufacture of glass fibre boats, packaging, cosmetics and toiletries, assembly and distribution of motor cycles, generators and outboard engines, and distributors of consumer durables and non-durables. John Holt & Co. (Liverpool) Ltd., are an intermediate holding company engaged in cargo handling. Both are subsidiaries of Lonrho Africa Ltd. The archive includes the administrative, financial and property records of the many companies taken over by John Holt & Co. (Liverpool) Ltd., as well as the records of the various John Holt Group divisions. There is also a large photographic collection of ships, cargoes, staff and properties in Nigeria. Whilst the bulk of the collection is uncatalogued, the photographs have been sorted and listed on database (see Vol. II chap. 9). The Museum also holds models of the *Balmore* (1900), *Jonathon Holt* (1910) and *John Holt* (1926).

Records

The bulk of the records originated in the secretarial and property departments of the company. Progress has been made on the arrangement of the records, and the records sorted so far can be divided into the following categories:

Administration, c.1897-1991.

Financial, c.1963-1984.

Staff, c.1938-1964.

Property (including title deeds, conveyances and associated correspondence, UK and abroad), c.1813-1981.

Photographs (shipping, property and staff), c.1852-1964 (see chapter 13).

Miscellaneous, c.1893-1970.

Other companies owned or taken over by John Holt & Co. (Liverpool) Ltd., with records (mostly secretarial/administrative) in the collection, include:

J. Allen & Co.; Kay Aspinall; Bartholemew (London) Ltd.; R.N. Bollans & Co.; Bushell Maples & Co.; G. Buswell & Co., Ltd.; Camdere Ltd.; F.A. Wild Ltd.; Campbell Co. Inc.; William Dodd Ltd.; Dunrobin Products; Ess (International); Homeworthy Furniture (Northern) Ltd.; House of Aton (Lancs.) Ltd.; J.P. Lebegue & Co., Ltd.; Nathan's Equipment Ltd.; T.R.F. Pland Ltd.; L.A. Rix (Insurance) Ltd.; Sheer Pride Ltd.; Alfred Smith Insurance Ltd.; Carl Wolf (Agencies) Ltd.; Universal Mortgage Assurance Brokers Ltd.

B/JH   c.1813-1991   c.300 Boxes

References

Holt, C. *The Diary of John Holt and the Voyage of the Maria*. Liverpool, 1948.
Mather, D. *A Short History of the ships of John Holt and Company (Liverpool) Ltd. and the Guinea Gulf Line Ltd*. Liverpool, 1965.

Compiled by A. Glynn, D. Littler and J. Moore.

INDEX

Compiled by H. Threlfall

This is a cumulative index combining volumes I (Research in Maritime History No. 8) and II. Entries therefore refer to volume and page number; thus, II, 24 refers to volume II, page 24. All significant subjects, places and persons are included in this index. With the exception of *Conway, Indefatigable, Titanic* and *Lusitania*, ship names, however, have not been included.